ROBERT DUNCAN *and* DENISE LEVERTOV

ROBERT DUNCAN

and

DENISE LEVERTOV

---

*The Poetry of Politics,
the Politics of Poetry*

Edited by
Albert Gelpi
and
Robert J. Bertholf

STANFORD UNIVERSITY PRESS
Stanford, California   *2006*

Stanford University Press
Stanford, California

Library of Congress Cataloging-in-Publication Data

Robert Duncan and Denise Levertov : the poetry of politics, the politics of poetry / edited by Albert Gelpi and Robert J. Bertholf.
      p.   cm.
   Essays derived from a symposium held at Stanford University on November 7th and 8th, 2003, to mark the publication of The letters of Robert Duncan and Denise Levertov.
   Includes bibliographical references and index.
   ISBN-10: 0-8047-5130-7 (alk. paper)
   ISBN-10: 0-8047-5131-5 (pbk. : alk. paper)
   ISBN-13: 978-0-8047-5130-8 (alk. paper)
   ISBN-13: 978-0-8047-5131-5 (pbk. : alk. paper)
   1. Duncan, Robert Edward, 1919—Correspondence.   2. Levertov, Denise, 1923—Correspondence.   3. American poetry—20th century—History and criticism.   4. Politics and literature—United States—History—20th century.
5. Vietnam War, 1961–1975—Literature and the war.   I. Gelpi, Albert.
II. Bertholf, Robert J.

PS3507.U629Z85 2006
811'.54—dc22

                                                          2006017970

Contents

Preface   vii

List of Abbreviations   xiii

                                    I

1   Decision at the Apogee: Robert Duncan's
    Anarchist Critique of Denise Levertov   1
        Robert J. Bertholf

2   Robert Duncan and the Question of Law:
    Ernst Kantorowicz and the Poet's Two Bodies   18
        Graça Capinha

3   Better to Stumble to It: The Start of Duncan's
    Letters: Poems, 1953–1956   32
        Devin Johnston

4   Visions of the Field in Poetry and Painting:
    Denise Levertov, Robert Duncan, and John Button   43
        Donna Krolik Hollenberg

                                   II

5   My Stories with Robert Duncan   63
        Ellen Tallman

6   The People's P***k: A Dialectical Tale   71
        Aaron Shurin

7   The Hasid and the Kabbalist   81
        John Felstiner

III

8 *Chelsea* 8: Political Poetry at Midcentury 93
   Brett Millier

9 Poetic Authority and the Public Sphere
   of Politics in the Activist 1960s:
   The Duncan-Levertov Debate 109
   Anne Dewey

10 Prophetic Frustrations: Robert Duncan's *Tribunals* 126
   Peter O'Leary

11 Revolution or Death: Levertov's Poetry in Time of War 148
   Jose Rodriguez Herrera

12 The Vision of the Burning Babe: Southwell,
   Levertov, and Duncan 161
   Paul A. Lacey

13 Poetic Language and Language Poetry:
   Levertov, Duncan, Creeley 180
   Albert Gelpi

List of Contributors 199
Index 203

Preface

American poetry in the postwar years was a time of creative contention. The formalist poetics of the New Criticism—exemplified by John
Crowe Ransom, Allen Tate, and Cleanth Brooks, and by younger poets
like Robert Lowell, Randall Jarrell, and Richard Wilbur—was challenged
by several different kinds of experimentation with what was called open
and inventive form, as opposed to closed, or conventional form. The sections of Donald Allen's canonizing anthology *The New American Poetry*
(1960) mapped out the experimenters in groups: the Black Mountain poets (including Charles Olson, Robert Creeley, Duncan, and Levertov), the
San Francisco poets (including William Everson, Lawrence Ferlinghetti,
Robin Blaser, and Jack Spicer), the Beats (including Jack Kerouac, Allen
Ginsberg, and Gregory Corso), and the New York poets (including Kenneth Koch, Frank O'Hara, and John Ashbery). There was some overlap
and interaction between the groups, but the mapping was useful because
the groupings represented different places, different literary lineages, and
significantly different intentions in open form poetry and poetics.

Robert Duncan and Denise Levertov are linked, in anthologies and
literary histories, with the experimental poets of the Black Mountain
school. During the early and mid-1950s the Black Mountain poets coalesced in the pages of *Origin*, edited by Cid Corman, and in the *Black
Mountain Review*, edited by Robert Creeley. The group's clearest rallying
call and statement of purpose had come in Olson's 1950 essay "Projective
Verse," with its notion of "composition by field." The collective name of
the group derived from the Black Mountain College in rural North Carolina, where Olson was rector during its last years and where a number of
the poets were students or faculty, but also, and much more accurately, the
designation came from the constellation of the poets in the *Black Mountain Review*. "The Black Mountain poets" was a literary not a geographical

designation. The poets visited one another now and then, but not often, and it was not until the Vancouver Poetry Conference in the summer of 1963 that Olson, Duncan, Creeley, and Levertov were in the same place at the same time. The letter was the medium of communication. The crisscross of letters and poems knit the group together and created a sense of a shared venture. Their deep concern with the creative process and specifically with articulating just how the poem took form as a linguistic field from the many-leveled field of experience generated a remarkable epistolary record—notably between Olson and Creeley, published in nine volumes (which is not the complete correspondence) by Black Sparrow Press, and between Duncan and Levertov, published in a single large volume by Stanford University Press.

The friendship between Duncan and Levertov was particularly close. Duncan had been bowled over by her poem "The Shifting" in *Origin* in 1953 and then initiated the correspondence, but she had known and admired his early book *Heavenly City Earthly City* even before she emigrated to the United States in 1948. The poets met for the first time in New York in February 1955 when Duncan and Duncan's partner the painter Jess Collins were on their way to Mallorca, where they met Creeley for the first time. The Duncan-Levertov correspondence runs to almost five hundred letters. They wrote back and forth about their domestic lives as well as literary and artistic events, but above all their ongoing discussions explored the ways of the poem—its possible forms, its visionary character—and the binding responsibility of being a poet. For many years this exchange of letters, so frequent that they read almost like an epistolary novel, sustained the poems they wrote, often to and for each other. They led separate domestic lives on opposite coasts—Duncan in the San Francisco area and Levertov in New York and Maine—and consequently met in person infrequently. Nonetheless, their correspondence comprises a personal and poetic dialogue so urgent and intense that it reads like love letters whose bonded commitment was to the power of language and to the imagination's unflagging search for expressive form. As Levertov said to Duncan at the end of a poem-letter of April 1966,

> Love I send, but I send it
> in another word.
> > Longing?
> > Poetry.

In the course of the 1960s, however, the Vietnam War entered and transformed their world. To their consternation they found themselves by the end of the decade in increasingly sharp and sharply expressed disagreement about how poetry can and should cope with the violence and evil of the war, and more fundamentally about the agency of poetry in the political and social world. The rupture that came in the early 1970s was personally devastating, but their divergent views about the moral and aesthetic responsibilities of the imagination remain instructive and challenging because those vexed issues not only defined their poetic epoch but continue to be just as crucial—and as vexed—today. There is no richer or more revealing exchange between two major artists in modern American letters.

To mark the publication of *The Letters of Robert Duncan and Denise Levertov*, we, as coeditors of the volume, organized a symposium at Stanford University on November 7 and 8, 2003. Three poets with various allegiances with Levertov and Duncan—Robert Creeley, Eavan Boland, and Michael Davidson—opened and closed the symposium. Creeley—through his close ties with Duncan and Levertov and through his magnanimous and generous spirit—became a radiant center for all the proceedings. Moreover, as we listened to the papers by a wide range of critics, we recognized that the intersections and juxtapositions, the convergences and contrasts of insight and perspective gave the occasion at once an extraordinary openness and a pervasive coherence. This was the kind of "company" of poets and readers Creeley talked about so often.

Except for the essays by Robert J. Bertholf, Albert Gelpi, and Aaron Shurin, all the other essays presented here are revised and expanded versions of the papers delivered at the Stanford symposium. In one way or another, all the essays develop out of themes and ideas in the correspondence between Duncan and Levertov. The table of contents organizes the essays into three interrelated sections. The first section deals with several formative issues in the poets' growth and relationship. Robert J. Bertholf explores the anarchist principles behind Duncan's thinking about politics and his antiwar sentiments, all of which shaped his response to Levertov's active participation in antiwar protest. Graça Capinha's essay, which follows Bertholf's, gives serious consideration to the issue of how the teaching of Ernst Kantorowicz, who was one of Duncan's professors at the University of California, Berkeley, helped define Duncan's ideas about the laws of politics and the laws of poetry. In the next chapter, Devin Johnston discusses the poems in Duncan's book *Letters*; when Duncan read Levertov's poem "The Shifting" in *Origin*, he wrote the first poem of that book, "For A Muse Meant," which he sent to her, initiating their long correspondence. Levertov and Duncan lived in a world of poetry as well as in the world of the arts, and Donna Krolik Hollenberg centers her discussion on the artist John Button, known by both Duncan and Levertov. Levertov wrote a long poem about Button, and the discussion of that poem reveals much about her aesthetics and her ideas about poetic form.

The second section presents and reflects on Duncan and Levertov through more personal accounts. Ellen Tallman, who, with her husband Warren Tallman, organized the Vancouver Poetry Conference in the summer of 1963, tells informative and amusing stories about Duncan. From the point of view of having known both Duncan and Levertov as mentors, Aaron Shurin sets out the poets' responses to political views by reading their political poems against specific historical events of the 1960s and 1970s. Both Duncan and Levertov read in the spiritualist sources of Jewish mysticism and the Kabbalah and, as John Felstiner demonstrates in his chapter, each made different uses of the materials.

The third section examines various aspects of the split that ended the poets' close and intense association. The discussions of poetry and politics in the Duncan/Levertov letters was not the only such discussion, as Brett Millier demonstrates in her essay on the eighth issue of the magazine *Chelsea*, edited by David Ignatow, the theme of which was the relationship between politics, war, and poetry. Millier raises some of the same issues about political and war poetry—mainly how difficult it is to write such poetry—as Charles Simic raised in his recent review of the Duncan-Levertov correspondence (*New York Review of Books*, November 4, 2004). Anne Dewey, in her chapter, develops related themes as she defines the conflict between personal and public authority in building a foundation for a political stance in a poem. Peter O'Leary then shifts the attention to the poems in Duncan's volume *Tribunals*, as he raises more issues about the poet's control over his own texts in preparation for a reading of the prophetic themes in the poem "Before the Judgment, Passages 35." Jose Rodriguez Herrera finds in his analysis of the theme of "Revolution or Death" that part of the difference of views of Duncan and Levertov about political subjects derived from a different apprehension of the functions of language in the poetics of the two poets. Paul A. Lacey might agree with some of Herrera's conclusions, because in his exploration of Duncan's and Levertov's use of Southwell's poem "The Burning Babe," he finds that the poets come to different conclusions though they derive their poems from the same Southwell poem. And in the collection's final essay, Albert Gelpi lays out the argument that even though both poets shared the view of life and poetry as sacred events, their different stances toward visionary experiences produced a poetry that characterizes the conflict between Postmodernism (Duncan) and Neoromanticism (Levertov). The variety in the essays finally projects the variety, intensity, and complexity of the whole of the Levertov/Duncan correspondence.

We wanted to dedicate the volume to Robert and Denise, and we had hoped that Bob Creeley might write an afterword for it. But, saddened now by his absence, we dedicate it to the memory of Robert, Denise, and Bob, old friends and wonderful poets whom we were fortunate enough to know and count as friends. They would have eagerly engaged the authors of these essays in further and even heated discussion of the issues out of common concern—but each with differently inflected gusto, emphasis, and conviction.

Albert Gelpi and Robert J. Bertholf
May 13, 2005

Abbreviations

BB   Robert Duncan. *Bending the Bow*. New York: New Directions, 1968.

Bib   Robert J. Bertholf. *Robert Duncan: A Descriptive Bibliography*. Santa Rosa, CA: Black Sparrow Press, 1986.

CB   Denise Levertov. *Candles in Babylon*. New York: New Directions, 1982.

D   Robert Duncan. *Derivations: Selected Poems, 1950–56*. London: Fulcrum Press, 1968.

FC   Robert Duncan. *Fictive Certainties*. New York: New Directions, 1985.

GW   Robert Duncan. *Ground Work: Before the War*. New York: New Directions, 1984.

JL   Denise Levertov. *The Jacob's Ladder*. New York: New Directions Press, 1961.

L   Robert J. Bertholf and Albert Gelpi, eds. *The Letters of Robert Duncan and Denise Levertov*. Stanford, CA: Stanford University Press, 2004.

LA   Denise Levertov. *The Life Around Us: Selected Poems on Nature*. New York: New Directions, 1997.

LC   Denise Levertov. *Light Up the Cave*. New York: New Directions, 1971.

Letters   Robert Duncan. *Letters: Poems, 1953–56*. Ed. Robert J. Bertholf. Chicago: Flood Editions, 2003.

LF   Denise Levertov. *Life in the Forest*. New York: New Directions, 1978.

NES   Denise Levertov. *New and Selected Essays*. New York: New Directions, 1992.

OF	Robert Duncan. *The Opening of the Field.* New York: Grove Press, 1960.
P60	Denise Levertov. *Poems, 1960–1967.* New York: New Directions, 1983.
P68	Denise Levertov. *Poems, 1968–1972.* New York: New Directions, 1987.
PW	Denise Levertov. *The Poet in the World.* New York: New Directions, 1973.
RA	Denise Levertov. *Relearning the Alphabet.* New York: New Directions, 1970.
RB	Robert Duncan. *Roots and Branches.* New York: New Directions, 1964.
SA	Denise Levertov. *To Stay Alive.* New York: New Directions, 1971.
SD	Denise Levertov. *The Sorrow Dance.* New York: New Directions, 1966.
SP	Robert Duncan. *A Selected Prose.* Ed. Robert J. Bertholf. New York: New Directions, 1995.
TMS	Denise Levertov. *Tesserae: Memories and Suppositions.* New York: New Directions, 1995.
TS	Denise Levertov. *O Taste and See.* New York: New Directions. 1964.

I

Decision at the Apogee: Robert
Duncan's Anarchist Critique of
Denise Levertov

Robert J. Bertholf

I

From their first letters in 1953 through the ones in 1969, both Robert
Duncan and Denise Levertov were attuned to one another as poets and as
close friends; their conversations at times sound like lovers talking. They
engaged each other on many levels in their discussions of art and style, domestic arrangements, the books they were reading, the exhibitions they
went to see, and the people they knew. They were both dedicated to poetry and worked hard with one another to define "the poet." The nature of
the poem and its poetics appeared throughout the intense discussions over
the period when both poets published defining books of poems—Levertov, *With Eyes at the Back of Our Heads* (1960) and Duncan, *The Opening of
the Field* (1960). At one point, Duncan disagreed with Levertov's decision
to divide a manuscript into two parts, one part published by Lawrence
Ferlinghetti as *Here and Now,* and the second part by Jonathan Williams
as *Overland to the Islands,* but that issue was set aside in favor of the larger issues of the poetics and form in poetry. Duncan's reaction to Hayden
Carruth in his article "A Critical Difference of View" (L 729–33) and then
Levertov's reaction to Duncan, however, contained forebodings of an es-

trangement in the stern positions each established. Levertov delayed writing from October 1969 to late February 1970, and in the letter of 22 February she criticized sharply Duncan's attack on Carruth. Discussions of the life of the poem gave way to personal and emotional positions about friends as well as national political issues. At the same time, the war in Vietnam became a much larger national issue. That war and then the poets' responses to the war, perhaps, were national issues too large, too overwhelming to be comprehended by either personal affection or an encompassing poetics. All the discussions of possible poetries, notes on books and people, statements of principle, the lineation of affection and the aura of admiration come together, focused or infected, determined or misshapen by the personal and political reactions to the war in Vietnam. A fracture was inevitable.

Duncan's attack on Carruth's views of William Carlos Williams's three-part line and then his later attack on Levertov's poems are both startling; they bring to the surface some of Duncan's deeply engrained political and social views, and drive them forward armed with frequent reference to a poetics. From the late 1930s onward, Duncan was against war as a solution for society's diseases. He was aware of the arguments for pacifism, as well as the frequent comparisons between Fascism and Democracy.[1] Soon after World War II, he met up with William Everson at Pond Farm, Mary and Hamilton Tyler's farm near Guerneville, California. Everson had spent time during the war at the prison camp for conscientious objectors at Waldport, Oregon. In World War II Duncan made a claim to be a conscientious objector, but that claim was rejected. He was drafted and served in the U.S. Army for three months, mainly at Fort Knox; he wrote about his experience in the poem "A Spring Memorandum: Fort Knox." His poem "An Essay at War" about the Korean War and "Up Rising" about the war in Vietnam firmly established his antiwar positions as well as the strength of his convictions. He was passionately against the policies of President Johnson and passionately against the war. The theme of war permeates his late poetry, in *Ground Work: Before the War* and *Ground Work II: In the Dark.* In other discussions, he called himself an "anarchist poet." Underneath his poetics was an understanding of anarchist thinking that he acquired in the 1940s. When the correspondence between Duncan and Levertov registered the tensions of sincere disagree-

1. See, for example, Savage, Woodcock, Comfort, and Orwell, "Pacifism and the War: A Controversy"; or Calhoun, "The Political Relevance of Conscientious Objection."

ment, Duncan mentions Vanzetti, and then calls up the embedded anarchist principles as the basis for his critique of Levertov's poems about the war. Citing the telling passages from earlier letters will make it easier to discuss the anarchist principles, which show up in the letters from October 1971:

(Letter 374, 28 July 1966)

That God's intent in Purgatory is to liberate the individual volition is a lasting concept of the good on Dante's part. Vanzetti's *voluntarism* ultimately the nature of political good lies in our imagination of how to extend this volition in a wider and deeper range of the communal good: i.e. the concord of individual volitions. (L 542)

(Letter 386, 15 February 1967)

As too in the variable meters of Williams or the free meters [when they are most meaningful, having to do with that same volition of reality that Vanzetti means in his voluntarism] we strive for, we strive for meaning in the very beat. (L 568)

(Letter 424, 25 March 1969)

An answer that was not "revolution" was Vanzetti's voluntary state. Volition cannot commit itself to a future agreement or covenant anymore than it can bind itself to the past covenants; for it must spring afresh from the message of the here and now. When I first heard the Trotskyite slogan of "Perpetual Revolution" I thought it meant this volition ever ready to spring afresh, to strike out for freedom even from the parties that carried the name on their banners. (L 629–30)

(Letter 426, 1 May 1969)

Mostly I do not advance beyond the confines of my outrage at the war. . . . And my spirit leaps up at Whitman's each man his own law; which is also Vanzetti's: the volitional politic is NOT a movement, not, I am sure, in this light, a commitment but a freedom. (L 632–33)

In his own letters between 1921 and 1927, Vanzetti became more sophisticated in his thinking as his ability to write in English improved. Discussions and assertions of human freedom and liberty permeated his letters, and in fact were the foundation of his idea of volition, the freedom to make a choice, and then the perseverance to maintain the decision. "I was prompted by my nature to an ideal of freedom and of justice to all," he writes, "and this is the worst of the crime to my enemies" (Frankfurter and Jackson 196). He also mentions Pierre-Joseph Proudhon's idea of "volunteerism": "There is but one system, one philosophy through which I can explain to myself the causes of this universal tragedy and the possible remedies, which of course, should be prompted by the human volunteerism: It is the *Philosophy of the Miseria* by Proudhon" (Frankfurter and Jackson 231). At another point he writes: "But I wholly share of your confidence in Co-operatives, and, what is more, in real co-operatives, free initiative, both individual and collective. Mutual aid and co-operation and co-operatives shall be the very base of a completely new social system, or else, nothing is accomplished" (Frankfurter and Jackson 143). Cooperation and mutual aid among workers and groups of workers are integral parts of the vision of Vanzetti that Duncan brings over into his letters to Denise Levertov. Vanzetti was a volunteer for a direction, not a conscript or a person swept up in a huge emotional reaction to a situation. He joined what course of action he chose by free will. "Anarchy, the anarchists alone" he wrote, "could break these deadly cycles" of history and dominating governments to bring on "the greatest emancipation of the history" (Frankfurter and Jackson 309). Vanzetti's crusade for freedom became, for Duncan, a model for the power of volition.

That the individual is free to act as long as his actions do not impinge on the freedom to act of other people is a basic principle of the anarchist position. As George Woodcock says in his book *Anarchy or Chaos*:

It [this book] is based on the assumption that the most desirable human good is the social and economic freedom of the individual human being, and its theme is a society in which men will have liberty and space to develop their personalities and to advance in a world where there exist no longer the bonds of poverty and coercion, towards the complete man of the visionaries. (6)

The second principle is that essential freedom means living in a society without government. Structured government is corrupt, an institution based on the greed for power to maintain itself, mainly coercing people and taking away their individual freedoms. Vanzetti wrote, "I do not believe in the government, any of them, since to me they can only differ in names from one another, and because we have witnessed the utter failure of both the social-democrat governments in Germany, and the Bolshevik government in Russia" (Frankfurter and Jackson 143). Government, along with every economic monopoly, every other coercive structure, should be done away with, and replaced with a mutually cooperating association of groups which make agreements with one another to supply the needs of people to get along in life. Rudolf Rocker begins his book *Anarcho-Syndicalism* with the following statement about the state-manipulated economic system:

> Anarchism is a definite intellectual current in the life of our times, whose adherents advocate the abolition of economic monopolies and of all political and social coercive institutions within society. In place of the present capitalistic economic order Anarchists would have a free association of all productive forces based upon co-operative labour, which would have as its sole purpose the satisfying of the necessary requirements of every member of society, and would no longer have in view the special interest of privileged minorities within the social union. (9)

These are the two principles of anarchist thought that appealed to Duncan, plus a third: the necessity to destroy present social and economic systems in order to create new kinds of organization in which the freedom and integrity of the individual will flourish. As Herbert Read states it in *Poetry and Anarchism*:

> To make life, to insure progress, to create interest and vividness, it is necessary to break form, to distort pattern, to change the nature of our civilization. In order to create it is necessary to destroy; and the agent of destruction in society is the poet. I believe that the poet is necessarily an anarchist, and that he must oppose all organized conceptions of the State, not only those which we inherit from the past, but equally those which are imposed on people in the name of the future. (15)

The principle is very close to Coleridge's definition of the secondary imagination in *Biographia Literaria*: "It dissolves, diffuses, dissipates, in order to re-create" (167). The vitality of the imagination breaks down existing ways of seeing, projecting the forms of poems, and of organizing societies, and creates new ways of seeing, projecting poetic forms and organizing societies. Emerson's essay "The Poet," and his idea of the secret intelligence of the poet, are direct sources for Duncan's thinking, as are the processes of destruction/creation inside the activities of the Romantic imagination that Herbert Read has taken over into his political thought. But the discussion comes down to the place of volition, individual choice in thought and action in the community of others also acting individually, and then to the distinction of people acting cooperatively for the common good and people acting uniformly under the coercion of a movement or a government.

Duncan's political views and how he acquired them have not been much discussed. Because his political positions break through into his poetic attacks on Carruth and Levertov, setting out the sources and growth of his political ideas will help elucidate his long and sometimes dense letters to Levertov in October and November 1971. The following sketch of his contacts with anarchist thought will make the point that the references to Vanzetti and his position about Levertov's poetry are neither random nor whimsical, but were actually life-long concerns, principles of his poetics and his politics.

II

As an undergraduate student at Berkeley, Duncan became aware of the debate between the Stalinists and the Trotskyites. Though he was politically innocent, he was nonetheless attracted to Virginia Admiral, a young woman from Chicago who took the Trotskyite position seriously, and to Pauline Kael who was politically very active long before her career as a movie critic. He also met Hamilton Tyler, a man who had fought on the side of the Republicans in the Spanish Civil War and was an anarchist, as well as Lily and Mary Fabilli. Lily left school to become a labor organizer in Carmel, but from the start held political views close to the anarchist position, and Mary achieved a position as a poet and for a time was the wife of William Everson. Duncan was a member of the Young People's Socialist League and attended its meetings. By the spring of 1937, Duncan was writing to James Peter Cooney, editor of the journal *The Phoenix*. Cooney was a follower of D. H. Lawrence and an anarchist. He had farms in western Massachusetts and Georgia, farmed with horses, grew his own food, and tried to live independently from the contemporary economy. He and his wife Blanche published the *Phoenix* as a labor of love and an ideological necessity, as well as an homage to D. H. Lawrence's views of love and life. The couple welcomed Duncan when he came to stay to recover from his adventures in New York or Provincetown at their farm near North Adams, Massachusetts. Duncan published early poems in *The Phoenix*— "The Gestation," "The Protestants (Canto One)" (1939); and "We Have Forgotten Venus" and "Persephone" (1940).[2]

2. Blanche Cooney published a book, *In My Own Sweet Time: An Autobiography*, in which she remembers her life with James Peter Cooney. Duncan was a welcome guest in the Cooneys' household.

In the fall of 1938, Duncan left Berkeley and went to Black Mountain College, where he had been admitted as a student. In 1955, just after visiting Charles Olson at Black Mountain for one night, he recalled the first visit to the college:

I had not been there since sometime in 1938 when, having written from Berkeley I received an acceptance as a student and, as I remember, a part scholarship, and, precariously, set out, arriving there late one night, only to be turned away after the following day, firmly, with the notification by the instructor who had welcomed me that I was found to be emotionally unfit. Was it after the heated argument I got into the morning of that day concerning the Spanish Civil War? In my anarchist convictions, the Madrid government seemd to me much the enemy as Franco was.[3]

Duncan lived in Philadelphia, Annapolis, New York, and finally from September to December 1939 he lived with Connie and Jeff Rall at 75 Bedford Street, in New York City. Jeff Rall was a unionist, and he kept a library of anarchist literature that was available to the young Robert Duncan. He shows up in Duncan's poem "Under Ground":

> There may be
> here at the center of a chamber cut out
>   of context
> cenotaph for Jeff Rall who
>   in youth fell
> at Dunkirk, because war was more real
>   than Blenheim's
> in the Village. . . .   (OF 80)

Unknown to Duncan at the time, Rall was not killed at Dunkirk, and at the time of the publishing of *The Opening of the Field* was living in a small town south of Vancouver, British Columbia. He worked on a barge in the inland waterway. He wrote to Duncan after seeing his name in the *Industrial Worker*. Duncan wrote to him and in fact visited him in July 1961 and again during the Vancouver Poetry Conference, August 1963. In letter 144, 16 October 1959, Duncan quotes a long passage from a letter from Rall, in which he states his position firmly: "I'm still an anarchist, and belong to a small Libertarian League. I also write regularly for the *Industrial Worker*" (L 216). Duncan was loyal to old friends, and his friendship with Jeff Rall was based entirely on the anarchist attitude. The letter from Rall, Duncan

3. Duncan, "Black Mountain College," March 1955, Robert Duncan Papers.

writes, "has brought new confidence forward in me to revive the full force of what I desired to be as a writer when anarchism was an allegiance to a reality in daily life itself" (L 217).

In New York, Duncan met up again with Virginia Admiral, his friend from Berkeley, who knew Holley Cantine and Dachine Rainer, both anarchists who wrote for journals like *Now* and *Retort*. Everyone read the *Partisan Review*, which was the central literary journal for political discussions mainly about the fights between the Stalinists and the Trotskyites, antiwar movements, unionism, and anarchist views. Dwight Macdonald was an editor and through his efforts the debate between the Stalinist view and the Trotskyite view was much discussed until about 1944 when there was a distinct shift away from the communist view because of the sense that the revolution had been, in itself, a failure that generated another rigid bureaucracy to replace the one that it overthrew. The harshness of the Moscow trials alienated humanistic sympathies, and drove the discussion back to the values of democracy as a defense against both Fascism and Communism.[4] In 1944, Macdonald left *Partisan Review* to start the magazine *Politics*, where Duncan published his famous essay "The Homosexual in Society" (1944). Duncan met Jackson MacLow at an anarchist meeting, September 1943, and that meeting began a political association between the two poets that lasted for many years.

When he went to Florida to see Laura Riding, and when he worked as a dishwasher in a restaurant in Provincetown, he wrote to Pauline Kael, who had moved from Berkeley to New York City. These letters, as well as one to Dwight Macdonald, are long and passionate, and establish the basis of Duncan's political thinking.

(Duncan to Pauline Kael, 24 June–5 July 1944)

There will be a long period this afternoon (some two or three hours) when the dishes will fall off; the cook goes to sleep; Jennie who cuts the pies, ladles out the olives and tomato-juice, will sit down to chat with the cook's boy; and I will have a thing or two to say about Read's "Cult of Leadership," Ciliga's *Russian Enigma*, and some notes after reading this English pamphlet *Trade Unionism or Syndical-*

---

4. Duncan was aware of the controversy. See Dewey, *Freedom and Culture*; Fromm, *Escape from Freedom*; Ciliga, *The Russian Enigma*; Macdonald, "The Future of Democratic Values"; Rosenberg, "Myth and History"; Calhoun, "Can Democracy Be Socialized."

ism—notes suggested more by my own reflections than by those of the pamphlet which seems rather thin.[5]

I continue to feel that anarcho syndicalism is a sound approach to a free society but I must say it is in spite of what arguments and definitions this anarchist mag *Now* brings to bear. Herbert Read's "Cult of Leadership" is the unhappy result of so much misreading, abuse of the simplest common sense and marriage of irreconcilable elements that my tongue is quite tied in knots with fury. Step by step one has to go over the devils' network, untie fury's tongue. Read's support of anarchism reads like Darwin's *Origin of the Species* might have read had he referrd to the *doctrine of the divinity of Christ* and to Thomas Aquinas for proof and definition.[6]

(Duncan to Dwight Macdonald, 28 June 1944)

Ciliga's book ought to be prescribed reading for every minority Trotskyite and leftwards. Right of that point, that is for those who are genuine Bolsheviks it would only make them mad.

The accounts of Russian-Stalinist cruelties and injustices are incredible. They don't seem to make the main issue any clearer—it is quite explicit it seems to me already in Ciliga's historical account and his own political reflections. The unbelievable numbers of people killed, exported and enslaved is just that: unbelievable. It makes the book hard to accept. Altho I always knew that in Russia man had become "society's" slave that it is actually true—and true as dismally and on the gigantic scale which Ciliga indicates is—incomprehensible.[7]

(Duncan to Pauline Kael, 10 July 1944)

I started reading the Kropotkin again and got into bed reading Kropotkin and got up in the morning walking to work reading Kropotkin—against his confusions on the nature of arts—there are such basic principles of human behavior, ethical and social understanding at last found expressed that I have been beside myself with joy. The selections from his last work *Ethics* written after he was 75 quicken my pulse and set a new wave of ideas, of projected action into motion. Wld. you find out if the following books are available—I will also write Macdonald and ask—

Ethics—Origin and Development	L. McVeagh, New York, 1924
	350 pages
Mutual Aid—A factor in Evolution	Heinemann, London, 1902, 348 pages
Fields, Factories and Workshops	Putnams, 1913, 477 pages

5. Read, "The Cult of Leadership"; Ciliga, *The Russian Enigma*; Brown, *Trade Unionism or Syndicalism*.

6. Robert Duncan and Pauline Kael, Correspondence.

7. Dwight Macdonald Archive.

There are other letters to both Pauline Kael and Dwight Macdonald. While he was living in Provincetown with Leslie Sherman, the two hitch-hiked to Macdonald's summer house on Long Island to carry on the political discussions. Duncan wanted to start a group of people to comment on Macdonald's political positions in *Politics*, and so he wrote to Holley Cantine, Hamilton Taylor, and James Peter Cooney. The group never got started. Duncan wrote to Macdonald on 15 May 1944: "I am sending you the enclosed poem not merely because I have liked these first issues of POLITICS immensely; but it is in the context of the judgment that POLITICS presupposes that I feel the poem can most fairly appear." Macdonald did not accept the poem, but he did accept and print the essay "The Homosexual in Society."

Duncan's essay is only partially a statement about his homosexuality. In the preface to the essay, written fifteen years after its first publication, Duncan wrote:

My view was that minority associations and identifications were an evil wherever they supersede allegiance to and share in the creation of a human community good—the recognition of fellow-manhood. . . . I was trying to rid myself of one persona in order to give birth to another, and at the same time to communicate the process and relate it to what I called "society," a public responsibility. (SP 38–9)

A person has the personal freedom, the volition of free will, to make choices and to live by those choices as long as the choices do not prevent another person from making choices. The freedom of the individual to act on his own is the paramount assumption in the essay. Then the choices destroy one way of seeing and acting as they create other ways, thus asserting the same process of destruction/creation enjoyed by artists and poets as an activating motive for the individual. Social pressures are as oppressive to individual freedom as governmental regulations, so the freed individual must struggle to establish and maintain the position against great pressures. Duncan also wrote against the homosexual cult, specifically the group led by Parker Tyler and Charles Henri Ford and based in the offices of *View*, a magazine published in New York that advocated the interrelationships between poetry and the arts as an advocate for avant-garde movements. The cult of the homosexual was a cause, a group with a passionate involvement in its own idea, not a political movement, but a segregating organization that isolated the individual from society, and finally denied the individual freedom in the passion of the group. Duncan was always against the coercion of group action, or a movement with a cause, as fiercely as he was an advocate for individual volition and cooperative groups.

At the conclusion of the essay Duncan asserts his "devotion to human freedom, toward the liberation of human love, human conflicts, human aspirations," which is also an assertion of a basic anarchist position. In his "Reflections 1959" he quotes from the same letter by Jeff Rall that he quotes in the letter to Levertov, as if to confirm Rall's devotion to human freedom and his own to Rall and the anarchist views which informed their friendship. He continues:

To do this one must disown *all* the special groups (nations, churches, sexes, races) that would claim allegiance. To hold this devotion every written word, every spoken word, every action, every purpose must be examined and considered. The old fears, the old specialties will be there, mocking and tempting; the old protective associations will be there, offering for a surrender of one's humanity congratulation upon one's special nature and value. It must be always recognized that the others, those who have surrendered their humanity, are not less than oneself. It must be always remembered that one's own honesty, one's battle against the inhumanity of his own group (be it against patriotism, against bigotry, against—in this special case—the homosexual cult) is a battle that cannot be won in the immediate scene. The forces of inhumanity are overwhelming, but only one's continued opposition can make any other order possible, will give an added strength for all those who desire freedom and equality to break at last those fetters that seem now so unbreakable. (SP 47–48)

To assert the integrity of his position, the homosexual should renounce allegiances to any groups that threaten his individuality and assume the responsibility for his own volition; he should live openly in society.

When Duncan returned to the West in 1945, he lived with Hamilton and Mary Tyler in Guerneville, California, on their chicken farm. He went from the Cooneys' to the Tylers', both farms of old friends with anarchist views. Duncan wrote to Pauline Kael on 10 July 1944:

In the same mail I received a copy of the Kropotkin selections which I orderd from *politics*; Leslie orderd the Ciliga book. Macdonald says that the Ciliga is running out—there are very few copies left. I am going to order one for Ham Tyler. It is, I think I have stressd before, a book we all been waiting patiently for; Russia seen by a man who combines an honesty and integrity governd by a thorough political understanding. Compare the man's tone with Trotsky's.

Hamilton Tyler influenced Duncan's thinking about politics and a lifestyle which supported an anarchist position, so there is a strong allegiance that brought Duncan to Tyler's farm in 1945. In Berkeley and then San Francisco there were anarchist groups, the most famous of which was the Friday-evening discussions at Kenneth Rexroth's house. George Leite's literary magazine in Berkeley, *Circle*, had an anarchist focus. In its first issue the San Francisco journal *Ark* (1947) featured George Woodcock's essay "What Is Anarchism" and Duncan's article "Reviewing *View*: An Attack." Duncan published the first version of his poem "Often I Am Permitted to Return to a Meadow" in the second issue of *Ark II/Moby I*. Of all these goings-on, Rexroth's evening discussions kept Duncan in touch with current anarchist thinking.

As an anarchist, Duncan believed in the authority of the individual to act with and make decisions freely without compromising individuality. He also believed in mutual aid, cooperation among people and groups of people. As a poet he believed also in the company of poets working together as a contemporary group for a common cause—Creeley, Duncan, Olson, Levertov, and projective forms, for example—and he believed in a company of poets in a tradition as Ezra Pound had found in his book *The Spirit of Romance*. In Pound's and in Duncan's views the volition of the individual, as poet and anarchist, is fulfilled when an imaginative activity of one poet cooperates or corresponds with the equally valid imaginative activity of another poet. Duncan has multiple views here that he calls "pluralism." The enemy to equal imaginative actions is uniformity, a mass reaction caused by coercion, and the loss, therefore, of individual will.

III

Duncan's letters to Denise Levertov now have a context for discussion. However, one other point needs to be put in place. Levertov wrote a short note to Duncan on 29 October 1969, and then waited until 22 February 1970 to write again about Duncan's article "A Critical Difference of View." She sent a short note dated 4 April 1970 in reply to Duncan's response, spent the summer in Europe, and then wrote again on 26 October 1970. So by the time Duncan wrote the first letter critical of her poetry, Levertov had not written a substantial letter to Duncan since 22 February

1970. After the attack on Carruth, her own concerns of family, her own health, the reaction to the war, and her own poetry have supplanted the urgency of the correspondence with Duncan.

Duncan begins his letter of 16 October with a reference to Yeats's *Autobiographies*—"All creation is from conflict" (L 663)—as a way of casting the present conflict into an abstracted system of the interaction of contraries, as he had done in his essay "Man's Fulfillment in Order and Strife," and as he had done in his letters of disagreement with Robin Blaser over the Nerval translations. He moves immediately to the image of Levertov as Kali dancing in her red skirt, which appeared in the poem "Santa Cruz Propositions," and then makes the point that she was "possessed by the demonic spirit of the mass" (L 663). Herbert Read makes the point in his essay "Cult of Leadership" that joining a party (in this case the Nazi Party) relinquished the freedom of the individual and made the joiner a part of the mass movement of passion, individuality abandoned. Duncan made a similar point in "The Homosexual in Society" about joining a homosexual cult. In the subsequent letter to Levertov, Duncan again maintains that because she has given up her individuality to the cause, she has betrayed the position of the artist; she accepts the mass position, the passionate appeal, and no longer imagines or projects the very nature of the work, the evil, she is protesting—"The urgency that demands the poet to reveal what is back of the political slogans and persuasions" (L 666). And while both poets would agree that the powerful greed of the government was causing terrible tribulation, death, and slaughter on the people of Vietnam, Duncan would maintain that in joining the movement Levertov was helping to create another bureaucracy strong enough to confront the present government; that the direct result would not be the destruction of one form of government and economic system but the replacement of it with the same kind of government and economic system. This was the same argument that Vanzetti used, and that Dwight Macdonald also used in his *Partisan Review* article "War and the Intellectuals," in denouncing the October Revolution in Russia for installing a despotic, coercive government to replace the one it destroyed. That was the point Duncan had made earlier in countering Levertov's involvement with the People's Park movement in Berkeley. By joining the cause she joined an organization that was as corrupt and coercive as the one she thought she was protesting. She had misunderstood the multiple uses of power; and he accuses her of the "failure to project anywhere the force of Revolution, or Rebellion" (L 664).

She is left then with "empty and vain slogans because those who use them are destitute of any imagination of or feeling of what such greed, racism or imperialism is like. The poet's role is not to oppose evil, but to imagine it" (L 669). Duncan made the same point in recounting an anarchist meeting when he spoke out for the freedom of the individual to act: "To imagine what the good is and to imagine what evil is, what goods there are and what evils: this is releasing to our powers, it helps us prepare for actual works—and we're often mistaken in our imaginations" (L 275). In Levertov's case, moralizing and commentary interrupt the process of destruction/creation, and "the poems have been removed from the field they belong to poetically" (L 664), and "form as the direct vehicle and medium of content" (L 668) has been negated. The failure of the creative process and the failure of the imagination then lead to the failure of language, as the poet is outside the poems commenting on them, not inside the imagination of the poem projecting form in active language outward. By joining the movement and taking up the language of the movement, Duncan says, Levertov gave up her individual volition—the ability, then, to imagine evil—and took herself out of the actual process of destruction leading to creation. She was lost in a search for an authority to counter the governmental authority without destroying it. And finally, she betrayed the role of the artist. She exposes not the revelation of content, but "a moralizing reproof" (L 667) of the American government.

He is especially harsh in his statements about her involvement with the People's Park movement in Berkeley, which he understands—without having been there, Levertov notes—as one group of coerced people struggling against another group of coerced people without the assertion of any individual freedom. "I find that I am outraged not only by the hypocrites and self-deluded, but by the innocent. Those who think they can *merely* make a green place as a claim on University property. Well, yes. Their ignorance *is* outrageous. It requires so much willing refusal of facts" (L 673). Duncan's judgment is harsh, but it rests on actual anarchist principles.

He concludes that his views are not ideological, but rather are based on the readings he did in anarchist literature from 1939 onward; however, he has reshaped his views in this discussion of a "pluralism" into a literary argument that insists upon the imaginative integrity of the poem and the view of the artist as the projector of literary form. "Within the plurality of forces the Heraclitean opposites have the drama and pathos of a heightened figure upon a ground in which a multitude of figures appear" (L 674). Duncan had read the discussions about the role of the poet in political events, among them Herbert Read's:

When an artist, a poet or a philosopher—the kind of person we often describe as an intellectual—ventures to take part in the political controversies of his own time, he always does so at a certain risk. . . . He is a creature of intuitions and sympathies, and by his very nature shrinks from definiteness and doctrinaire attitudes. . . . Disenfranchised by his lack of residence in any fixed constituency, wandering faithlessly in the no-man's-land of his imagination, the poet cannot, without renouncing his essential function, come to rest in the bleak conventicles of a political party. It is not his pride that keeps him outside; it is really his humility, his devotion to the complex wholeness of humanity—in the precise sense of the word, his magnanimity. (*Poetry* 41, 42)

The contradiction remains, however, that this "devotion to the complex wholeness of humanity" could undermine and fracture the attunement between two poets. Even though they called a truce period of a "year-and-a-day" (L 707)—the length of time, that is, that Duncan would delay writing an essay on her poems—neither poet was able to compromise enough to heal the estrangement. They made attempts in unmailed letters; then Levertov read Duncan's comments in James Mersmann's book *Out of the Vietnam Vortex*, in which Duncan was highly critical of her positions on the war. She wrote back: "I felt our friendship twice broken, deeply betrayed" (L 711). By the time Duncan changed his position and wished for reconciliation, after he had read new poems by Levertov, Levertov wrote: "The sad thing is that your letter came *at least* 2 years too late. I don't find it in me to respond with the warmth & gladness you expected. There can be a statute of limitations on emotional commitments" (L 717).

Duncan remained as firmly committed to his belief in the authority of individual volitional acts to create an imaginative company as Levertov did in her powerful feelings against the war in Vietnam. Personalities, affections, and loyalties of the spirit can be negated in such intense confrontations, as indeed they were in the case of these two poets.

Works Cited

Brown, Tom. *Trade Unionism or Syndicalism*. London: Freedom Press, 1942.

Calhoun, Arthur W. "Can Democracy Be Socialized." *Retort* 3.1 (Fall 1945): 24–27.

Calhoun, Don. "The Political Relevance of Conscientious Objection." *Politics* 1.6 (July 1944): 177–79.

Ciliga, Ante (Anton). *The Russian Enigma*. Trans. Ferenand G. Renier and Anne Cliff. London: Routledge, 1940.

Coleridge, Samuel Taylor. *Biographia Literaria*. Ed. and intro. George Watson. London: Dent, 1962.

Cooney, Blanche. *In My Own Sweet Time: An Autobiography*. Chicago and Athens: Swallow Press and Ohio University Press, 1993.

Dewey, John. *Freedom and Culture*. New York: Putnam's, 1939.

Duncan, Robert. Papers. Poetry Collection, State University of New York, Buffalo.

Duncan, Robert, and Pauline Kael. Correspondence. Bancroft Library, University of California, Berkeley.

Emerson, Ralph Waldo. "The Poet." In *Emerson's Essays*, intro. Irwin Edman. New York: Crowell, 1951, 261–91.

Frankfurter, Marin Denman, and Gardner Jackson, eds. *The Letters of Sacco and Vanzetti*. Intro. Richard Polenberg. Harmondsworth, UK: Penguin, 1997.

Fromm, Eric H. *Escape from Freedom*. New York: Holt, 1941.

Macdonald, Dwight. Dwight Macdonald Archive. Sterling Library, Yale University.

———. "The Future of Democratic Values." *Partisan Review* 10.4 (July–August 1943): 321–42.

———. "War and the Intellectuals: Act Two." *Partisan Review*. 6.3 (Spring 1939): 3–20.

Nietzsche, Friedrich. *Thus Spake Zarathustra*. Trans. Thomas Common. Mineola, NY: Dover, 1999.

Pound, Ezra. *The Spirit of Romance*. London: Dent, 1910.

Read, Herbert. "The Cult of Leadership." *Now* 1 (1943): 9–19.

———. *Poetry and Anarchism*. London: Faber and Faber, 1938.

Rocker, Rudolf. *Anarcho-Syndicalism*. Pref. Noam Chomsky. Intro. Nicolas Walter. 1938. Reprint, London: Pluto, 1989.

Rosenberg, Harold. "Myth and History." *Partisan Review* 6.2 (Winter 1939): 19–25.

Savage, D. S., George Woodcock, Alex Comfort, and George Orwell. "Pacifism and the War: A Controversy." *Partisan Review* 9.5 (September–October 1942): 414–21.

Trotsky, Leon. "Art and Politics." *Partisan Review* 5.3 (August–September 1938): 4–10.

Woodcock, George. *Anarchy or Chaos*. London: Freedom, 1944.

Wreszin, Michael. *A Rebel in Defense of Tradition: The Life and Politics of Dwight Macdonald*. New York: Basic, 1994.

———, ed. and intro. *A Moral Temper: The Letters of Dwight Macdonald*. Chicago: Dee, 2001.

Yeats, W. B. *Autobiographies*. London: Macmillan, 1955.

Robert Duncan and the Question of Law: Ernst Kantorowicz and the Poet's Two Bodies

Graça Capinha

When we approach Robert Duncan's writing, the unavoidable first conclusion seems to be that it presents a challenge. His work unfolds as a challenge to different kinds of power but, prior to anything else, it becomes a challenge to our own power over the world's categories and orders, and over our consciousness of language and of self. Robert Duncan's poetry is, according to his own view, an experience in language—a live and organic experience of words and senses, of their infinite and complex associations of forms, a live and organic experience of their infinite and complex associations of bodies. In "Notes on Poetics Regarding Olson's *Maximus*," Duncan claims:

Metrics, as it coheres, is actual—the sense of language in terms of weights and durations (by which we cohere in moving). This is a dance in whose measured steps time emerges, as space emerges from the dance of the body. The ear is intimate to muscular equilibrium. . . . But, if the muscular realization of language is the latest mode of poetry, the beginning point was muscular too, localized in the discharge of energy expressed in the gaining, first, breath, and then, tongue. The gift of spirit and of tongues. (FC 70, 72)

Duncan's poetry is an experience in the order of bodies and/or forms, but, simultaneously and paradoxically, it challenges that order constantly.

The first questions that arose when I first started reading Robert Duncan seriously are unchanged ten years later—and they are methodological questions. How does one deal with a poetics that is looking for absolute freedom and possibility, an asystematic/nonclosed vision of reality, a discontinuous, fragmented, incomplete, and decentered model of language—a poetics that is trying to give voice(s) to a discontinuous, fragmented, incomplete, and decentered model of subject—and still argue for a wholeness of organic form, "a gift of spirit and of tongues," "a coherence in our moving"?

How does one deal with all this, when analytical tools and literary models still demand causality, sequentiality, continuity, totalizing conclusions, and closed scientific narratives? Within the dominant scientific/rationalistic paradigm, literary studies and the humanities, in general, have always occupied a subaltern (both subordinate and marginal) position in the hierarchy of the discourses of knowledge for lack of all these "qualities." Even today, when the other sciences seem to have *discovered* the humanities and "the question of narrative," they (sciences within the dominant scientific/rationalistic paradigm) still describe that field of knowledge, patronizingly, as lacking that kind of order in discourse that would make our knowledge "respectable." Things are changing and we are all aware that a paradigmatic transition is happening (Bachelard; Santos). But it will take a long time to develop "acceptable" models of language and of subject that will include discontinuity, fragmentation, incompleteness, and decentering—and still be able to provide meaning and knowledge (Deleuze and Guattari; Bernstein; Lecercle). Our methodological approach to Duncan's work is therefore a challenge: our methodological models must change, and literary scholars must adapt and change too, and so be transformed with (in) the research process itself.

Robert Duncan saw the contemporary discussion about the transition of paradigms of thought and the emergence of a second epistemological break as a process initiated at the fin de siècle and the first part of the twentieth century, something that was at the root of the Modernist project itself. In "Rites of Participation," Duncan wrote:

The dissolving of boundaries of time, as in H.D.'s *Palimpsest*, so that Egyptian or Hellenistic ways invade the contemporary scene—the reorganization of identity to extend the burden of consciousness—this change of mind has been at work in many fields. The thought of primitives, dreamers, or the mad—once excluded by the provincial claims of common sense from the domain of the meaningful or significant—has been reclaimed by the comparative psychologies of William James, Freud, Lévy-Bruhl, by the comparative linguistics of Sapir or Whorf, brought into the community of a new epistemology. (SP 98)

Creative scientists, for instance Lévy-Leblond, are still struggling today to bring science back to history and society, back to culture and its discourse density. Creative scientists are still fighting for this new epistemology that the Modernist project envisioned. Duncan claimed that his work was within this very same project, refusing the dominant hegemonic paradigm as the unique and sole paradigm to expand (or "extend") his consciousness and his poetry. He said in "The Truth and Life of Myth," however, that "where Philosophy raised a dialectic, a debate, toward what it calls Truth; Poetry raised a theater, a drama of Truth" (FC 4). His is a world of representation that deals with "fictive certainties." In working with these representations, there is always the risk of discovery, since "Writing preserves in itself the first version" (FC 37). The problematics of language and representation dominate the philosophical debate.

Robert Duncan's poetry could easily be defined as epistemological research, experimental work (the search for an unlimited experience in words) toward possible paradigms of language and of knowledge. Yet Duncan's poetry is never a problematics of "either/or," but always, in a very postmodern and Kierkegaardean way, of "both/and." He works toward a language capable of dealing with complexity and with multiple and superimposed layers of meaning—the Blakean struggle of contraries. He includes causality, sequentiality, closure—along with the impossible totalization of both the object and the subject that are, of course, interchangeable realities.

The poet used the *jigsaw puzzle* and the *mobile* as metaphors to define his project of the *grand collage*. He saw his poetry as an act of participation in a major *grand collage* of all the possible wisdoms, of all the possible knowledges within languages, within societies, within galaxies, within the universe—in motion. This is the all-inclusive and infinite Whole in motion—expanding—that he called "the Law" (with a capital *L*). His poems, as mobiles, are images that result from random association within the mobile that the whole of his work is, within other mobiles, and so on, ad infinitum, as if in a fractal system. His *grand collage* moves among the infinite possibilities opened by the philosophical processes. In the essay "Changing Perspectives in Reading Whitman," and while relating his writing to Whitman's and Dante's, Duncan gives one of the many definitions of the Law, showing how individual action is individual power, and, simultaneously, obedience to the action of the whole: "Law is hidden in us, for it—our share of the Law—is what we must create as we create our selves. To be individual is to recognize one's nature, or the Nature in one, to be conscious and conscientious in thought and action" (FC 172). This concept of Law—"one's nature" and "the Nature in one"—is at the origin of medieval jurisprudence and it is a concept related to the Christological legal figure of "the king's two bodies" (the Body natural and the Body politic/mystic), studied by Ernst Kantorowicz. This historian was Duncan's professor of renaissance and medieval studies, from 1948, when Duncan came back to study at the University of California, Berkeley, to 1951, when Kantorowicz was dismissed from the University of California for refusing to sign a loyalty oath. In an interview, Duncan told Ekbert Faas:

Robin Blaser, Jack Spicer, and I, as poets, are all variously students of Kantorowicz and share through his teaching the sense of creative ground in history that is also in poetry. The concept that to form is to transform, is a magic then, and that metaphor is not a literary device but an actual meaning arising from, operating in, and leading us to realize the co-inherence of being, that we perceive forms because there are correspondences. (Faas 281)

The relation to history is fundamental. In "The Truth and Life of Myth," Duncan defined history as "a poetry of events" (FC 38), and the above-mentioned "creative ground in history" can only mean the community itself: the creators/makers of events, of history, and of language, the parts of the whole in motion—transforming and being transformed, in a social process perceived by the poet as a ritualistic process (and thus religious) that is, in its nature, both individual and collective. *Poiesis* therefore is understood in its etymological sense—to make. Metaphor combines form and meaning at an ontological level: a "meaning arising," leading to "the co-inherence of being." In what magic, ritual, the sense of the sacred are concerned—these were at the origin of medieval jurisprudence, as Kantorowicz shows in *The King's Two Bodies: A Study in Medieval Politi-*

cal Theology, a work first published in 1957. In Roman law, there was no distinction in jurisprudence between the knowledge of things divine and the knowledge of things human. In the Middle Ages, long before the seventeenth-century epistemological break between the two cultures and the two discourses (science vs. art and the humanities), jurisprudence was defined not only as a science but also as an art—and art was, for the jurists, "Imitation of Nature": "Of this art, said Ulpian, we jurists may be called the priests, 'for we worship Justice' (*Iustitiam namque colimus*), to which a late gloss added explainingly: *ut Deam*, 'as a goddess'" (Kantorowicz 139).

In the Middle Ages, the worshipping of Justice was therefore the worshipping of a goddess who was, simultaneously, nature, art, and knowledge/science. In an interview with Faas, Duncan said something very similar to Ulpian's words: "We are not poets . . . other than by occupying the office of poet. And that office is a holy office. We are in a holy office when we sit in front of a piece of paper" (Faas 273).

Poets, then, like jurists, are priests, and their holy office is to worship poetry/art, a goddess, divine and human, natural and politic. Furthermore, according to Kantorowicz's study, the medieval juridical concept of the king's duplication (Body natural and Body politic) was connected to theology, and mirrored the duplication of natures in Christ (Kantorowicz 58). Kantorowicz provides an illustrative excerpt from a medieval document:

> . . . that by the Common Law no Act which the King does as King, shall be defeated by his Nonage. For the King has in him two Bodies, *viz.*, a Body natural, and a Body politic. His Body natural (if he be considered in itself) is a Body mortal, subject to all Infirmities that come by Nature or Accident, to the Imbecility of Infancy or old Age, and to the like Defects that happen to the natural Bodies of other People. But his Body politic is a Body that cannot be seen or handled, consisting of Policy and Government, and constituted for the Direction of the People, and the Management of the public weal, and this Body is utterly void of Infancy, and old Age, and other natural Defects and Imbecilities, which the Body natural is subject to, and for this Cause, what the King does in his Body politic, cannot be invalidated or frustrated by any Disability in his natural Body. (Kantorowicz 7)

The Body natural (physical) manifests a mere representation/form of the true Body—which is the power, that is, the political and mystical Body. The natural body gives nothing but a testimony of this presence, and is one with this presence. Duncan's model of language begins here: words seen as forms and as bodies, which are representations/metaphors of "the Word"—a power that is not visible, a Body politic both social and historical. In Duncan, however—as in Durkheim (1912)—the social is religious: the process of social construction is ritualistic, and thus sacred in that it means the survival of the community. In Duncan, the sacred/mystical and political power of the Word are manifested in words (the present forms of language) and in the poet (the present form of man). The poet cannot be separated from the word of the poem, the same way that, according to Kantorowicz, the king cannot be separated from the word of the law. Through historical research, Kantorowicz finds the origin of this fiction—just like Duncan, through the archeology of the mythopoeic (words, forms, myths)—in medieval religiosity and in the duplication of natures in the figure of Christ, both God and man. Both theological and ontological powers are in the nature of the model of language.

Kantorowicz argues that in the secularization process, especially during the Elizabethan period, between the sixteenth and the seventeenth centuries—but already at the beginning of the Renaissance and of humanism—the sacred idea of the mystical/political body of the king (the Law) was gradually displaced by the abstraction of the State and by the empty concept—a fiction—that was *dignitas*. The Christological model of the king's two bodies becomes only a form with another form inside, a representation (the Body natural) of power (the Body politic) that has lost its real substance (mystical/divine); from now on, the Body politic is nothing but another representation: a law without Law. Man is at the center of a concept of monarchy—but this man, claims Kantorowicz, has become an instrument of man's own fictions/myths. *Dignitas* is unreal, a fictional form emptied of substance. *Dignitas* comes not from within but from without (Kantorowicz 445). According to Duncan (but also Dante and Shakespeare), law becomes a form without the true content of the Law (divine Body: the Spirit, Love). In this sense, the secularization process meant the loss of our humanity. Human action becomes separated from the sacred action of the Whole in expansion ("in via," Augustine said [Augustine 2.8.22]). There is no process in the concept of *dignitas*, no possibility of human transcendence, except material transcendence.

In "The Sweetness and Greatness of Dante's *Divine Comedy*," Duncan calls Dante "the first of modern poets" (FC 149), precisely because he does not separate the Real from Love (one single body of creation in creation—*Poiesis, Logos*, Law). According to Duncan, the sweetness of the language in Dante comes from the supreme beauty that Dante knew to be the order of all the orders in the universe—Love/Law. The Law includes all the laws, but these are nothing except errors (and the Law includes everything, even error) if they remain only human, without any relation to the Law of nature and of the universe. To forget that "beauty is the property of Heaven" is the origin of all evil in Dante's *Divine Comedy*, says Duncan (FC 156). This is the error, argues Kantorowicz, that Dante was denouncing in his political treatise *Monarchia*. The most interesting idea in Dante—but also in Shakespeare, when rationalism was emerging—is the prophetical dissidence in the position taken by the poet, exactly at the time when the humanistic and secular paradigm was emerging in the laws that would give form to the new social and political order of the Renaissance and of modernity.

Dante was interested in a monarchy free from the pope's jurisdiction. In his *Monarchia*, he defends the monarchy truly centered in the human: *Homo instrumentum humanitatis* (Kantorowicz 451). His Universal Emperor possessed an intellect independent from the soul, but he could not accept the new humanistic appropriation of the intellect by the State, while the care of the soul was appropriated by the Church. Dante separates humanism from Christianity, isolating the "human" as a value in its own right (intellect and soul)—perhaps Dante's most original accomplishment in the field of political theology, says Kantorowicz (465).

It remained to the poet to establish an image of kingship which was merely human and of which MAN, pure and simple, was the center and standard—MAN, to be sure, in all his relations to God and universe, to law, society, and city, to nature, knowledge and faith. *Homo instrumentum humanitatis*—this twist of the theological-legal maxim might well serve as a motto for penetrating into Dante's moral-political views, provided that the opalescent notion of *humanitas* be perceived in all its numerous hues. (Kantorowicz 451)

Robert Duncan focused on these "hues" in a totally inclusive poetics marked by the diversity of humanity—Adam as "a whole body of man" (Kantorowicz 467). Like Dante, Duncan was at the center of the philosophical and intellectual debate of his time, but it is the intimate relation between their political and philosophical views and the models of language that both poets will develop that distinguishes their thought. "A whole body of man" can only find expression in the numerous hues that writing configures. Hence writing is complex, where fragments and opposites are in permanent tension with narrative; where diverse discourses of knowledge give form to a diversified mosaic (or mobile), trying to reflect the infinite heterogeneity of human experience; and where responsibility and authenticity are demanded from the individual.

The emancipatory nature of these poetics relates unquestionably to a model of language that can only be defined as action. The transformation/expansion of consciousness and of knowledge can only be achieved through the transformation/expansion of language—and the transformation of language interferes with our consciousness of the world and of ourselves. The relation between poetic action and political action, the Augustinian *Logos* as the Law, the need to go back to the root of poetry—*poiesis*, "to make"—to participate in the community of the human that each word carries inside (the part in the whole and the whole in the part constitute another example of Body natural and Body politic/mystic in an inclusive unity, inter-acting). In Dante's words:

Now since our present subject is political, indeed is the source and starting point of just forms of government, and everything in the political sphere comes under human control, it is clear that the present subject is not directed primarily towards theoretical understanding but towards action. Again, since in actions it is the final objective which sets in motion and causes everything—for that is what first moves a person who acts—it follows that the whole basis of the means for attaining an end is derived from the end itself. . . . for it would be foolish to suppose that there is one purpose for this society and another for that, and not a common purpose for all of them. (Dante 5)

The Law is the action in all action—the whole possibility for any action: Augustine's "via," Aquinas's "the mover," and Dante's Love/Real. For Duncan, this action is "our share of the Law—what we must create as we create our selves" (FC 172). This action is the acknowledgment of the cosmos as an open field within which all the possible fields are generated. "Composition by field is the concept of the cosmos as a field of fields," he says, in "Changing Perspectives in Reading Whitman" (FC 168). This field of fields empowers language and the Body mystic/politic empowers the natural body of the poem and the poet.

Nearly three centuries after Dante, Shakespeare creates another example of dissidence in the emerging paradigm of (this time) rationalistic thought, argues Kantorowicz in *The King's Two Bodies*. *Richard II* tells the tragic story of the king's loss of his political body, which was, at that time, nothing but the fiction of *dignitas*. At the end of the tragedy, Richard II remains nothing but a man—without the power of *dignitas*, naked, his image fragmented in a broken mirror. His human frailty, however, finally unveils to him his true Nature, the nature of any man, "the Nature in us" (FC 172), the sacred Law of his mere existence.

In this play, God, the King, and the Fool become one in the virtual space of the mirror. Only when it is broken will this mirror let the pure being free, without any reflection, true human nature finally liberated. This metaphor of the broken becomes very useful for comprehending Robert Duncan's poetry. It must be broken as a metaphor in order to break the illusion that the representation creates for us. There is only the visible form, the Body natural. If the mirror/language is broken, reality is finally unveiled, and within the breakage, beginnings, ends, and totalized whole reveal themselves. To break the mirror, to break language, is an emancipatory action. In the lack of limits, in the multiplication and proliferation of fragments, the possibility emerges for the true diversity of "hues" in human nature. In Shakespeare's play, losing *dignitas* also means losing the Name. After being deconsecrated, Richard II has no Name. He has lost the shield that protected him from his human frailty, madness, and suffering. Knowing that he is going to die, Richard II finds his ultimate identity in the dignity of being a man. "Over against his lost outward kingship he sets an inner kingship, makes his true kingship to retire to inner man," argues Kantorowicz (37). The meeting with his mortal Body natural is simultaneously the meeting with the Body of the true Law, with the sacred principle of eternity (creation) inside his physicality.

Robert Duncan refers to Dante and Shakespeare, in "The Sweetness and Greatness of Dante's *Divine Comedy*," as "two suns in our poetic world" (FC 142). Like his "two suns," Duncan is trying to recuperate the consciousness of the sacred/mystical Body for the Body natural that language and poetry—but also himself, the poet—are. He knows that there is no power without a form, a representation. But to be a representation of a representation, the form of nothing but a fiction, is for Duncan—as well as for Dante and Shakespeare, and also for Kantorowicz—the ultimate error on which Western civilization and language stand. Duncan argues: "To be individual is to recognize one's nature, or the Nature in one, to be conscious and conscientious in thought and action" (FC 172). Reporting on an anonymous Norman pamphlet writer from the twelfth century, Kantorowicz said about this action:

> In short, the . . . vision of the king as a *personae geminata* is ontological and, as an effluence of a sacramental and liturgical action performed at the altar, it is liturgical as well. His vision is, on the whole, more closely related to the liturgy, to *the holy action which itself is image and reality* at the same time than to the distinction of functional capacities and constitutional competencies, or to the concepts of office and dignity as opposed to man. (Kantorowicz 59; my emphasis)

This statement defines the ontological and liturgical vision of political and poetic action in Robert Duncan, so an action is simultaneously "image and reality," that is, Body natural and Body politic. Bearing this liturgical definition in mind, Duncan will always be in search of a true humanism, a humanistic paradigm that will ultimately be antihumanistic, against the kind of empty humanism that became our dominant, rationalistic paradigm of thought and of language. And this is why his poetics and his poetry search and demand a second epistemological break (humanism/ rationalism being the first epistemological break at the core of our idea of "modernity"), a break that will reunite two forms of discourse and two rationalities that have long been separated. As Kantorowicz shows, reason and imagination, science and art, two forms of discourse and two rationalities, were united at the core of a divinely human jurisprudence from which our present (even if adulterated) legal system was born. Through scientists like the Portuguese neurobiologist António Damásio, Descartes has been corrected because there is no possibility of rationalization (of reason, of consciousness, and of language) without emotion (Damásio 2000). Finally, for Duncan the "creative scientists" are speaking of "emotional intelligence" and of imagination as the inevitable tool for the creation of knowledge (FC 6).

Robert Duncan has a holistic view of poetics, a philosophical, religious, scientific, and political perspective on art and poetry. Ulpian's ideas, as they appear in Kantorowicz's books, could be defined as a postmodern view, but his is simultaneously a very archaic vision and consciousness of the human condition. The artist/poet must—as a man of Law—know things divine and human, but he must be a scientist, observing—to imitate/integrate—Nature; and he must be a priest, in office, worshipping Justice as a goddess.

The ultimate definition of the Law in Duncan is the Goddess, always present in his writing, in metaphors such as "the Lady," "the Queen Under the Hill" (OF 7), the "Mother" (OF 25): poetry as the Augustinian *Logos*, the Law to which the poet must, to use both Duncan's and Aquinas's vocabulary, "bear testimony" to the Goddess. In the poem "The Law I Love Is Major Mover," Duncan defines the poet's relation to this Lady/Word: "for She is fair, whom we, masters, serve" (OF 10). The poet, like the king, in his *persona geminata* (in the oneness of his two bodies) obeys the Word (Goddess/Law/*Logos*/Love) that form(ulate)s him but, paradoxically and simultaneously, he commands that Word: he gives It a form. Like a shaman, in a co-primordial process, the poet/king thus traces his *passage* (his "eyes"/"I's") through the time/space (field) where all times/spaces (fields) exist:

> The shaman sends himself
> The universe is filld with eyes then, intensities,
>   with intent,
>   outflowings of good or evil,
>   benemaledictions of the dead,
>
>   but
> the witness brings self up before the Law.
> It is the Law before the witness that
>   makes Justice. (OF 10)

Ernst Kantorowicz speaks of "a king-making Law and a law-making King" (Kantorowicz 155). In Duncan's poetics, this medieval conception of power becomes a poet-making Poetry/Word and a poetry/word-making Poet. In Duncan, the poem/poet is the Body natural manifesting the Word/Body politic. The poem/poet is an instrument and a function. His "major mover" clearly echoes Aquinas: "insofar as the soul is the mover of the body, the body serves the soul as instrument" (Aquinas 3.9.8, a.2).

Kantorowicz traces the historical path from these archaic forms to the seventeenth century. From this time onward there is "a law without a

Law," which means that the community has no consciousness of the true power, of the power that is within the whole of creation (the *Logos*, for "In the beginning was the Word," says John's Gospel).

The bricolage process deep in Duncan's agonistic poetics—the most representative text of which is "The Truth and Life of Myth" (FC 1–59)—is anchored in these concepts of Law and Power. These are the Christological and liturgical foundations of the legal system in our Judeo-Christian civilization. While trying to understand the formation of European political theology during the Middle Ages, Kantorowicz is also opening the path for understanding how the new secular juridical forms emerge from this political theology (how did we move from the Law to the law). His conclusions are very pertinent to Robert Duncan's own quest of the sacred. Duncan, as well as Dante, wanted to understand how, in this historical juridical process, our nature was not sacred, that is, but was also part of a Whole, part of an eternal act of creation that is infinitely "opening the field," expanding in possibility, and liberating form (of the universe, of words, and of ourselves). Humanity forgot both individual power and responsibility to participate in the action, or in the creative movement of energy—in the community, in history, in politics, in our own consciousness. Individual power and responsibility to respond to the Word disappeared. In "The Law I Love Is Major Mover," Duncan calls it "Syntax," and he will make a statement in this poem that will be repeated in numerous moments of his work: "Responsibility is to keep / the ability to respond" (OF 11, 10).

Humanity is asleep, seeing neither the true body, nor the true body of language. And the whole of his work will reflect on this question. The Body natural / the Flesh of language is nothing but a form given to the Law—given to energy, to spirit, to truth, to power—whatever you want to call "It" (which is another of Duncan's metaphors, and the title of one of the sections of the preface to *Bending the Bow* [BB vi–viii]). He discusses the two bodies of the poet and the two bodies of language—with Augustine and Aquinas, Ulpian and Plowden, Dante and Shakespeare—but also with the latest scientific discourses in mind, with quantics, contingency, indeterminacy, relativity, chaos, genetics, and psychoanalysis. In any case, he is aiming at composing a *grand collage* that will be eminently emancipatory, in search of a *passage* to alternative models of language, a *passage* to alternative models of subject/object, to alternative models of extending human consciousness.

Duncan's poetry participates creatively (trans-*form*-actively) in the dance of the whole of the primordial energy/matter in expansion. His search is both archeological and genealogical, looking for the passage of human language and of human consciousness that are inscribed both in history and in the knowledge that was being built *in* and *through* language. Only like this, Duncan argues, will humanity be able to understand what defines the community of the human and how that definition was being built throughout the centuries, because myth and poetry are at the origin of the process, in the ritual that unites the part and the whole, the individual and the community. His interest in the archaic, the mythological, and the recognition of the magical (transformative) power of language, and so the recognition of the mythopoeic in science, in politics, in society (myths as forms given to reality and to knowledge) substantiates his poetics. The importance of looking at the marginalized, the unproved and the disapproved discourses, moreover, makes clear that many powers are present in the definition of this hierarchy.

This is the emancipatory nature of Duncan's project and this is why his project becomes an agonistic project that questions the discourses and the common sense in power, and a project that is always looking for new possibilities to participate in the transformation of the world. But agonistic also means "in agony." His is a struggle for life and creation in face of death and stasis. *Poiesis* means "to make," to make new forms/fictions to live by, in order "to re-orient our possible knowledge of what is" (FC 6). Again, in "The Truth and Life of Myth," he describes this rite of participation: "I wrestle with the syntax of the world of my experience to bring forward into the Day the twisted syntax of my human language that will be changed in that contest even with what I dread there. And recently I have come to think of Poetry more and more as a wrestling with Form to liberate Form" (FC 8).

So that the tribe may survive.

Works Cited

Aquinas, Thomas. *The Summa Theologica of St. Thomas Aquinas*. Trans. Fathers of the English Dominican Province. London: Burns, Oates, and Washbourne, 1923.

Augustine. *On Free Will.* In *Augustine: Earlier Writings*, trans. J. H. S. Burleigh, vol. 6. London: SCM Press, 1953.

Bachelard, Gaston. *La Formation de l'esprit scientifique.* Paris: Vrin, 1972.

Bernstein, Charles. *A Poetics.* Cambridge, MA: Harvard University Press, 1992.

―――. *Log Rhythms.* New York: Granary, 1999.

Damásio, António. *O Erro de Descartes: Emoçã o, Razão e Cérebro Humano* [*Descartes' Error: Emotion, Reason, and the Human Brain*]. Lisbon: Publicações Europa-América, 1995.

―――. *O Sentimento de Si: O Corpo, a Emoção e a Neurobiologia da Consciência* [*The Feeling of What Happens: Body and Emotion in the Making of Consciousness*]. Lisbon: Publicações Europa-América, 2000.

Dante Alighieri. *Monarchy.* Ed. and trans. Prue Shaw. Cambridge: Cambridge University Press, 1996.

Deleuze, Gilles, and Guattari, Félix. *Kafka: Pour une littérature mineure.* Paris: Minuit, 1975.

Durkheim, Émile. *Les Formes élémentaires de la vie religieuse: Le Système totémique en Australie.* Paris: Alcan, 1912.

Faas, Ekbert. *Young Robert Duncan: Portrait of the Poet as Homosexual in Society.* Santa Barbara, CA: Black Sparrow Press, 1983.

Kantorowicz, Ernst. *The King's Two Bodies: A Study in Medieval Political Theology.* 1957. Reprint, Princeton, NJ: Princeton University Press, 1985.

Lecercle, Jean-Jacques. *The Philosophy of Nonsense.* London: Routledge, 1994.

Lévy-Leblond, Jean-Marc. *Aux contraires: L'Exercice de la pensée et la pratique de la science.* Paris: Gallimard, 1996.

Santos, Boaventura de Sousa. *Toward a New Common Sense: Law, Science, and Politics in the Paradigmatic Transition.* New York: Routledge, 1995.

―――, ed. *Conhecimento prudente para uma vida decente: "Um discurso sobre a ciência" revisitado.* Porto: Afrontamento, 2003.

CHAPTER 3

Better to Stumble to It: The Start of Duncan's *Letters: Poems, 1953–1956*

Devin Johnston

> I make poetry as other men make war or make love or make states
> or revolutions: to exercise my faculties at large.
>
> —ROBERT DUNCAN, "PAGES FROM A NOTEBOOK" (1953)

Robert Duncan's distrust of mastery and accomplishment is well known: for him, poetry is "exercis[ing] the faculties at large," "journey work to the stars." As he asks in "Pages from a Notebook," "Why should one's art then be an achievement? Why not, more an adventure?" (SP 14). The full implications of this emphasis on poetry as process and experience have yet to be reckoned with. In the early 1950s, Duncan's growing engagement with these values resulted in a period of tremendous creative freedom and productivity. His comments from a late interview are significant in this regard: "The fifteen year break that I wanted between *Bending the Bow* and *Ground Work* (and the title *Ground Work* itself) I wanted to be back where I was when I was writing *Letters* and making things up" (Duncan 1985, 85).

In *Letters*, Duncan lays the groundwork for his approach to community, poetics, and politics, setting himself against mastery in all three spheres. Beyond craft, mastery raises questions that now seem central to that psychoanalytic era. In the wake of Freud, figures as diverse as Lionel Trilling, Allen Ginsberg, Jackson Pollock, and Robert Lowell were thinking through the relation between art and sublimation, creative production and neuroses. Like them, Duncan was asking—and would continue to ask all his life—what part poetry plays in civilization. Does poetry reflect the sublimation and mastery of desire, or something more primal? What might poetry accomplish or disrupt, cultivate or ravage?

In such questions, one may be tempted to hear the rhetorical oppositions that have run through American poetry in the past century: traditionalists and experimentalists, raw and cooked, Romans and barbarians, Houyhnhmns and Yahoos. In his own terms, Duncan was certainly immersed in what he later called "the different and differing orders of poetry that involve often incompatible ideas" (FC III). He often trumpeted an ideology of open form, sorting poets of fearful constraint from those of expansive enthusiasm. Yet Duncan also insisted that such strife and contention must be maintained rather than won; through disorder, one begins to arrive at "the nature of Poetry itself" (FC III).

At the outset, *Letters* would appear to be not only a playful book, but a sociable one. As correspondence, the poems define (or rather, revise) the author's poetic community: among the dedicatees are Denise Levertov, Philip Lamantia, Charles Olson, Helen Adam, Michael and Jo Ann McClure, Robert Creeley, and James Broughton. These are not only friends, but members of the poet's "company," to borrow Creeley's term. A company falls somewhere between a canon and a circle of companions, determined by taste as well as affection, at once elect and circumstantial. It might include the dead as well as the living: in the first poem of *Letters*, Duncan declares his intention to "brew another cup" in that "Marianne Moore - / E.P. - Williams - H.D. - Stein - / Zukofsky - Stevens - Perse - / surrealist - dada - staind / pot" (Letters 3). Gone from his dedications were the names of many Berkeley associates who marked a more local engagement. Duncan's company was increasingly determined by aesthetics rather than geography, keeping company in print more than place.

Origin, edited by Cid Corman, proved central to this new company. Duncan would later compare the real fellowship of its contributors, in their shared concern for "the immediate presence of the form in every locality of the poem," with the Imagists and Surrealists (L 396). When Duncan received *Origin* 6 in the summer of 1952, he found among familiars a poet new to him: Denise Levertov. The poem that caught his eye was "The Shifting" (later retitled "Turning"):

> The shifting, the shaded
> change of pleasure
>
> soft warm ashes in place of fire
> —out, irremediably
>
> and a door blown open:
>
> > planes tilt, interact, objects
> > fuse, disperse,
> this chair further from that table—hold it!
> > Focus on that: this table
> > closer to that shadow.   It's what appals the
> > heart's red rust.   Turn, turn!
> > Loyalty betrays.
>
> It's the fall of it, the drift,
> > pleasure
> source and sequence
> > lift
> > of golden cold sea.   (Levertov 114)

In the intensity of his excitement over this poem, Duncan wrote the first of the poems that were to become *Letters*, "An A Muse Ment" (retitled "For A Muse Meant"). Duncan sent the poem to Levertov as a letter, signed only "R.D." Without context, Levertov initially mistook this pounce for an attack on her poetry, though Duncan quickly assured her of his admiration. He later explained the properties of her poetry that sparked his imagination: "Music, the care of the word, and the immediacy of the movement of the poem to the movement of the image, these awaken an awe and a certainty that have increased with study. She had mastery, but she was not a Master, she was a Servant of the Language, a guardian of inner orders— not self-expressive but self-informing" (SP 160). In a letter to Levertov, he added that he found in her poem what he had been seeking in Mallarmé: "a form that might be like clouds or fumes, having strands, the inconclusive active in it" (L 431).

Such accounts speak eloquently of Levertov's poetics, but say little about "The Shifting" specifically. In the years to come, Duncan would successfully adopt a form "like clouds or fumes" in poems such as "A Storm of White" from *The Opening of the Field* (1960), with loosened strands of syntax breaking across lines so as to capture a sequence of perceptions. However, in the angular lines and dense punning of "For A Muse Meant," no such formal response is evident. One might observe that "The Shifting" involves a subtle but decisive change in a domestic environment, one of Duncan's great subjects. Yet here there is no celebration of hearth and household, but a hearth gone cold and a door blown open. The poem assures us of no constancy: we steady ourselves through perceptual attention to shifts and shaded changes ("hold it! / Focus on that . . . "). The pleasures arrived at are not domestic, but those of the "golden cold sea."

Was Duncan tempted to read "The Shifting" as a herald of the New American Poetry, as it would soon be called? The "door blown open," the disorienting fusion and dispersal of everyday things, and the title itself would invite such an emphasis. Yet such a poetry would seem to presage some loss or destruction: the hearth—suggestive of home, culture, and storytelling—is out "irremediably." The new pleasures will be less intimate, less familiar, and less comfortably constrained by civilization. As we shall see, this aspect of "The Shifting" proves central to Duncan's thinking in the early 1950s: as he writes in "Pages from a Notebook," "apparent entireties of domestication are in themselves undomesticated Africas. Our love is both the storm and the hearth of our emotional being" (SP 15).

When he happened on "The Shifting," Duncan was moving toward the completion of a long poem titled "An Essay at War." Levertov's extinguished fire immediately makes an appearance, with the nod of attribution, "it has all been said before":

> There is only the cold hearth.   The ashes
> waste   .   it has all been said before.
>
> The fire was the war.
> We said burn with it.   We said

> surrender all that we value to it,
> to the burning   .   to the war
> of words,   of the senses.
>
> We did not make sense.
> We made words dance.   Dance,
> we said.   What is left is the hearth.
> Dance by the light of the war. (D 22)

At the very heart of household, the hearth, one finds a destructive force, an aggression that takes the form of war or love or poetry. In the "war / of words," Duncan suggests, poetry does not stand outside or above these other spheres. In an advertisement for *A Book of Resemblances*, in which "An Essay at War" first appeared, Duncan wrote of the early 1950s as

a period of transition, of falling and failing in love, and also of America's falling and failing in war. The Korean War and obsessive homosexual love presented for me corresponding references of lies and defeats, waste and loss. . . .

It is the period at the same time of falling and failing in poetry—"An Essay at War," deriving its impulse from Williams's *Paterson*, strives to contain as beauty the flaws and inadequacies in the feeling of things—appropriate to the "police action" in the Orient—a pathetic fallacy? (Duncan 1962)

"Pathetic fallacy" is John Ruskin's term to describe the tendency of poets and artists to attribute human feelings to nature. According to Ruskin, this fallacy is caused by "an excited state of the feelings, making us, for the time, more or less irrational." It results in a "falseness in all our impressions of external things" (Ruskin 64, 65).

The correspondence Duncan celebrates, between historical "lies and defeats" and "falling and failing in poetry," would more aptly be described as a fallacy of imitative form. Both fallacies indicate a failure of discrimination through an excess of sympathy. The fallacy of imitative form, in particular, was often invoked by New Critics to describe the failures of Modernism. As Yvor Winters writes, "the author must endeavor to give form, or meaning, to the formless—in so far as he endeavors that his own state of mind may imitate or approximate the condition of the matter, he is surrendering to the matter instead of mastering it. Form, in so far as it endeavors to imitate the formless, destroys itself" (Winters 64). Without formal constraints, Winters implies, the poem can achieve no distance from its subject. Without such distance, how can the poem offer a moral or political critique?

In the early 1950s, Duncan sought no such moral high ground, as his wry question—"a pathetic fallacy?"—indicates. Rather, he increasingly emphasized the poem's unavoidable participation in the circumstances of its creation, seeking no mastery beyond it. As he writes in "For a Muse Meant," "Better to stum-/ *b'l* to it":

> :   A great effort, straining, breaking up
> all the melodic line   (the lyr-
> ick strain?)   Dont
> hand me that old line we say
> You dont know what yer saying.
>
> Why knot ab   stract
> a tract of   mere sound
> is more   a round
> of dis abs cons
>   t r a c t i o n
> —a deconstruction—
> for the reading of words.
>
> (Letters 2)

By stumbling, by moving against accomplishment, by letting in errors, Duncan sought contact with an alphabetic and sonic ground. Here, he gives equal weight to the poem as patterned energy (an *abstract knot*) and the poem as amusement or distraction (*why not*).

The title *Letters* meant not only a correspondence, but also an alphabet. Duncan suggests as much in a letter to Olson (dated 14 August 1955) regarding the progress of his book: "Gradually recent work is coming into book shape. Once I had the title *Letters*, it was clear. From the Letter to Denise Levertov (but I mean to remove the 'letter' aspect, any dedications, in order to make clear the letters vowels and consonants of it) thru to a projected second letter to Denise" (Duncan 1994, 97). As it turns out, Duncan kept the dedications in the original edition of *Letters*. Yet "For A Muse Meant" is dedicated—not *to*, as one would expect in correspondence—but *for*. His "deconstruction" involves the dissolution of point in field, figure in ground, words in an alphabetic fundament. In the same issue of *Origin* in which "The Shifting" appears, Duncan had also read Olson's poem "A Discrete Gloss." It includes the following lines:

> When the field of focus
> is not as admitted as the point is,
> what loss!   (Olson 119)

At the outset, "open field" entails not only a sense of the page as a field of composition, or field as a natural space; it also rejects any privilege given to a single point of focus.

By "making clear the letters vowels and consonants" implied by his title, Duncan was conceiving of poetry as a primary act of creation. In his preface to *Letters*, he cites the *Zohar* as "food for the letters of this alphabet" (Letters xii). According to the *Zohar*, the cosmos was constructed out of an alphabet, each letter serving as an atomic particle in Creation. Duncan elsewhere distils from the *Zohar* an image of "the Child Creator of the Universe playing with the letters of the alphabet" (Duncan 1981, 94). This child's play proves central to Duncan's sense of poetry: far from a refinement of ordinary language, poetry returns us to a primal act of making and discovery. As he writes in an imitation of Gertrude Stein from 16 June 1953:

Not a derangement of the senses but, yes, there is an occult other sense of meaning in all disarrangements (Dis in his arranging). What was it I imagined the language to be? Not mythy (except as there in the actual mythy evening, an atmosphere or preconception at best of the darkness of the actual night). Not visionary (except as the seen is real in its intensity; this is a scene wordwise).

But a hut of words primitive to our nature. The Language in its natural disarray. (D 77)

Though counterrational, Duncan claims no vatic authority and asserts no vision beyond what is seen (recall Levertov's "hold it!/Focus on that"). What is seen is darkness, or language in a state that precedes the rational ordering of thought. Such a state is not pure or cleansed of associations; rather, in "natural disarray," it spills over our categories. In "For A Muse Meant," Duncan illustrates this disarray with an inventive list that includes "a copy of the original," "an animal face," and "a fake seegar" (Letters 3). These items are, to various degrees, oxymorons: a copy jeopardizes the privileged status of an original; we can speak of an animal's face only anthropomorphically; "fake" negates the cigar it qualifies. Even such everyday expressions defy conceptual order.

In this respect, the broad sweep of Duncan's "deconstruction" in the early 1950s is breathtaking. As his preface to *Letters* makes clear, he seeks to dispel all that stands as illusion: the ghosts of history, the "glamorous tyranny of religion, of science, of democracy, of industry, of capitalism" (xi); as well as orthographic conventions, literary tradition, and even the authority of individual inspiration. As he continues, "I attempt the discontinuities of poetry. To interrupt all sure course of my inspiration" (xii). Following Artaud, Duncan depicts civilization as not only dead, but also necrophilic, in love with its monuments of decay. Such a state can only be countered by quick desire, excitement, and invention. Following Olson, Duncan thus locates breath as the source of poetry:

> :   in
> s p i r e d / the aspirate
> the aspirant almost
>
> without breath
> it is a breath out
> breathed—an aspiration
> pictured as the familiar spirit
> hoverer
> above
> each loved each
>
> a word giving up its ghost
> memorized as the flavor
> from the vowels (the bowels)
> of meaning
> (BE STILL THY BRATHE AND HEAR THEM SPEAK:)
> voices? images? essences
> as only in
> Yeats's 'desolation of reality'.   (Letters 1)

Here, "inspiration" returns from a mysterious creative agency to an intake of breath; "aspiration" returns from a desired goal to the exhalation that accompanies speech. Only by turning from acculturation to physiology can we arrive at the ground of poetry, the essences that constitute the "desolation of reality."

"Desolation of reality" is a strange phrase for Duncan to isolate, so accustomed are we to his celebrations of myth, fictiveness, and imaginative power. It comes from a section of Yeats's "Supernatural Songs," entitled "Meru":

> Civilisation is hooped together, brought
> Under a rule, under the semblance of peace
> By manifold illusion; but man's life is thought,
> And he, despite his terror, cannot cease
> Ravening through century after century,
> Ravening, raging, and uprooting that he may come
> Into the desolation of reality . . .

For Yeats, the strictures of civilization suppress (and repress) our psychic natures, covering all that is primal with illusions. As the poem concludes,

> Hermits upon Mount Meru or Everest,
> Caverned in night under the drifted snow,
> Or where that snow and winter's dreadful blast
> Beat down upon their naked bodies, know
> That day brings round the night, that before dawn
> His glory and his monuments are gone.   (Yeats 289)

Substituting "drifted snow" for "lone and level sands," "Meru" rewrites "Ozymandias" to other ends. "Ozymandias" warns of the ravages of time on our civilizations and accomplishments. On the other hand, "Meru" promises the collapse of civilization through our own psychic "ravenings." "Raven" is a violent word indeed, meaning to plunder or devour (having the same root as *rapine* and *rape*, with an emphasis on the appetites). As Yeats noted in a letter to Mrs. Shakespear, "The Fire = The purging away of our civilisation by our hatred" (Jeffares 259).

As Duncan was well aware, Sigmund Freud was climbing toward similar conclusions regarding the conflicts between pleasure and reality, between the demands of instinct and the restrictions of civilization. *Civilization and Its Discontents* was published in 1930, just a few years before Yeats composed his "Supernatural Songs." According to Freud, the preservation of civilization depends on replacing the drive toward pleasure with an avoidance of suffering. This goal in turn requires that we displace our libido, finding substitutes not easily baffled by the strictures of civilization. In Yeats's phrase, these displacements preserve "the semblance of peace / By manifold illusion." Among the secondary pleasures of displacement, Freud includes intellectual and creative work. He writes of such satisfactions, "their intensity is mild as compared with that derived from the sating of crude and primary instinctual impulses; it does not convulse our physical being" (Freud 26–27). He goes on to suggest that such displacements are not open to anyone, but presuppose "the possession of special dispositions" (27).

Duncan was as intensely engaged with Freudian thought as any poet of his time, albeit argumentatively. In contrast to the displacement and specialization of libido that Freud emphasizes, Duncan struggled to define poetry as a primary activity, arising from the "desire for speech" (Letters ix) that is not secondary to libidinal desire. As he writes in the preface to *Letters*,

It is a superstition of our time to read out of Freud that art is made out of a borrowing from sexual energies; and the professors or doctors lecture to expose the system of debits and credits whereby the artist manipulates the fund of energies. What happens when immediate excitements are postponed, when sexual responses are transmuted into hate and love, when talk is reserved to re-emerge as poetic speech? These are specializations of the individual creature, spiritual lusters or armories which I see as alike to the shells or furs or combs apparent in the animal world. Specializations of action. And then a will in living or a consciousness. I confound the two, having in mind a process which sets self-creation and self-consciousness in constant interplay. (Letters ix–x)

Duncan suggests that we confound specialization by reading and writing at once, by manifesting energy in multiple directions. Like Yeats, he is perhaps more sanguine than Freud in his celebration of psychic energy: as Yeats writes, against the hoops of civilization, "man's life is thought." Though Duncan often emphasizes amusement and delight in *Letters*, these are not "finer and higher" satisfactions, as Freud characterizes creative work. For Duncan, amusements are childish rather than refined. He seeks in poetry a state in which instinct has not been sacrificed to conscience, nor happiness to guilt; a state of primal pleasures in language, but primal terrors as well.

Letters is a book of great tensions and contradictions. Along with all it dismantles, it marks the beginning of a household for Duncan, in and out of poetry: as "Upon Taking Hold" ends, "The joys of the household are fates that command us" (8). His household, as we are often told, holds joys, delights, and amusements from things homemade and made up. Yet the life force of thought moves against all that is civilized and sheltering, despite our terrors. Back of the human, as Duncan would say, is an animal: back of the housecat is a lion, back of the poem is an owl. The owl may give "his hoot for joy as he flies" (44), but he is also ravening. Back of the hearth is a door blown open, and Levertov's "golden cold sea." Back of civilization is Mount Meru, "Caverned in night under the drifted snow."

Works Cited

Duncan, Robert. "Eleven Letters to Charles Olson." *Sulfur* 35 (Fall 1994): 87–118.

———. "The H.D. Book Part II: Nights and Days Chapter 11." *Montemora* 8 (1981): 79–113.

———. "An Interview: Robert Duncan / Michael McClure." By Michael McClure. *Conjunctions* 7 (1985): 69–86.

———. Unpublished advertisement (1962) for *A Book of Resemblances*. Quoted in Bib.

Freud, Sigmund. *Civilization and Its Discontents*. Trans. James Strachey. New York: Norton, 1962.

Jeffares, A. Norman. *W. B. Yeats: Man and Poet*. New York: St. Martin's Press, 1996.

Levertov, Denise. "The Shifting." *Origin* 6 (Summer 1952): 114.

Olson, Charles. "A Discrete Gloss." *Origin* 6 (Summer 1952): 119–21.

Ruskin, John. "Of the Pathetic Fallacy" [*Modern Painters*, vol. 3, pt. 4, chap. 12]. Cited in *The Genius of John Ruskin: Selections from His Writings*, ed. John D. Rosenberg, 61–72. Boston: Houghton Mifflin, 1963.

Winters, Yvor. *In Defense of Reason*. Chicago: Swallow Press, 1947.

Yeats, W. B. *The Poems*. Ed. Richard J. Finneran. New York: Macmillan, 1983.

Visions of the Field in Poetry and
Painting: Denise Levertov, Robert
Duncan, and John Button

Donna Krolik Hollenberg

"Poetry is a response to the daily necessity of getting the world right,"
Denise Levertov wrote in an epigraph to a draft of her poem "A Cure of
Souls" (Poetry Mss.). She wrote this draft in the spring of 1962 on the back
of a flyer announcing a show by the ailing landscape painter John Button.
The poem begins, "The pastor of grief and dreams // guides his flock towards / the next field // with all his care" (P60 92), and, although John Button is not mentioned in it, he had been on her mind for some time. He was
a mutual friend of hers and Robert Duncan's, whom she had met in New
York City in the 1950s. Levertov loved his work, particularly his paintings
of clouds floating above city rooftops, which contrast effects of light and
sky with urban structures. Inspired by these paintings and by Duncan's vision of the poetic field, she had written the poem "Clouds," in November
1960. Now, in the spring of 1962, she thought Button was dying of cancer
and she wrote another poem inspired by him and his paintings that she
sent in a letter to Robert Duncan. This poem was never published, for rea-
sons that will become clear. However, the process of writing it led Levertov
to clarify her approach to writing, to differentiate her concept of the field
from Duncan's, and to express more of her experience in the next phase of

her poetry. Although she would return much later, in ekphrastic poems, to the lyric mode of "Clouds," by the late 1960s a documentary impulse would become central in the poetic sequences that marked her maturity as a social poet.

Like other poets who reached adulthood during World War II, Levertov and Duncan examined their warrant for composing poetry with particular care. They considered themselves in the tradition of the High Modernists Pound, Williams, and H.D. (among others), yet they discerned problems with this legacy in the postwar moment and questioned the relation of individual action to social change with new energy. They were dissatisfied with "academic verse" influenced by T. S. Eliot, because it affected an ironic urbanity which, they felt, was too often smug and complacent (von Hallberg 30 ff.). They allied themselves with Charles Olson and other practitioners of open-form verse with whom they were included in Donald Allen's anthology, *The New American Poetry* (1960). Both of them were conversant with Olson's concept of "composition by field," in which individual agency is subordinated to a field of impersonal forces in the environment and their visions of the field were informed by Olson's ideas, particularly those (derived from Pound) which resonated with their Romantic sensibilities.[1]

The contemporary poets they respected, the Objectivists and the Deep Imagists, for example, were exploring and redefining the connection between the imagination and reality. As Jerome Rothenberg put it, in those days they all debated the nature of "the really real" (Interview). Was it external reality mediated by language? Was it internal reality, the superior reality of the dream? What part did tradition (literary, religious, mythic) play in it? If internal reality was the most authentic, could one consciously seek it out or should one, as Levertov thought, aim for "clarity and fidelity to . . . [lived] experience" ("An Argument" 116). In particular, she was concerned that the Deep Imagist project, whose visionary proclivity she shared, lacked "moral backbone" and the "sharpness of necessity" (L 266).

1. For a discussion of Olson's concept of the field compared with that of Pound and Zukofsky, see Anne Dewey; for a discussion of Duncan's Romanticism in relation to Pound and Olson, see Christopher Beach. Beach's point, that Duncan privileged "an openness to a mystical or spiritual consciousness, or to sensual and erotic impulses generally figured by representations of the feminine" (Beach 4), applies to Levertov as well.

In the early 1960s, Duncan and Levertov had a shared concept of the poet's task. They saw themselves as servants of Poetry's power not as masters of it, a self-positioning in relation to cultural tradition that had formal implications. Though they practiced open-form verse, both disliked the lack of craftsmanship in the work of some of the Beats included in Allen's anthology and they opposed any simplistic agenda of "form smashing," such as the one proposed in the *Nation* where Levertov was later interim poetry editor (L 273).[2] In his 1961 essay "Ideas of the Meaning of Form," Duncan took care to distinguish between formal conventions arising out of conformity and those arising out of "psychic need." Concerned that the "rational man," whether he be churchgoer or atheist, made himself "immune to revelation," Duncan saw "fact and reason" as defensive strategies, as means by which we protect ourselves "against a vision of life where information and intelligence invade us, where what we know shapes us and we become creatures, not rulers, of what is. Where . . . we are part of the creative process, not its goal" (SP 33–34). For poets who feel as he does, such formal matters as "movement and association" are "not arbitrary but arise as an inner need" (36). Similarly, in her 1961 essay "A Note on the Work of the Imagination," which was inspired by a dream, Levertov took care to distinguish between the Imagination and Fancy. She alluded to Ruskin's observations about Turner's paintings to make the point that the "total imagination," an entity larger than the self, manifested itself in "the life of dream." As she put it, "What joy to be reminded by truth in dream that the Imagination does not rise from the environment but has the power to create it!" (PW 206). She wrote to Duncan that she was grateful to him for "the re-entry into [her] life of the magic, the 'romantic,'" which she had temporarily put aside under the influence of Williams, Creeley, and Pound (L 434).

Clearly, both poets were influenced by the rise of "psychological man," as Peter Homans termed the growing influence of psychoanalysis and psychology in American life after World War II. In "The H.D. Book," which he sent to Levertov as he wrote it, Duncan made clear his familiarity with Freud's ideas. Levertov had been reading Jung in the 1950s as well as seeing a Jungian therapist who helped her to analyze her dreams. In fact, she had in mind as "the pastor of grief and dreams" who guided his flock to

2. Levertov was poetry editor of the *Nation* for three months beginning in April 1961.

a "new field," mentioned earlier, a particular Jungian analyst. Their letters in the early 1960s reveal that both poets thought that, in Levertov's words, the connection between "intellectual value and significance . . . depended upon the copious flow of mythical association of ideas and their power to permeate the moment" (L 361). Both were also friends and readers of Norman O. Brown, whose psychoanalytic reading of history and antirepression psychology urged people to rediscover a real, "naked" self that exists beyond institutions and roles, the sources of which lay in the future creation of fresh and new values.

Further, they both lived with a sense of doom or catastrophe, rooted in personal-historical sources, that was enmeshed in their poetry. Duncan's mature work begins with his book *The Opening of the Field* (1960), in which the first poem, "Often I Am Permitted to Return to a Meadow," is a recapitulation of the "Atlantis Dream" reported in "The H.D. Book." There he describes himself as belonging to a doomed Atlantean generation "that would see once more last things and destruction of the world" in a wave of water from which he rescues himself by playing with words so that in "the Atlantean phantasy and the Atlantis game or play, the most real emerged only in terms of what was most unreal" (unpaginated). As Peter O'Leary has pointed out, this dream, more than any other interior experience, "constitutes the personal-narcissistic-religion in his life and work" (85). In his 1958 grant application to the Guggenheim Foundation, Duncan described the idea of "the field" governing his prospective book as three-fold: it is "known intimately as the given field of my own life, intellectually as the field of the language (or spirit), and imaginatively as the field given to Man (of many languages)" (Bib 54).

In a 1976 interview, Duncan pointed out that this dream space originated in the open fields around his Stinson Beach home, a space which he then orchestrated (Power 23–55). Perhaps the most famous rendition of it occurs in "Often I Am Permitted to Return to a Meadow," where the field is

> an eternal pasture folded in all thought
> so that there is a hall therein
>
> that is a made place, created by light
> wherefrom the shadows that are forms fall.   (OF 7)

This poem is also marked by a sense of Duncan's creative arrival. It records a kind of permission, or at least a "traumatic recognition that Duncan is in the center of the creative meadow" employing "the disturbance of words within words'" to stave off chaos (O'Leary 90). The meadow is a "made place" but it is not only his. It has come from without, has been given to him in a dream, and serves to distract him and us from the chaos that bounds it.

Similarly, by 1960 Levertov was increasingly becoming aware of the part catastrophe had played in *her* life, particularly the psychological implications of growing up in England before and during World War II in a family of Jewish-Christian background who were avid antifascists. By the late 1950s she had been in America long enough to want to recover her European roots. She expressed this desire in several poems in *The Jacob's Ladder* (1961), the book in which "Clouds" appears.[3] Also, beginning in the late 1950s, Levertov was recording dreams related to the Holocaust in her diary and, because of the arms race, the threat of nuclear annihilation was very much on her mind. In response to Duncan's having described his "Atlantis dream" to her, in 1962 she shared her own recurrent childhood dream. In it, she is in a "great barn, filled with sweet-smelling hay & candle-glow, & around the walls all kinds of animals sitting in almost human pose, or as dogs sit . . .) and I with them, and all in an atmosphere of mutual love and joyful peace. And then suddenly all blackens to a crinkling, crinkled blackness, corrugated like iron & blackly twisting like burning paper." Commenting plaintively on this dream, she continued, "I felt fearful, thinking, is it true that we are of a generation that is to see an end in holocaust?" (L 362). On a more personal level, in this period she was also coping with the recent deaths of her father (1954) and her husband's mother (1960), and with the declining health of her husband's father who had become increasingly confused. In addition, she and her husband Mitchell Goodman were experiencing marital problems.[4] This diffuse array of fears and difficulties is the context for Levertov's poem "Clouds," as well as for her unpublished poem, titled in manuscript "Paintings by John Button."

Although Button and Levertov traveled in different circles in New

3. Besides the title poem, cf. "The Well," "A Window," "During the Eichmann Trial."

4. This is well documented in Levertov's diary and in such poems as "The Ache of Marriage."

York (he was associated with the New York School of poets and paint-ers),[5] they were both close to Robert Duncan, who had been at Berkeley in 1947–48, at the same time as Button. Button had also attended Dun-can's lectures at Borregaard's Museum in San Francisco and he admired the paintings of Jess Collins, Duncan's partner (L 284). In the late 1950s, But-ton was introduced to Levertov in New York by the painter, Albert Kresch, another mutual friend. When Button went to paint in Mexico in 1959, he befriended Levertov's mother, herself an amateur painter. Thus he entered Levertov's circle of intimates for a period.

Button shared artistic proclivities with Levertov as well. He was an artist who persisted in a realist style even during the height of Abstract Ex-pressionism. After moving from California to New York in the early 1950s, he had studied at the Hans Hoffman School and been influenced by the Abstract Expressionists, but he preferred to grow up alongside them and was allied with other "painterly realists" such as Fairfield Porter and Jane Frielicher. Unlike the action painters (a group of Abstract Expressionists of whom Jackson Pollock was the most famous), who painted their reactions to emotional stimuli, the painterly realists painted their reactions to the natural world. They wished not to make inner reality objective, but rath-er to internalize the outer world. Further, as Gerrit Henry has noted, the painterly realist "paints not only *what* he sees, but *how* he sees. The picture becomes not a record of itself, as with the Abstract Expressionists, but a re-cord of perceiving" (112). This emphasis upon recording one's perception of the external world, on making reflections visible, is similar to Levertov's definition of "organic form" as "a method of apperception, ie. of recogniz-ing what we perceive," which she was in the process of formulating in this period (PW 7).

Button is best known for paintings of the corners of buildings in New York, "seen from an odd angle below, jutting out into . . . technicol-or skies" (Katz and Jackson, unpaginated). In his work, "light is the ba-sis of the composition and the source of the poetic mood. The light in-forms large areas of color to build a deceptively clear and simple image. He is related to Winslow Homer and Edward Hopper by his constructive use of light and by the romantic awareness of the moment frozen in time. Through his intense pictorial observation he can elevate . . . the buildings

5. Button was a close friend of Frank O'Hara, who paid tribute to the friendship in his 1957 poem "John Button Birthday" (O'Hara 268).

on a city street into an enduring vision" (Katz and Jackson). Button explained his aesthetic values in a letter about a painting by Bonnard as follows: "What makes it good? Who knows, the incredible surface, the astonishing color, the light that pours out of it, or the feeling in it. Bonnard seems to have looked at the little breakfast table and its window, fixed his heart on all of life, and painted. He, Matisse, and de Kooning are certainly my ideals" (Doty, unpaginated). As Bill Berkson has noted, "A similar merger of attentiveness, technical resolve, and sentiment at once calibrated and far-reaching appears palpable in the landscapes and street scenes Button himself painted from the mid 50s on" (Doty). Berkson continues:

Button was an aesthete in the strict sense of one who maintains a moral—or even religious—preference for the beautiful. His allegiance to New York was modified by an inherent civility that brought all things under a harmonizing touch. . . . The scaled-up perceptual intimacy his best paintings assert is part of what the realist wing of the New York School developed, beginning in the 50s, as a counter-thrust to—as well as an absorption of—abstraction's headlong specifyings of applied paint.

Perhaps it was this "scaled-up perceptual intimacy" that Levertov responded to in Button's work as well as his civility and his refusal to give up the representational image. In these respects, Button's artistic vision coincided with Levertov's more than with Duncan's. In fact, Duncan allied his concept of the field and of open form explicitly with that of the Abstract Expressionists. He said in an interview, "I actually got to see Jackson Pollock painting one of those great canvases. It must have been in the 50s. . . . What struck me again and again was that Jackson Pollock was in the middle of the painting, literally in the middle—not in front of it or in back of it, in the middle of it—and that's the way I feel in a poem too" (Power 26). In the same interview an analogy is made between Pollock's idea of being "in" the action of the painting and Duncan's desire to live "in the swarm of human speech" (Power 26). Also, Duncan's acceptance of, in his own words, "the accidents and imperfections of speech," on the grounds that they "awake intimations of human being," is analogous to "the Abstract Expressionist's acceptance of accident as a factor in the creation of the canvas" (Power 26K).

Levertov did not share this affinity with Pollock and his group. With the exception of Mark Rothko, whose work she admired, she did not like the work of the Abstract Expressionists (Kresch interview).[6] In a letter to Cid Corman, praising his new book of poems, *The Responses*, she wrote:

Don't care for the cover design though—I'm anti-Kline, Altoon, Laubies, etc etc. That stuff does nothing for me. Kline has an occasional raw violence, an expression of energy; yes; well, o.k. No doubt it does him good but I'd sooner do my own or go look at Goya or whatever. Some of Al Copley's stuff, the best of it, had what they called a fine nervous line which was nice to look at; but he's strictly an amateur really. No real conviction. And the others, all I've seen—they founder along behind Kline glorifying every accident, so damn busy making something out of nothing. As far as I'm concerned it's a case of "The Emperor's New Clothes."[7]

One can read Levertov's "Clouds" as a response to Duncan's "Often I Am Permitted to Return to a Meadow," mediated by her appreciation of Button's paintings. There are thematic and stylistic similarities with Duncan's poem even as the tone echoes Button. Like Duncan, Levertov has an intuition of trouble, which she depicts initially as clouds "rising urgently," over "roofs and hermetic / grim walls." She associates this trouble with signs of the death of an intimate relationship. Then she brings to mind a visionary space that helps her to counteract this intuition, a "vision of a sky / close and enclosed, unlike the space in which these clouds move—" (JL 48). This visionary space is covertly associated with Button's colorful paintings of clouds above urban rooftops. She may well have had in mind his painting *Yellow Sunset*, reproduced in Figure 1, as well as others.

Upon intense inspection, she sees that the "gray mist" is more nuanced and colorful than it first appeared. It is

> a field of freshest deep spiring grass
> starred with dandelions,
> green and gold
> gold and green alternating in closewoven
> chords, madrigal field.   (48)

That is, her meditation on the clouds, undertaken with Button's paintings in mind, took a corrective turn inward:

> . . . leaning
> into myself to see
> the colors of truth

6. Robert Rosenblum places Button on a continuum between Friedrich and Rothko.

7. Denise Levertov, letter to Cid Corman (1956).

FIGURE I. John Button, *Yellow Sunset,* 1958 oil on canvas (?), by John Button, b.1929–d. 1982. Reproduced by kind permission of the Estate of John Button.

> I watch the clouds as I see them
> in pomp advancing, pursuing
> the fallen sun.   (47)

The stylistic similarities with Duncan's poem include repetition of some of the first and last lines, which increases the musical quality of the poem (Duncan thought of poetry as musical thought). Levertov's painterly sense of chiaroscuro, her modeling in light and dark, was central also to Duncan's conception of creativity. As he put it in "Ideas of the Meaning of Form," "I am glad that there is night and day, Heaven and Hell, love and wrath, sanity and ecstasie, together in a little place" (SP 23).

However, there is a subtle difference in the conceptualization of subject formation implied in these two poems that would eventually take Duncan and Levertov along different paths. Duncan's concept of "a field folded" (a field he was opening in his poems) implies a view of identity, derived from Whitehead's *Process and Reality*, in which persons are not seen as entities but rather as "events in the universe" (Power 35). "You've got to be flooded by the world," he said in a later interview, "*how* to be flooded by the world becomes the question of the artist" (Cohn and O'Donnell 530). This view led him, in the late 1960s, to begin an unbounded serial poem, "The Passages Poems," which he continued working on until his death. Levertov watches the clouds, "as I see them," emphatically repeating the personal pronoun. She prefers to "stand fast in [her] place," as she put it in the first of "Three Meditations" composed in the same period as "Clouds" (JL 31). As epigraph to her first meditation, she chose a passage from Charles Olson in which he claims that "the only object is / a man, carved / out of himself" (31). In the body of the poem she stresses the numinous aspect of this claim, turning as a model to the religious poet Caedmon, who was chosen to sing God's praise despite his humble station. Like Button, who said, "I cannot erase my self from the picture. . . . I cannot give up the representational image either. . . . neither can I indulge myself in the mere illustration of personal visions" (Katz and Jackson, unpaginated), Levertov continued to insist upon the integrity of the self even when she began writing poetic sequences that were more overtly politicized.[8]

When Levertov returned to thinking about John Button's paintings in the spring of 1962, she had already written her sequence "During the Eichmann Trial" (1961). The trial, reported in major newspapers around the world, was a turning point in awareness of the Holocaust as historical memory and moral burden after the war. It brought to view the principles of personal responsibility and accountability in the hope that, in the future, if a person was assigned a task similar to Eichmann's, the knowledge of history's verdict would stop him. The trial also had the indirect effect of registering a grave moral indictment against the free world: that it stood by passively and did not offer refuge while a people was being slaughtered. Levertov followed the testimony closely in the papers. Her poem reflects both horror at the human details it revealed and a heightened sense of moral responsibility. She published the first section, "When We Look Up," in the *Catholic Worker*, a left-wing paper that was deeply ashamed of the Church's silence during the Holocaust. The epigraph in the first section, "When we

8. Joseph Conte distinguishes between procedural poetic sequences, like Levertov's, which retain their base in an organic theory of continuity and development, and serial poems, like Duncan's, which are discontinuous and incomplete. He argues that they are "complementary responses to post-modernity" (15).

look up / each from his being," grounds moral responsibility in human connection (JL 63). The quotation is from Duncan's "Variations on Two Dicta of William Blake," a celebration of the unitive power of the imagination when people engage each other fully. The second and third parts of the poem were published later that year.

"During the Eichmann Trial," Levertov's first overtly political poem, was groundbreaking because it broke the taboo against speaking openly of the Holocaust, especially if the speaker had no direct involvement. But it was damned with faint praise by reviewers and even by some of her friends.[9] She was particularly disappointed that George Oppen did not like it (DuPlessis 57–58). In his positive reaction to the poem, Duncan was an exception. He recognized Levertov's deep need to witness the Holocaust through her imagination as a condition of her own spiritual survival despite all of the attendant difficulties and risks. The tepid response to her Eichmann poem was not the only snub she had received. By the spring of 1962, Levertov had been under attack from other quarters as well. When she wrote the second, unpublished poem inspired by Button's paintings, she was perhaps overreacting, she thought, "to the academic world as experienced in Michigan with its overemphasis on the 'right,' the 'well done,' the polished and balanced and clear" (L 347).

In her diary, Levertov had also expressed dissatisfaction with her ability to access troubling personal experience in her poems. Though she felt she had achieved new insights in therapy, and that consequently her poems came increasingly from a "submerged world," her therapist had suggested that she needed to "shake off the influence of her father in her work in order to achieve something truly original." She rejected this view at first but then she acknowledged that "there has been all my life some sense of inner censorship, of not writing in all honesty for fear of what the parents might say if they saw it. This has of course lessened with the years but it is not all gone" (Diary, 1963). It is worth noting, in this connection, that she thought it amusing and "yet sad" that her mother had taken a liking to Button, whose homosexuality she would have disapproved of had she known of it (L 284). That Levertov confided this to Duncan, whose groundbreaking essay "The Homosexual in Society" (1944) had connected the battle for social acceptance of homosexual love with a general battle

9. It was damned with faint praise by James Wright and Gilbert Sorrentino, for example.

for freedom and expression shared by other persecuted groups, indicates that she admired the emotional honesty and courage of openly gay men in those pre-Stonewall years.

Perhaps the most immediate context for the unpublished poem about Button's paintings was the pressures of Levertov's personal life, which had increased significantly. Not only was she was a wife and mother, but she and Mitch had assumed responsibility for her father-in-law, who lived with them briefly before he entered a nursing home. Given this situation, it is not surprising that she wished she could write like Robert Duncan, in the midst of whatever was happening, or like the Beats, relaxed by drugs or alcohol. In fact, she confided to Duncan that she had written the unpublished poem while "not quite sober," to see if that would help her (L 347).

The conflicting demands upon her as a woman artist are clearly and poignantly evident in the unpublished poem that she sent to Duncan:

> If John Button is to die soon
> how is it that my future
> spreads out with only
> the general shadow on it?
>
> He who (I think) loves Duncan as I do—from afar;
> He who paints clouds, roofs, walls, bodies
>   as I in dreams would or try to reach
> in words
>   "the clouds as I see them—
> rising
> urgently, roseate in the
> mounting of somber power"
> (and his name got left out of the poem
> because a You got in who was not he)
> who walked on Mexican mountains with my mother
> . . .
>
> I tell you I said the clouds were "surging
> in evening haste over hermetic grim walls—"
> I had nothing to tell me the haste was in him
> I saw the hasting clouds as through my own
> dusty late-afternoon windows. No thought that
> death was whitely pursuing
>   "in pomp advancing, pursuing the falling sun."

Duncan had not yet told me that Button had had cancer
and that (he may live in the shadow of that thought)
he heard it had reoccurred. He does not know
(if this is true)—
                        The future,
intricate valley of hillocks and boldly spangled shadows!
Where I'm to be and he is not?

John Button, if that's the truth, yet
you've found love,
a calm in the midst of
the dark brickwork, the sun
always swinging, sweeping
the spun-out beautiful shadows
in its wake

(and I have so far to go).

Don't feel (if this is true)
I pity you. You've made
that luminous and defined
presence, multiplied,
you were born to make.   And I?

The kids that play ball week-ends in the parking lot—
my crumbling father-in-law trying or pretending to
        try to remember when he was last here and what
        day of the week it is, weeping
false tears of remembrance at a picture of me as
        a small, fat, eager child in a cane chair
        in my garden of brick walls
—I've made nothing of these and so much else,

nothing to say: (if this is true)
this was life for me in 1962, with a new desk
        (not replacing my old one but added space, an
        other desk—oak, Pennsylvania carving, circa 1901),
a son my own size, a husband
moving erratically towards . . .
        . . .

—nothing, yet,
of the oppression and charm of letters,
coldness of wonder, tedium of female cycles, intricate
waterfall of dream and breathing daily
death and rebirth—going to bed in tears,
waking grumpy or full of decision or simply
reborn, nothing yet.

The clouds are on your side, Button,
the bricks
have glowed for you, you've spoken
for the roofs and the old grim walls of warehouses.
From hermetic silence your silent
song has gone forth.   (L 343–44)

References to "my crumbling father-in-law," "a son my own size, a husband / moving erratically towards . . . nothing," make clear that, compared
with John Button, Levertov felt she had much to achieve as an artist. Unlike herself, whose future "spreads out with only / the general shadow on
it," Button had made "that luminous and defined / presence, multiplied"
he was "born to make," and thus his approaching death is not pitiable.

Feeling her life as an artist at risk, Levertov is in a state of "empathic
unsettlement" with respect to Button in this poem. That is, she puts herself in the other's position "while recognizing the difference of that position and hence not taking the other's place" (LaCapra, quoted in Gubar
243). Susan Gubar has claimed this to be the position taken by many post-
Holocaust writers who are "determined to use proxy-witnessing as a means
of cultivating identifications that at least imaginatively traverse racial, sexual, national, and historical barriers" (Gubar 243). Of course, Levertov is
not writing about the Holocaust here, but her concerns about death in the
context of "the general shadow" and her other poems of the period, as well
her desire to unmask herself, make this imaginative strategy applicable.

In reply to her request that he tell her whether "it works as a poem,"
Duncan helped Levertov to see that this poem, in his words, "becomes a
most human note of [her] relationship to the poem 'Clouds.'" He wrote
that the passage about "old man fumbling for tears [her father-in-law] is
the nexus in experience around which the poem has tried to organize, as
in 'Clouds' the organizational experience is in the actual moment of cold,

fading, and fear" (L 345). He continued in that letter to Levertov by saying that the second poem made him realize how "splendid, how condensed a thing" is her first poem, "Clouds." In the intense exchange that followed, in which she confessed to have been drinking while writing the second poem, he commented further, that while the poem accurately recorded her state of confusion, she is "not a 'drunk with words' poet" (L 349). Duncan continued: "it's of the very nature of your calling in the art that a clear-eyed 'in back of your head' care is the key." Levertov appreciated Duncan's critique, commenting that she hoped to "use some of the components of the Button poem" later (L 355). She continued, "I feel the most basic error was that I was packing into a single poem elements that were really meant to go into several." She would, of course, use some of these elements in her poem "The Old Adam," which was originally titled "The Father-in-Law."

While Levertov's second poem about Button's paintings remained unfinished, in the process of writing it she learned much about her own vision of the field. She shared with Button, more than with Duncan, the evocative sense of a cut-off point from which can be glimpsed transcendent "vistas of . . . space more accessible by feeling than by foot" (Rosenblum 130). As she put it, responding to the poignant polarity created by the shallow foreground in his paintings:

> The clouds are on your side, Button,
> the bricks
> have glowed for you, you've spoken
> for the roofs and the old grim walls of warehouses.
> From hermetic silence your silent
> song has gone forth.   (L 344)

That is, the connections between earth and sky, body and mind, are more recuperative in Levertov's poetry than in Duncan's. When "Duncan speaks of his dream meadow as a place of first permission, that 'first' is as much cardinal as it is original. Its originality . . . has been lost through catastrophe. . . . The catastrophe creates gnostic prospect . . . —but only through a suffering and an illness from which there is no hope of recuperation" (O'Leary 112). In both of Levertov's poems inspired by Button's paintings, the visionary field has a more pronounced epiphanic quality. She would develop this quality twenty-five years later in poems about paintings that enabled her to bridge the gulf between a despairing political awareness and an "imagined destination of faith'" (Levertov, quoted in Hollenberg 520). Also, in writing "Paintings by John Button," Levertov had expressed painful experience in poetry more personally than before, an ability that would soon prove crucial in *The Sorrow Dance* (1967), where the "Olga Poems" provided an important transition to her poems protesting the Vietnam War. When she achieved full maturity as a social poet in the notebook poem that became "Staying Alive," she described this poem as a record of "one person's inner/outer experience in America during the sixties" (P68 107). Without losing her grasp of mythical patterns or of depth and elevation, Levertov incorporated documentary evidence into this poem, thereby accomplishing the "daily necessity of getting the world right."

Works Cited

Beach, Christopher, "Objectivist Romantic: Ezra Pound and the Poetic Constellations of Robert Duncan." *American Poetry* 6.1 (Fall 1988): 3–24.

Brown, Norman O. *Life Against Death: The Psychoanalytic Reading of History.* Middletown, CT: Wesleyan University Press, 1959.

Cohn, Jack, and Thomas J. O'Donnell. "An Interview with Robert Duncan." *Contemporary Literature* 21 (1984): 513–48.

Conte, Joseph. *Unending Design: The Forms of Postmodern Poetry.* Ithaca, NY: Cornell University Press, 1991.

Dewey, Anne, "History as a Force Field in Pound, Zukofsky, and Olson." *Sagetrieb* 13.3 (Winter 1994): 88–116.

Doty, Robert M., ed. *John Button: Exhibition and Catalogue.* Manchester, NH: Currier Gallery of Art, 1989.

Duncan, Robert. "The H.D. Book." Pt. I, chap. 5. *Aion: A Journal of Traditionary Sources* (Dec. 1964): 5–29.

DuPlessis, Rachel Blau. *The Selected Letters of George Oppen.* Durham, NC: University of North Carolina Press, 1990.

Gubar, Susan. *Poetry After Auschwitz: Remembering What One Never Knew.* Bloomington: Indiana University Press, 2003.

Henry, Gerrit. "Painterly Realism and the Modern Landscape." *Art in America* 69.7 (September 1981): 112–19.

Hollenberg, Donna Krolik. "'History as I desired It': Ekphrasis as Postmodern Witness in Denise Levertov's Late Poetry." *Modernism/Modernity* 10.3 (Fall 2003): 519–30.

Homans, Peter. *Jung in Context: Modernity and the Making of a Psychology.* 2nd ed.

Chicago: University of Chicago Press, 1995.

Katz, Paul, and Ward Jackson. "John Button." *Art Now: New York* 1.6 (June 1969): [5–29].

Kresch, Albert. Unpublished interview with Donna Hollenberg. 2002.

Levertov, Denise. "An Argument." *The Floating Bear* 1 (1961): 115–17.

———. Diary. Special Collections, Stanford University Libraries.

———. Letter to Cid Corman (1956). Harry Ransom Research Center, University of Texas, Austin.

———. Poetry Mss. Special Collections, Stanford University Libraries.

O'Hara, Frank. *The Collected Poems.* Ed. Donald Allen. Berkeley: University of California Press, 1995.

O'Leary, Peter. *Gnostic Contagion: Robert Duncan and the Poetry of Illness.* Middletown, CT: Wesleyan University Press, 2002.

Power, Kevin. "A Conversation with Robert Duncan About Poetry and Painting." *Line*, nos. 7–8 (1980): 23–55.

Rosenblum, Robert. *Modern Painting and the Northern Romantic Tradition: Friedrich to Rothko.* New York: Harper and Row, 1975.

Rothenberg, Jerome. Unpublished interview with Donna Hollenberg, 2002.

Sorrentino, Gilbert. "Measure of Maturity." *Nation*, 10 March 1962, 220–21.

von Hallberg, Robert. *American Poetry and Culture, 1945–1980.* Cambridge, MA: Harvard University Press, 1985.

Wright, James. "Gravity and Incantation." *Minnesota Review* 2 (Spring 1962): 424–27.

II

CHAPTER 5

My Stories with Robert Duncan

Ellen Tallman

My stories with Robert Duncan start in 1946 when I was eighteen and a music student at Mills College, Oakland, California. My best friend was Marthe Larsen—later to be Marthe Rexroth—and so it was that we went to the Wednesday night anarchist meetings at the Workman's Circle on Steiner Street in San Francisco where Kenneth Rexroth was the literary and organizational center of this Anarcho Pacifist Libertarian Circle. My first sight of Duncan, as well as Robin Blaser and Jack Spicer, was at these meetings.

Though these Wednesday nights were organized by Rexroth to give the historical development of the anarchist movement, Duncan's passion was literary discussion. His talks on Joyce's *Ulysses* and *Finnegans Wake* and on anarchist themes from Henry James were met with complaints from the very vocal and antiliterary Italian anarchists—some who came a long way on a weeknight from Petaluma, Cotati, and other outlying districts to talk anarchism, not literature. The Italian anarchists that Marthe and I particularly remember were Bessie, Tony, and Leno, who worked hard at farming and politics and didn't appreciate Robert's discourses on literature or anyone's talk on sexuality, which was another frequent subject at these meetings. Henry Miller, who occasionally attended, had a group of his own in Big Sur where there was less contention (so we heard), but not the big gatherings, fund-raisers, great music, and food that the San Francisco group had.

During this period right after World War II, pacifism remained one of the major issues at our meetings. There was no argument that government was the source of most of our world's troubles, and according to my journal notes of a meeting at that time, that there were "viable alternative forms of *voluntary* organization, out of which an Anarchist society would become a more and more living entity; that we need consciousness of our *evolution* through the study of Darwin, and that we need to be ready to take on complex *voluntary* responsibilities—order not from above—but a natural order informed by Darwin." My journal entry continues,

> Anarchism
> A revolution without authority
> That destroys power wielding institutions
> And replaces them by voluntary
> Cooperative institutions.

Denise Levertov describes Duncan as a "passionate Anarchist or Libertarian" in her brilliant essay "Some Duncan Letters—A Memoir and A Critical Tribute" in Bertholf and Reid's *Robert Duncan: Scales of the Marvelous* (1979). And perhaps he was. But more visibly at this time, Robert was a passionate student, auditing, if not attending, many English literature classes and various language courses. In particular, he, Robin, and Spicer were present for the famous medieval history courses by Kantorowicz. As Robin said, "We went for the Byzantine thing," which included their struggling with Latin and being tutored in Greek. It was in this period that Robert was giving readings of "Medieval Scenes" and "The Venice Poem" at the writer's conference meetings (run by Blaser and Spicer), at the Bancroft Room in the library, and even in the *Daily Californian* newspaper office, where Spicer and I were on staff. Robin reports that at Kantorowicz's last class before he left to teach at Princeton, as he walked out of the room at the end of the lecture, he tapped Robert, Jack, and Robin on the shoulders (they sat in aisle seats, one behind the other), and said, " I would take you three with me, but you are all poets."

It would be hard to exaggerate the effect that Robert had on the world around him with his wealth of interests in literature, history, art, languages, and the occult. He had been raised by theosophists who had adopted him by theosophical methods, which included his having to be born at a given hour, date, year—with his future already known at his birth—that future including his being a poet and homosexual. Robert referred to the occult, including Blavatsky, Yeats, the Golden Dawn, Waite's tarot deck in conversation and in his readings as if his listeners knew and understood his world. It was certainly easy to be overwhelmed by the enormity of what we *didn't* know. And it was just as dazzling to experience Robert's ability to sustain a kind of dual attention in which he would deftly interweave these references to the most esoteric and arcane information with astute and often devilish commentary on what was going on around him—his walleye affording him the ability to observe people without their knowing.

When he was in his talking-talking mode, which was also his teaching mode, he usually spoke in a monotone that seemed deliberately not inflected. Anaïs Nin, in her third *Diary*, describes an early meeting with Robert in New York when he was working for her, in the following quotation:

Robert talked obsessionally, overintently, overwillfully as if he wanted to hypnotize me. His stare gave me a desire to escape, relax. Later, when we became friends, I remember how the fixity of his stare and uninterrupted flow of words still distressed me. It was as if he were impelled by a fear of getting lost, interrupted, confused, and must maintain a monologue, not a dialogue, as if a dialogue might endanger him in some way. (159)

Robert spoke about his exhilarating, intoxicating, exhausting speaking at a later time in his life. I don't know whether this came from a poem or was a proclamation in the moment, but I made note of it: "Am I strapped to the manic wheel of speech, or am I free to speak if others are free to listen?" And as I write now, at his insistence: "Tell them about someone giving me Benzedrine at your wedding and how I talked through the night until your parents had to drive me home."

Surrounding us at this time—1949–1950—were not only the politics of anarchism and of poetry, but also the politics of love, with Robert leading the way for homosexuals to live more openly (and avoid the draft, the violence)—and in his own life moving into life-long love with Jess, which Robin Blaser describes:

Duncan met Jess in 1950 in San Francisco. In 1951, he left Berkeley and moved to San Francisco where he rented the ballroom of the Old Spreckles mansion. With Jess learning, Duncan's interest in Art went into high gear. They began there and continued in Stinson Beach what became two enormous scrapbooks of art reproduction—stunning—from art books (Skira, etc.) cut out—and arranged on the principle derived from Andre Malraux's *Museum without Walls*—but their own museum without walls.

Those scrapbooks were a wonder, as an aspect of their building an imaginary world. Their GIFT. (Tallman, unpaginated)

When I graduated from Berkeley in 1949, I left for the University of Washington in Seattle, where I did graduate work in English and met and married Warren Tallman, who was doing his Ph.D. in English—also at the University of Washington. Together, we moved to Vancouver where we both began teaching English at UBC, raising our children and thinking about how to build our own "imaginary world."

The fall of 1959 marked the beginning of building the "imaginary" in our lives—for what would unfold by way of poets and poetry in Vancouver and the course of Canadian poetry for decades to come. I was visiting the Rexroths in San Francisco, and Robert was there for dinner. He said, "Why don't I come to Vancouver and read?" In December 1959, he read in our basement. We packed in thirty to forty students and a few faculty. And in Warren's notes: "Robert brought a batch of books including Jack Spicer's *Billy the Kid* and *J* Magazine and his own City Lights *Selected Poems*. Read for over 3.5 hours without a break—took the money from the basket including the 40 bucks we put in for change."

That was Robert's first of many stays in Vancouver. Warren recorded eighteen visits in the next twenty years, some as long as six weeks. And Duncan was the first of many poets who came to Vancouver to work, teach, give readings, and to play. It seemed there was nearly always a poet staying with us, giving readings, teaching: Creeley, Spicer, Ginsberg, McClure, Snyder, Jonathan Williams, and more and more. Robert Creeley (who always forever was Warren's best friend) came to teach for a year or more, and Robin Blaser, close friend from the Berkeley days, moved to Vancouver to write and teach. He and I, with our partners, bought a house that we have lived in since the 1970s.

When Duncan arrived on visits, we evolved a ritual: From the airport we went to the Valetor Cleaners where Robert would leave a suitcase full of dirty shirts—they did a better job than in San Francisco, he said. Next, we'd go to the liquor store (although Robert didn't drink, we did), then to the greengrocers and the Safeway. In all of the stores we would clog up the aisles with Robert's incessant talking which gathered much attention, as the talk was loud and his appearance dramatic because he always wore the three-tiered black cape that he brought back from his visit to Creeley in Mallorca. He wore that amazing cape winter and summer during the 1960s. Maybe the 1970s too.

When Robert was out of teaching mode and into his more intimate mode about friends, adventures, his life and work with Jess, he was both a compelling talker and comprehensive listener. He talked at length about his evolving, absorbing relationship with Denise Levertov—a relationship we now, most fortunately, can read in the Stanford University Press edition of their correspondence. I didn't meet Denise until the Vancouver Poetry Conference, July 24–August 16, 1963, which Warren and Robert Creeley arranged.

For the conference, we had a houseful of poets and friends staying/visiting with us—Charles Olson, Allen Ginsberg, Philip Whalen, Don Allen, and Bob and Bobbie Creeley who lived a block or so away, and Robert and Jess who had rented a house nearby with their friends Hilde and David Burton—all gathered for the evening, as often happened after the long days of teaching and readings. (Amazing interactions in this crowded space. Olson's bedroom next door to Ginsberg's, and Olson, who talked in his sleep, awakening to Ginsberg, crouched on the floor next to his bed with a writing tablet, trying to get Olson's words. "It's not enough that you steal all the attention," Olson shouted [Ginsberg had been on the front of a recent issue of *Time* magazine], "but now you want to steal my dreams!" And then Ginsberg, with no hint of apology, "Yes, Charles, I do want to steal them.")

Another night, as everyone began to gather back at the house, Don Allen asked, "Why are people dressing up? Why the new shirts? Why the trimmed beards on the bathroom floor?" Someone replied, "Denise Levertov arrives tonight." Don still pursuing it, "But why dressing up?" . . . "She would be our conscience," someone (I wish I knew who), replied.

This reply ("She would be our conscience") is central to one of the areas of fire and fascination between Robert and Denise—conscience, consciousness, the known and unknown: the adventure for Robert in *not* knowing and the consequent quest for what *could be*; and for Denise—the movement toward *knowing* what was right, what *ought to be*, and living accordingly. Denise (in her *Scales of the Marvelous* article) describes Robert's insistent fascination with the dream, the fairy tale, the (Freudian) mistakes, the gifts of chance as all ways of avoiding coming solely from his "diamond needle intellect." And though sympathetic to his need, she articulates clearly her difficulty with Robert in this realm:

Related to this was my distrust of Robert's habit of attributing (deeply influenced as he was by Freud) to every slip of the tongue or unconscious pun not merely the revelation of some hidden attitude, but it appeared to me—and it seemed and still seems perverse of him—*more validity* than that of what the speaker meant to say, thought he or she said. To discount the earnest intention, because of some hinted, unrecognized, contradictory coexisting factor has never seemed to me just; and to automatically suppose that the unrecognized is necessarily *more* authentic than what has been brought into consciousness strikes me as absurd. (*Scales* 96)

For Robert, in his constant talking and constant teaching, "the intellectual adventure in living, in writing the poem, is in *not* knowing; and the right chaos, the right vagueness are jointly required for effective harmony." "Transgress the boundaries," he would add. These points he would make often whether teaching in the living room, in the classroom, in workshops, even in helping my mother, an accomplished violist and music teacher, to understand and appreciate contemporary music. Mother resisted modern music, but she would take Robert and me to concerts, and surrender happily to his lectures. "The right chaos," he would begin. "The right vagueness. Transgress the boundaries." This was his teaching mantra.

I hadn't known about Robert's intense listening and formal interest in music until I started staying with Jess and him for visits in the 1970s and early 1980s. He played versions to compare, of the same sonata, concerto, not too often symphony, and brought his depth of musical knowledge to the various forms he played for us. Lou Harrison, composer, in *The Scales of the Marvelous*, says: "Duncan has no formal musical training that I know of, but this has not prevented in him an astonishing knowledge of the whole art of music, including an understanding of much of its lovely esoterica" (*Scales* 210).

The last of my notes of Robert's teachings are from Cortez Island, B.C., in 1978, where I was running groups in a residential psychotherapy program for Cold Mountain Institute. In a session on poetry and violence, a student asked Robert if he thought wars would ever end. I quote my notes for his answer:

I don't know, but there will be a third world war which could start in Palestine. The danger is of three tribes clashing in a holy war and the tribes are the Jews, the Muslims and the fundamentalist Christians—that they are all sharing a very small piece of real estate—bitter, bitter battles over the oil and the commercial inter- ests of the larger powers—Russia, the United States, etc. They will perhaps attach themselves to these warring holy tribes.

How it would end he did not prophesy.

In the same residential program, Robert gave a week-long po- etry class, in which he worked with participants' poems as if they were dreams—helping them to see what they might have intended in the poem, and as he said, "Seeking the unknown (revealing what they knew and didn't know)."

He started the first class in a swaying dance motion, rooted in one place, saying: "a stammer . . . a stutter . . . stops with singing . . . " Which was both his introduction to himself and his stammer and to a poem, as he intoned it in different rhythms, in different inflections, and spoke about how only in magic and practices of magic did you go into the sounds of language, the power of soundings, incantations; and that we would be working with poetry as if it were contemporary music, where the bound- aries are gone—where cough has sound. "You are a writer when you write in the journal, and begin to see your journal as series. Everything goes into the book. Rescue from the dream everything to go into the journal."

I want to close with the playful, devilish, demonic Robert who per- haps did not get enough attention in these pages. Illustrative of this per- sona is one of his often-repeated stories—that Jess had a huge Black Book (hidden), in which he wrote down Robert's sins, lies, transgressions—all his wickednesses. Jess, of course, magically knew these without being told. I believe that the presence, the continual mention by Robert of the hidden Black Book of sin (Robert's word) was one of the contributions to the se- renity of their domestic life—keeping the dangerous known unknown— keeping the dangerous unknown known.

This was a worthy game, a wild playing field in the midst of the serious, brilliant works they created.

Works Cited

Duncan, Robert. *Selected Poems*. San Francisco: City Lights Books, 1959.

Harrison, Lou. "A Note About Robert Duncan and Music." In *Robert Duncan: Scales of the Marvelous*, ed. Robert J. Bertholf and Ian Reid. New York: New Directions, 1979, 200–202.

Levertov, Denise. "Some Duncan Letters—A Memoir and A Critical Tribute." In *Robert Duncan: Scales of the Marvelous*, ed. Robert J. Bertholf and Ian Reid. New York: New Directions, 1979, 85–115.

Malraux, André. *Museum Without Walls*. Vol. 1 of *The Psychology of Art*. Trans. Stuart Gilbert. 3 vols. Bollingen Series, no. 24. New York: Bollingen Foundation, 1953.

Nin, Anaïs. *The Diary of Anaïs Nin, 1939–1944*. Ed. and preface Gunther Stuhlmann. 3 vols. New York: Harcourt Brace Jovanovich, 1969.

Tallman, Ellen. "Conversation with Robin Blaser" (2003).

CHAPTER 6

The People's P***k:
A Dialectical Tale

Aaron Shurin

In the war of letters between Robert Duncan and Denise Levertov—
the essential contention around poetry and politics, agenda and surrender,
that marks both the evolution and devolution of their thirty-year correspondence—one might be easily persuaded to side with one or the other,
to hunker down in position held by fierce idealism or sanctimony, as it
may be, and rest in that resolve as though the contention had been con-
cluded. As an act of politics such determination might be persuasive; as
a poetics it may be seen as a preliminary if not suspicious position, and
against practice per se. The social forces that pressure the creative use of
language have not yet given ground to the imagination; the agony of how
to speak into, over, through, or from history is a compositional struggle
engaged by each generation, each poet, each reader.

How do we claim forebears? How do the articulations of our heroes
dramatize our own contentions? When is poetics, or how may it be, the
third position in a dialectic? Any of us—students and teachers alike (and
many of us are both)—participate *experientially* in aesthetic dialogue as we
claim affinities, derivations, literary genealogies based on friendships, personal communication, affection, or argument. The Duncan/Levertov cor-

respondence distills both poetics and action into a high-minded critique of personal practice—it is mostly Denise's practice that is critiqued—and the wave of righteous intelligence animating Duncan's defense of the imagination is often hard to counter. The embrace of discovery, accident, Freudian shame or slip, wayward invention, chance; of surprise and contradiction, danger and tangent ("I can't help it, I'm a tangent queen!" a brilliant, talkative friend once said to me) are so fundamental to postmodern procedure as to be almost unquestionable. And yet the Patriot Act impinges; the war in Iraq, 9/11, Palestine, abortion rights, AIDS: any confidence in aesthetic solution must be provisional, unless none of these key inciters means anything to you. (I recently listened to an Argentine writer, who had been "disappeared," whose brother had been terminally disappeared, discuss her struggle to find the formal shape for a fictionalized memoir which might raise a response [and what kind of response do we seek?] greater than that offered by a litany of facts.) If we question the efficacy of Levertov's solutions—how was her poetry altered by her convictions and how do we measure the failure or success of those alterations?—her sense of urgency is hard to question. Duncan's "grand collage," which includes worlds of destruction *and* instruction, is a bliss of a magus overview we might seek to attain as poets but fail to meet as nervous humans.

If Levertov came to see writing as an argumentative means to action, Duncan saw it as an already active mode, wherein contentions aren't argued or answered so much as rendered visible, as *made*. Both were profoundly communal writers, both teachers in the literal and general sense. How might a student of either or both—and how is a reader a student?—come to a synthesis mutually engaging? To honor positions taken with such vehemence one can offer vehement attention. To read their correspondence richly as if it mattered *now* is to argue with *oneself.* The following is a necessarily personal account in which *The Letters of Robert Duncan and Denise Levertov* are at risk.

As part of my literary biography, I often joke to those in the know that I'm the bastard son of Robert Duncan and Frank O'Hara, an heir to seemingly irreconcilable poetic territories: diction high and low; mythopoeic drama and breezy urban rhythm; Esclarmonde de Foix in her holy fortress and Lana Turner in her turban; communal San Francisco and vigorous, imperial New York (I was born and raised in Manhattan, have lived my adult life in S.F.). But the truth is I'm the love child of Denise Levertov and Robert Duncan. Each was my longtime poetic mentor, teacher, beloved friend, spiritual guide, and muse. For each I was apprentice, acolyte, amanuensis, confidant, communer, and fellow traveler.

From early 1969, when I met Denise, to Robert's death in 1988, they were the highest comrades of my poetic community; their work awakened me to the power and possibility of American poetry, and called me forward into my own imagination and practice. If our friendships swelled or faded as did their own, mastery notwithstanding, the work was resolute. Such graces of encounter are not casual. As in the familial paradigm (Robert died the same year as my father), individuation is the synthesis of deep obedience and disavowal: in the crisis of these poets' unfolding aesthetic and political conflict my own writing was tested and proved—and still is.

In the spring of 1969 I was nearing the end of my undergraduate days at Berkeley, a tenure reaching from the close of the Free Speech Movement (in which my brother Isak, to whom Levertov's "Relearning the Alphabet" is dedicated [RA 110], was arrested) through vivid, multiple protests against the Vietnam buildup, conscription, and university racism, along with various unnamed armed conflicts (my twenty-first birthday found me under curfew-driven house arrest as national guardsmen patrolled each civic corner; I remember the fact, but who can remember the reason why?), as well as through the Summer of Love, the great Human Be-in, the Fillmore, the Avalon, Hendrix, and Joplin; through, too, uncountable nights charting my own adventurous forlorn and ecstatic forays into gay life in the City; all seeming to culminate, then, in the epochal war-at-home known as the battle for People's Park. How can the spring of 1969 in Berkeley be registered without such coordinates, the *feel* of cultural seismology and the pressure of localized national events? So when Denise's poetry class answered the call to come work at People's Park, each of those historical ganglia was waving, charged, and for each of us, I think, symbolic action was fed by these cumulative empowerments and disempowerments.

It must have been a bright sunny day, that May 14 Denise describes in "Staying Alive" (SA 43–44), because I remember the sheen on the green as we rolled out great swaths of sod like a carpet to cover the ground of the park. The school quarter had been peppered with demonstrations and student strikes and we'd often, if I remember correctly, met off campus; that we should go together to work at the park was testimony to our support of Denise's political conviction as well as our belief that the common purposes of poetry made a place for voice in the space of action; "the personal is political" extended its alliterative syllogism to include "poetry." Denise describes scooping up debris to haul away to a dump, and who could help imagining that a red wheelbarrow might have been involved?

That specific domestic conflict was galvanizing, and in a particularly San Francisco way the poetic community came alive to its civic urgency, and called together a resplendent literary gathering to raise money for the park. On Monday, June 2, the great California Hall was the site of an over-flowing "Poetry Reading for the People's Park," with appearances by Levertov, Duncan, Brautigan, Ferlinghetti, Snyder, McClure, and others. The scene was raucous, celebratory, serious, committed, with overtones of literary history and an aura of cultural significance, fed by the political drama of the immediate weeks and orchestrated by Denise's role as MC.

What fate, I can almost hear Robert ask, was at work in bringing Denise to that role on that stage that night, where her uses of poetry and her use by poetry met their boundaries and overflowed? The chaotic (post-Beat?) impulses of the Bay Area cultural scene were different than those of the Movement that was framing her current practices, and her sober streak hardened in direct proportion to the gospel-like fervor, the shrieks and laughter, the carnal carnival of the gathered masses. As she felt the crowd inch beyond her control—beyond her intentions as if the poem itself refused to obey her projections—where she would bring it back to a political formulation exactly as the audience was riding its imagination—a face came over her face that was a borrowed face, a stern righteous visage that wasn't a poetic face yet was exactly what Robert saw or feared he saw as the face of her war poems.

As if on cue, up onto the stage from somewhere in the audience jumped an eight-foot pink felt penis, who grabbed the mike and announced to the crowd that he was "the People's Prick," bouncing around like a giant bunny on LSD. The audience roared their approval (the other operative syllogism extended "free all political prisoners" into "free love")—but not Denise. She was outraged. She was affronted. She knew better. She tried to take back control, hectoring the audience to behave with a puritan, if not Stalinist, regard that made it clear that Emma Goldman's revolution was not *her* revolution. But the *audience* was *not* hers. The Prick defied her, danced around her, as her sense of offence congealed and straightened her unbending spine into something far more disturbingly erect.

I no longer remember how events progressed after that, but for me the image of the clash between the embodied pleasure principle and the officer of the doctrinaire has stood precisely for the poetic trouble Robert envisioned when he cautioned Denise that her public poetic thinking was "a force that, coming on *strong*, sweeps away all the vital weaknesses of the living identity; the *soul* is sacrificed to the demotic persona that fires itself from spirit" (L 607), and, later, "The poet's role is not to oppose evil, but to imagine it. . . . Is it a disease of our generation that we offer symptoms and diagnoses of what we are in the place of imaginations and creations of what we are." (L 669), or, even at the very beginning of their correspondence, "The feeling of what is false for me is the evident *use* of language to persuade" (L 34). And how, in the end, can we not be reminded of Duncan's Freudian complaint, which so enraged Denise, that read into the skinned penises of "Life at War" "an effect and tone of disgusted sensuality" (L 749).

He would not be alone, here, in registering the break between Movement politics and the sociopolitical implications of cultural and personal exploration, which found their catalysts in the emerging women's and gay liberation movements—even if this insight did not succeed in liberating poetry from the rhetoricizing projections of those very countering insurgencies. Yet there my poetry fled, bounding into the communal arms of gay comrades, who fought both the male domination of the power brokers of the revolution and the homophobia and heterosexism that fed it. The rhetoric was heavy; the poems groaned under its weight. But if I'd understood the problem that lay within the People's Prick scenario, it went only so far as to resurrect (re-erect?) issues of pleasure—the life of Eros and the social registrations of its repression—from the peace movement's cemetery, but not yet entirely to question the poem's obedience to my instructions. The American people's red army may have been mutated, but if you read the poetry in my first book (and you needn't) you will find that I was frequently writing like a new pink officer of the doctrinaire.

The spring of People's Park marked the beginning, not the end, of my friendship with Denise. In fact, she had given me every sense of poetry's immediacy and magic; the California Hall reading was a small event in a large apprenticeship. We both moved east that summer, and stayed in proximity for years. The finesse of her poetic line—its rhythmic and perceptual discriminations—remains for me, with Creeley's, the definitive American investigative verse line (though the writing I *refer* to largely predates the war poems). The disciplinarian that seemed in evidence later was not so in evidence earlier; instead there was the most joyful, appreciative, wonder-seeking and wonder-giving person I'd yet met. This is the same writer Robert adored, a poet whose aural and visual access to a sensory world places her in the company of H.D. and Dickinson, of Colette and Virginia Woolf, a writer capable of an audible hush into which a melodic apprehension of experience is raised precisely into language.

I've found, in rereading letters, that sympathy to gay ideology as it was forming was not intuitive to her, though her sympathy to *me* was, and we discussed in person and through correspondence the arguments and articulations of gender construction and sexual liberation. She was frankly confused, and interested in being educated; from her few responses I must have offered my own (communally derived) convictions and cant about male domination and power. (A letter from 1972 has probing questions from her about homosocial theory, and naive ones about homoerotic formation and even wicked hairdressers.) We visited regularly, and spoke with great emotional intimacy, and each visit for me was a privileged occasion. By the time I moved to San Francisco in the summer of 1974 we'd been in less frequent contact; a letter sent in 1975 shows we'd been out of touch for a while. It contains a reference to the idea of, and the seeds to, her poem "Writing to Aaron," which appeared in *Life in the Forest* (LF 5), and which raised a consonant pang in Robert—"And that's how we lost touch for so long" (L 714). And when, in 1976, my first book was published, I sent it to Denise with expectant pride. The irony of her response was bitter: "Some of your poems are too emphatically homosexual for me to identify with, as you surely realize," she wrote. "When I seem to detect a note of propaganda it turns me off completely. But when you are simply writing poetry and transcending opinion then I can respond. This may sound inconsistent from one who has written 'political' poetry, but I believe my political concerns to be less parochial in theme."[1]

Her analysis of dogma infecting my poetry per se could have come

1. Unpublished personal correspondence, January 26, 1977.

right from Robert's critique of her own writing, though the second part was hers alone, and the wound it opened between us never really healed. She was telling me, in fact, that it wasn't a poetic argument that most mattered to her: the argument was political and revolved around the supremacy of her own ideology. Parochial! If I (thought I) was busy tying up racism, misogyny, homophobia, and warmongering into a unified theory of oppression, her authoritarianism split the weave, and unraveled me where I was most in need of support, where my own personal sense of oppression was, in fact, most tenderly situated. This double face of her response had the power of revelation: of a true homophobia in her nature ("too emphatically homosexual") that called forth the same stern disapproving persona who so vehemently opposed the People's Prick.

It occurs to me now that Denise's ruffled recalcitrance may have hidden the fact that I had recently met and formed a friendship with Robert Duncan. I must have told her, and she must have felt in a paranoid way— as she certainly did later—that this new association implied a censure and maybe even a kind of gay alliance.

I'd met Robert on a Market Street trolley in 1975, capping an imaginative sequence begun earlier in the week. I'd had a dream in which a rainbow loop of light appeared to me on a clifftop, raising such howling winds that I was nearly driven over. A hand appeared from a nearing car to steady me, and bring me safely into the presence of the enormous, pulsating light. I awoke and named that light "Jehovah," and wrote a poem that seemed to me, then, all my own, with the sense of finding my true way into poetry for the first time. The next day, in a bookstore, I chanced upon *The Opening of the Field,* and opened directly to the poem "A Natural Doctrine," in which a rabbi Aaron of Baghdad "came upon the Name of God and achieved a pure rapture." "But it was for a clearing of the sky / . . . my thought cried," writes Robert, and, "the actual language is written in rainbows" (OF 81). Just a few days later I spied him on the bus, introduced myself, recounted in the most astonished way the correspondences between my dream and the poem, flush with the magic of circumstance, synchronicity, or fate. I remember distinctly that Robert was unimpressed by the linkage, as if this foretelling were a matter of course, utterly quotidian. But he was just enough impressed with me to invite me come to visit him, which I soon did.

I brought with me my first chapbook publication, and read it aloud; Robert's response was gleeful and warm.[2] The piece united themes of ritual transvestism, gender deconstruction, and plain ol' drag, and even by that time the writing was willing to be "fabulous"—to test the bounds of content permission and diction—in a way that was directly related to my reading of Duncan. His response, and our connection, I would say, was not based on some perceived or evident gay fraternal alliance but rather on this common understanding (my understanding under the wing of his) that the writing would be permitted to go where it needed to go, unabashed. It could never be "too emphatically homosexual," only because it could never be "too" *anything* in terms of limit or censure. This revelatory position in relation to permission was the foundation of my understanding of Robert's poetics, the key to his cosmic orchestrations and orchestral modulations—and remains so.

For me, from then, the conflict was resolutely resolved in terms of the poem's form being isometric with its (emerging) content, and a belief that when the poem is infected by the right-thinking politics which is dogma—replacing flexible *at*tention with inflexible *in*tention—it dies on the vine. Though Robert knew of my friendship with Denise, and I remember early on his addressing the issue in terms that were insufficiently clear to me so I may only have nodded sheepish assent, it was not really a subject of our conversation. By the 1980s it was clear that Denise was staying away from San Francisco, possibly so as not to have to contend directly with Robert. (A letter from 1980 states, "I just can't take that SF scene—was there in secret last summer & don't dig it."[3])

But then something came into view that challenged *my* political will, that threatened to deliver the politic back into the poetic in a way unmatched in the previous fifteen years: AIDS. By the late 1980s AIDS had ravaged San Francisco, seizing the territory of both action and imagination, and how to write about or into AIDS became, for me, an unavoidable confrontation, and challenged explorative composition with its insistence of thematic content. Advocacy, action, information, were demanded; the very nature of the epidemic spewed information and viral activity. At a loss as to how to meet this troubling matter in poetry without resorting to

2. Shurin, *Woman on Fire*.
3. Unpublished personal correspondence, July 13, 1980.

didacticism, I turned to prose to help me carry the more direct address-es—the portraiture and narrative of events—that were consonant with my experience, built largely around the struggles and insights of friends, of "comrades," I want to say, "returning to the rhetoric of an early mode" (RB 89). But when I finally found the means to write complexly about AIDS through poetry it was not dogmatic and was not presumptuously moralizing; the piece ("Human Immune") carried elegiac weight through a *formal* ideology, built on an epidemiological model: each stanza grew by design larger than the previous, subsumed it, so that without realizing it the reader was brought *inside* the epidemic, as if surrounded by the virus. And I spoke not from my own first person, but from a range of subject/ob-ject, singular, and plural points of view to suggest the invariability of risk and loss. I spoke, in fact, as just such a People's Prick who in an earlier era jumped onstage to announce the pleasure principle, but here the pleasure was inextricably conjoined with pain: "I squirted them with kisses. On his back at the edge of the couch to die of pleasure . . . "[4] To say the words that couldn't be said to address the content that had to be spoken—the sacra-mental profane—with a phallic imperative, to "penetrate into their histo-rian's hearts and foist upon the reader authenticity of the marvels."

The oracle, whose exact charge was to speak into the unspeakable, had stepped forward and demanded ground. "I want that energy while speaking, place yourselves close by me, excessive behavior swell discourse in proportion." Since the disease itself was not a moral occasion, the poem needed to voice *not-myself* arising from *not-my-moral-circumstance*, and would range in accordance with the full multiphasic ceremony of public and secret acts. The permission I needed to write the poem could not have come from hounding the penetrating organ off the stage.

The test and retest of esthetics informed by convictions, the vision of art's purposes and possibilities in relation to or *as* action, remain the core processes enacted by—and *engendered* by—the Duncan/Levertov corre-spondence. If sympathy to Robert's poetics excited my own writing, the passionate advocacy and determination to speak into *un*necessary silence I'll trace to both mentors—and the poetics of their contention is dialec-tically *in* me. I've only ever counted such dual inheritance as one of ex-traordinary luck: their immediate graces mine to learn from, their tensions

4. Shurin, *Unbound: A Book of Aids*, 58.

played out in the parameters of my work. The spiraling conversation is acute: "a mind hovering ecstatic / above a mouth in which the heart rises" (GW 168), writes Robert, and Denise will answer, "The poem ascends" (JL 37).

Works Cited

Shurin, Aaron. *Unbound: A Book of Aids*. Los Angeles: Sun and Moon Press, 1997.
———. *Woman on Fire*. San Francisco: Rose Deeprose Press, 1975.

CHAPTER 7

The Hasid and the Kabbalist

John Felstiner

"The Hasid and the Kabbalist": this title sounds promising and provocative, yet maybe it misleads, since Denise Levertov and Robert Duncan are poets too richly complex to be saddled with a single term. And neither was Jewish, or outright Jewish. And anyway Hasidism, an eighteenth-century popular movement of mystical piety and enthusiasm, and Kabbalah, an esoteric medieval system of theosophical Judaism, certainly share common elements, as Levertov and Duncan knew well enough. Still and all, my title may turn up some revealing lights and angles.

To begin with, we have well-known benchmarks. Denise's 1958 poem "Illustrious Ancestors" ends up "thinking some line taut between me and them"—"them" being her father's ancestor Shneour Zalman, founder of Habad Hasidism, who understood the language of birds, and her mother's ancestor Angel Jones of Mold, a Welsh tailor-mystic. Denise's book *The Jacob's Ladder* bears an epigraph from Martin Buber's *Tales of the Hasidim*, and a later poem calls up the magic flying peddler her father witnessed as a child and Chagall painted. She liked Zalman's concrete immediacy: asked by his son, "What do you pray with?" meaning "What's the basis of your praying?" he replied: "With the floor and the bench."

We also have Robert from Mallorca in 1956, writing Denise about headaches with the *Zohar*, Kabbalah's central text. Later he denounces a sneering critic "ignorant of the world of Jewish mysticism, and generations of a living community to which Denise Levertov's imagination here belongs, and into which, through her father, rabbi and then Christian priest, translator of the Zohar, she was born." Duncan prizes the miraculous grace in everyday things, à la Rilke and Denise's broom vendor, "one of the Hidden Ones," with divine wisdom through whom, he says, "the Chassidic masters speak not only to the Jewish community but to our common humanity." In February 1974, when I mentioned to Robert that I was going to teach American poetry in Jerusalem that fall, his immediate and only comment was, "You *must* study Zohar!"

Finally one more item, marking the closeness of both Hasidism and Kabbalah to Levertov's consciousness, as well as to Duncan's. In 1987 I wrote Denise responding fervently to her latest collection, and also sent along my just published essay tracing the manifold sources of Paul Celan's "Near, in the Aorta's Arch," a poem stemming in part from the great twentieth-century recoverer of Kabbalah, Gershom Scholem, whom he'd read in May 1967. With Egypt and Syria threatening Israel's borders, Celan's poem says, "Mother Rachel / weeps no more," Rachel being Kabbalah's figure for the Shekhinah, God's luminous presence lamenting with His people in exile. The poem ends with a *Hellwort*, a Hebraic "brightword" set free in the blood: "*Ziv*, that light"—since Scholem identifies *Ziv* as "the light of the Shekhinah."

Denise generously wrote back acknowledging my fervency. If I may repeat her as ever shapely and shapefully handwritten sentences:

What you say in response to my poems would make any poet feel glad no matter who said it—but to have the mind that wrote the "*Ziv*, that light" essay thus respond is a treasure indeed. What a marvelous piece. I think of the thrilling detective work on Coleridge by J. Livingston Lowes that so excited me when I discovered "The Road to Xanadu" when I was 18 or so, (prowling around the dear Ilford Public Library as was my wont) and see how much further and deeper such a hunt goes when informed by the spirit which, in Kabbala and Hasidism, heightened the dryer exegetical Rabbinical traditions & illuminated texts with the poetic imagination.

Of course Denise herself knew whereof she spoke when it came to height-

ening—and materializing—mystical intimations with the poetic imagination. Incidentally, though I'd first seen her at Stanford in 1966 in a red
pomegranate dress, speaking her antiwar poem "The Pulse"—"the glit-
ter / of all that shines out of itself"—I didn't really know her in 1974. But if
I'd told her then that I was going to teach in Israel, rather than "Study Zohar!" she'd more likely have told me: "Make the government behave!"

Turning back now to Robert Duncan, I'd like to touch on his Kab-
balism, his poet's more-or-less occult apprehension of godhead, by way of
two only-recently-published letters. Prompted by Donald Davie, in the fall
of 1973 I designed a verse translation workshop at Stanford—and why not
invite an accomplished practitioner to open his art to us? I'd met Robert at
Al and Barbara Gelpi's: Would he come and talk about translating Nerval?
Yes, he'll be glad to come, but as it happens, he has his own French translator right now in San Francisco, Serge Fauchereau: Might they *both* come
and in our presence work together on Duncan's poetry? By all means! "But
Robert," say I, "I still have only the twenty-five dollar honorarium for the
two of you."

Moving through "Structure of Rime V" with Serge in my class, at
one point Robert intones an archaic mystery or procreation ritual: "Their
prayers rise from the ground and hold me to the everlasting promise, to the
Adam!" Whereupon Fauchereau speaks his version—*Leurs prières s'élèvent
du sol et m'élèvent vers la promesse éternelle, vers l'Adam*—and Duncan takes
fire from this. The added spur of *vers*, "toward," and those progressional
verb forms, *s'élèvent* breeding *m'élèvent*, discovers a new possibility. Why
not (I recall him exclaiming) make it move this way, through consonance:
"Their prayers *rise* from the ground and [not "hold" but] *rouse* me to the
everlasting promise, to the Adam!" A French intervention, *s'élèvent . . .
m'élèvent*, opens the way to new music along with its bonus of an erotic lift:
"rise . . . rouse," urging him toward Adam's divine origin.

Translators can seldom claim such authority. What's more, it's a nice
instance of Duncan "re-visioning": we can't know the sense or direction of
a poem "until the process speaks," he'd written to Denise. "It comes sure
enuf then, the hand's feel that 'this' is what must be done." To borrow from
Antonio Machado: *Caminante, no hay camino. Se hace camino al andar.*
"Wayfarer, there is no way. You make a way as you go."

And there was more to come, translationally speaking. Shortly after

Duncan's visit, I wrote thanking him and seized the moment to pass along something I'd attempted years before, which might intrigue him: a version of Rainer Maria Rilke's *Archaïscher Torso Apollos*.

Wir kannten nicht sein unerhörtes Haupt,
darin die Augenäpfel reiften. Aber
sein Torso glüht noch wie ein Kandelaber,
in dem sein Schauen, nur zurückgeschraubt,

sich hält und glänzt. Sonst könnte nicht der Bug
der Brust dich blenden, und im leisen Drehen
der Lenden könnte nicht ein Lächeln gehen
zu jener Mitte, die die Zeugung trug.

Sonst stünde dieser Stein enstellt und kurz
unter der Schultern durchsichtigem Sturz
und flimmerte nicht so wie Raubtierfelle

und bräche nicht aus allen seinen Rändern
aus wie ein Stern: denn da ist keine Stelle
die dich nicht sieht. Du musst dein Leben ändern.

Archaic Torso of Apollo

We never witnessed his unheard-of head
in which the eyeballs apple-ripened. Yet
his torso still glows like a streetlamp's globe,
and inside, turned down low a while, his gaze

holds fast and shines. Otherwise the bend
of the breast could not blind you, or a smile
wind through the gentle twisting of the loins
into that core that kept the seed alive.

Otherwise this stone would stand distorted
and cut short under the shoulders' sheer fall
and would not glimmer so, like wild beast fell,

and not be breaking out from all its edges
just like a star: for there's no place on it
that does not see you. You must change your life.

In this sonnet from summer 1908, Rilke regenerates an ancient torso in the Louvre, a remnant fragment of a Greek sculpture of the mythic god of poetry, music, prophecy, and the sun.

On first looking into this German lyric's possible English music, Duncan rose and roused to the occasion in two vigorous letters of February 1974. To climb back up the ladder of translation, a kind of Jacob's ladder, drew him toward what originally drew Rilke: divine radiance, "that light" which in Judaic mysticism emanates from God. Robert's letters on this sonnet say that "Rilke's daring in the first place is to go into a fascination," and that "the oracular mode of Rilke's form—the music of the poem projects a vision in being seen, a lure of the god. . . . "[1]

Well, somehow since then it took me twenty-seven years to publish Duncan's two precious letters. Now they've come out in *Mantis*, the Stanford English Department graduate student magazine, and David Goldstein and I have given *Parnassus* an essay on the letters. In them, Robert's ear for vocalic cadence carries the day. In translating Rilke's lines, because only musical truth begets spiritual, he says, "We rightly work to keep the hypnagogic repetitions and returns of tones." "Hypnagogic" makes the difference here, "sleep-inducing," for Robert after what he calls "a visionary and oracular dream" in Rilke. His two letters abound with words for the Orphic—or rather Apollonian, or Neoplatonic, or Kabbalistic—enthusiasm of his encounter: "colloquy . . . invitation . . . beckoning . . . signalling . . . compelling . . . fascination . . . a fascination . . . lure . . . lured me . . . drawn me . . . search . . . effort . . . labor . . . struggle."

I believe, in fact, that Robert Duncan kindled to this encounter because within the "communion of poets" he so valued, the task of translation brought him closer, really *closest*, to Rilke's own inspiration. "Rilke's daring in the first place is to go into a fascination, call upon it, call it to him. . . . I think I want to get—likewise—a fascination, now not of the torso which I don't face; but of the poem which in its turn fascinates." In

1. Cited from Robert Duncan, "Rilke in Duncan-Land," *Mantis: A Journal of Poetry, Criticism, and Translation*, no. 2 (2001): 38–44.

other words, wrestling the *Archaïscher Torso Apollos* into his native tongue gives Robert more luminous, more numinous access to the gaze of the god than simply reading the German or composing his own poem might give. This I believe: translation can *do* this.

Listen to his use of the verb "lure" just before saying the poem's music projects "a lure of the god." "The light is dimming," he says. "And your translation has (as all translations must) lured me into that unsettled interregnum between two rules." Clearly the lure of the god inspirits the lure of the poem. And Duncan's two rules (a cunning anagram, "lure" into "rule")—his two rules may be those of German and English language, of oracle and devotee, divine and mortal.

Divine and mortal: "I have come to think of Poetry more and more as a wrestling with Form to liberate Form," Duncan wrote in 1968. "The figure of Jacob returns again and again to my thought." This is not Jacob's dream of a ladder but another night, and it's not a dream. Nightlong he wrestles the angel and at dawn, crying "I will not let thee go, except thou bless me," Jacob gains the blessing of a new name, *Isra-el*, God-wrestler.

Robert closes his long first letter saying he "had a great time" at the seminar, yet even then a last thought presses further: "We always think it's our feelings or ideas or experiences that we struggle to translate. But it's words that are translatable and untranslatable. The poem is a language-feel, a language-idea, a language-experience we arrive at in the first place. Only to say we come right to the primary difficulty in coming to the very word of it."

Now, a different sort of faith, more Hasidic than Kabbalistic, lies in Denise Levertov's love for Rilke, her tutelary spirit. His "reverence for 'the savor of creation'" inspired her, his "intense joy in the visual"—witness her psalmic title *O Taste and See*. Often she invokes the ninth Duino elegy, wherein Rilke cries out:

> Earth, isn't this what you want: to rise up
> *invisible* in us?

Take, for instance, Denise's poem "For Instance," recalling some "fragment / of lichened stone" from her youth, a "gleam of East Anglian afternoon light, and leaves / dripping and shining." Movingly she ends this poem with Rilke's German, *Erde, du liebe . . .* , "Earth, you beloved . . . "

Seeking the sources of her attentiveness, her (Hasidic) readiness for mundane epiphany, we find one even deeper than Rilke. Denise's father, Paul Levertoff, a Russian-born Jew turned Anglican priest, kept tapping his Hasidic and Judaic roots. There exists, by the way, a frayed old poster in Hebrew and English from a church wall, announcing that *HaRav Dr. Paul Levertov* will lead songs and psalms every Sunday at 11 A.M. and celebrate Holy Communion *in Hebrew*. In 1928 he published *St. Paul in Jewish Thought* (Denise gave me a photocopy of this alas! unobtainable little book), which at one point speaks of a certain Jewish quality vital to Christianity: "This union of a deep faith in God with the highest concentration of human energy." Then he goes on, uncannily, to as much as foretell his five-year-old daughter's eventual poetic creed: "Jewish materialism is *religious* materialism, or, rather, realism. For every idea and every ideal the Jew demands a visible and touchable materialization." Given "the highest spiritual truth," a Jew must "see and feel its real working. He believes in the invisible . . . but he desires that this invisible should become visible and reveal its power; that it should permeate everything material."

Naturally it's no mere coincidence, given Denise's uniquely fortunate home education, that this desire should permeate poem after poem, where ever and again we "see and feel" the "real working" of "spiritual truth," especially in moments when light, that Kabbalist emanation of divine presence, touches the ordinary world around us:

> Trunk in deep shade, its lofting crown
> . . . an answering gold—

> . . . Sunlit
> children wait for the green light.

> Zones of flickering
> water-diamonds
> converse with almost-still
> glint of leaves along the poplar-row.

I'm particularly partial to Denise's 1988 poem "In California," written and first published at Stanford, which like a biblical Psalm joins praise to anger; joins dawn light "emblazoning" palm and pine to pesticide "poking" at weeds and moss; poises "Scripture of scintillas" against bulldozers, "babel of destructive construction," and finds a phrase for it all: "Fragile paradise."

"Who can utter" the praise or shame of all this? she asks psalm-wise at the end. A phrase from her collection *The Jacob's Ladder* answers this question in specifically Jewish mystical terms:

> each part
> of speech a spark
> awaiting redemption . . .

And although she didn't usually insist all that literally, as Duncan did, Levertov right on into Postmodernism held poetic utterance to be a primary, a sacred task.

Her glints and glimpses of light became shadowed and vulnerable, joyful alertness turned dreadful, as environmental degradation or (call it) desecration drastically worsened. One precarious thus precious moment occurs toward the end of "An English Field in the Nuclear Age" (1982). Levertov offsets imminent-seeming disaster with "haze and halos of / sunbless'd particulars." Simply she urges

> how among
> thistles, nettles, subtle silver
> of long-dried cowpads,
>
> gold mirrors of buttercup satin
> assert eternity as they reflect
> nothing, everything, absolute instant,
> and dread
>
> holds its breath, for
> this minute at least was
> not the last.

Sometimes, the evening before a class, I'd walk across the green field behind my house to Denise's apartment to record her voice. Especially in her British-tuned intonation, cadence, and emphases, Levertov's craft enlivens these lines: the vocal, tactile materialism of "thistles, nettles" right alongside "subtle silver," the startling run-on that links "subtle silver" to "long-dried cowpads," the metaphoric find of "gold mirrors" and "buttercup satin" claiming to "assert eternity," then the breath-taking, heart-stopping breaks where "dread // holds its breath," while an exquisite timing metes out one more moment saved.

Of course this poem's "acts of passion," "transubstantiate," remind me what an error it would be to isolate the Hasidic or diminish the Catholic strain in Levertov. She rejoiced in William Carlos Williams's "Franciscan sense of wonder"—"the stiff curl of wildcarrot leaf," the "small cheeping birds / skimming bare trees / above a snow glaze." Yet isn't it a continuous stream, on down from the jubilant Psalms of earthly Creation? As Denise once remarked, "The Hasidim were a lot like the Franciscans"—or, as her dad might have said: "The Franciscans were a lot like the Hasidim."

III

CHAPTER 8

Chelsea 8: Political Poetry at Midcentury

Brett Millier

Late in 1959, a little-known poet and aspiring editor named David Ignatow sent handwritten letters to a hundred or so of his fellow poets asking for contributions to a special issue of the little magazine *Chelsea*, to be devoted to political poetry.[1] His letter noted "a marked absence of a kind of poetry which had great prominence in the early 20s & 30s, and which gave to American poetry generally a flavor & background of high charge." "We sorely miss it today," he noted, lamenting that in its place we meet "monotonous sameness . . . in our present day literary journals." He was interested, he said, "in getting together the best political poetry being written today by our best American poets. In my opinion, the stuff is being written but with no place to publish. Political poetry, I feel, is one way to break out of the impasse into which American poets have gotten themselves by their exclusive concentration on metaphysical and self-conscious

1. I am grateful for the help of several research librarians in tracing the development of *Chelsea* 8; in particular, Rob Melton, of the Mandeville Special Collections Library at UC-San Diego; Nancy Kuhl, of the Beinecke Library at Yale; and Tara Wenger, of the Harry Ransom Humanities Research Center at the University of Texas, Austin.

introspective poetry."[2] He noted the political activism of poets abroad, and the relative vibrancy of the resulting British, European, and South American poetry. Given this characterization of the contemporary poetry scene, his initial list of potential contributors is fairly predictable. He wrote to Richard Wilbur and Donald Hall, to Richard Eberhart and Donald Justice, to Philip Booth and Galway Kinnell, among others—and he asked everyone he could about which European poets he might attract to the issue. He also wrote, sending essentially the same letter, to Charles Olson, the former rector of Black Mountain College and mentor to a great many young poets of quite different styles.

The United States in the winter of 1959–60 was of course on the eve of a presidential election which, in the minds of most of these poets, seemed likely to pit the dominant materialistic, conformist, and militaristic mode (in the reviled figure of Richard Nixon) against an undefined hope for an open and innovating future, in the figure of John F. Kennedy, or perhaps (at this point in the campaign) Adlai Stevenson. The election was much on the minds of poets as they scanned their stores of finished poems for those with explicit political content and responded to Ignatow's request. Several mentioned Nixon specifically (Philip Booth commented: "Your *Chelsea* issue sounds like a purely right idea for Slippery Dick's big year at the polls" [23 April 1960]), and there is a fascinating flurry of correspondence concerning a poetic "insult to Nixon" by Theodore Roethke, which he apparently read among friends and eventually sent to Ignatow with an hysterical note directing him to publish the poem prominently and send it on to several major figures in politics and journalism. The poem is not extant, though the letter is.

But most of the poets made much less reference to contemporary political events and personalities in their letters to Ignatow, whether they enclosed poems for his consideration or not. One assumes that a significant number simply did not respond to his request and tossed out his letter (for that reason it is not clear exactly to whom he wrote and when; Ignatow kept no carbons). A good handful responded cursorily—with either "Here are some poems; YOU tell me if they're political," or "I don't write political poems," or "I have no poems on hand right now." The letters are a study

2. Though Ignatow clearly sent this letter to many poets, only a few copies are extant. The above quotations are from his letter to Langston Hughes, dated 22 January 1960.

in the range of poets' circumstances and feelings on the subject, as some regarded the request as essentially a commission, and others felt compelled to explain their position on the subject of art and politics, often with irony. "I have, as it happens, a desperate need for the supplementary income I get from selling poems," wrote George Starbuck. "If I happen to write a good poem of unmarketable virulence before your deadline, I'll send it to you" (30 March 1960). John Ciardi found the premise banal: "I, for one, think some sort of social poetry is inevitable" (27 January 1960). "As you can see from my delay in replying," wrote Donald Justice,

> I have been pondering political poems. I would very much like to write one. I started an ode, so-called, to old Ike once several months ago but got nowhere, the subject matter was too unexcitedly unexciting; I got a little further with a sort of ironic piece deploring the absence of any public statues in Iowa City and half-finished a rather rhetorical report by a Martian returning home—but I have nothing to show for all this except scraps of paper and hope for the future. . . . Meanwhile, I'm sorry; I'm still, though I hope temporarily, stuck back in my childhood, up in the attic, and can't get downstairs and out into the street where the air, though smoggy, is at least healthier psychologically. (22 March 1960)

Justice here defends himself against Ignatow's charge that contemporary American poetry is fatally self-involved. This is, after all, the winter after the publication of Lowell's *Life Studies*, and poets everywhere were reexamining their childhoods in search of material. Oddly, there is no mention of Lowell whatsoever in the correspondence related to this issue, and if Ignatow wrote to him, Lowell did not respond.[3] Edward Brunner's impressive 2001 study of mainstream American poetry in the 1950s, *Cold War Poetry*, explicitly and convincingly argues that as "World War II as a defining instance [was] replaced by the cold war as a perpetual condition," and as criticism of the United States and its military actions were suppressed, the "bomb poem," as he calls poems about the threat of nuclear annihilation, took refuge in the "family poem" (featuring children as vulnerable potential victims of the bomb and other less clearly defined threats). Thus the breakthrough into confessional poetry represented by *Life Studies* was political, a kind of turning inward of political concern (xi, xiii–xiv). Jus-

---

3. In January of 1960, Lowell was home in Boston after his post–*Life Studies* breakdown and hospitalization, hard at work on another commission, this one for the Boston Arts Festival: "For the Union Dead."

tice's response here implicitly supports Ignatow's (and Brunner's) initial characterization of the poetry "scene" as having disengaged itself from political concerns. Another poet (signature indecipherable) wrote from Jerusalem, "I must say I was surprised to hear of the nature of your project—it seems to me that as far as poetry is concerned, there is hardly anything political being written. The poets once bitten have become twice shy" (29 April 1960).

Several other poets took the occasion to question and complicate the premise of any anthology of "political poems." "I have no idea what you mean by 'political' poetry," many said. A young French painter-poet (later painter–art critic and curator), Jean Jacques Lebel, articulated one end of the spectrum of opinion, echoing Ignatow's explicit reference to the political poetry of the 1930s: "I agree with your diagnostic, poetry is sick with metaphysical (or just plain) egotism," he wrote.

But are politics capable of remagnetizing it, of making it objective, of giving it the genius it lacks? I don't think so. Most political poetry is allegoric mercantile patriotic crap and then false poets used it to justify false socialism, governments have grabbed it for their propaganda, the N.Y. Chief of Police writes verse, I hear, that is political poetry that I despise. What I care for is poetry made of what Nietzsche calls *le sentiment de liberté*. May I translate a quotation from the great Octavio Paz: "Poetry, in itself, is only worthwhile if it has a sense of liberation. But, in general, social poetry is mistaken for political poetry. Social poetry happens not only to be bad poetry (which is no disaster, it's only one more lousy poem added to the pile): it's also very bad politics." . . .

"If poetry gets down on its knees in front of reality," wrote Lebel, "it is no longer poetry" ("Friday 1960"). Later Lebel did send a poem to Ignatow, "Coleur de mon sang," with the following explanatory note. "I do not believe in what Mallarmé calls circumstantial poetry. Poetry questions reality, it is impersonal, unpolitical, out of this world. Why then did I write *Coleur de Mon Sang*? [Because] Everything was collapsing" (n.d.). Lebel went on to a career of thoroughly *engagée* painting and criticism; Ignatow's letter apparently prompted him to articulate his developing principles.

But Ignatow's letter also prompted a wonderfully characteristic response from Charles Olson himself. Numerous other poets mention Olson in their replies to Ignatow, and while he is ultimately not himself represented in the volume, his very nearly indecipherable letter is positively

Poundian in its elliptical and oracular authority, and ultimately had a profound effect on which poets Ignatow included. Olson energetically rejects Ignatow's contention that political poetry has not been evident in recent years, and speaks of it in remarkably contemporary terms:

Right off the top don't quite get what you propose as "political", especially as of the history of English poesy, like
                and/or that you are talking abt. the drop, since the
'30s, of the social subject—like the old "Left". . . .
I lead [*sic*] to you, simply that both Duncan and myself, say, have been for years doing nothing but poems almost of—in his case, *polity*, in my own *polis* (the Maximus, now coming out as Volume 3 in March etc)
And Ginsberg, like—altogether political no? in such as Death to Van Gogh's Ear—or much of the "protest" of the Beat persons is political, no?
Just for my own stimulation wld you write me back—with examples, like (I have been myself a "politician", and like I say have spent 10 years already on the Maximus poem, and see no end to it yet, like;
        No 2: I see no reason not to think that exactly the "political" is what is (a) conspicuously corrupt as in present existence (both scale-wise: bipartisanism; world-wise: universalism etc) and (b) that as a point d'appui for man or for the poet the political is defunct.
        3: the restoration of that "vision" (that man lives among public fact as among private fact, and that either is solely a face of the double of the real) is conspicuous and crucially demanded

and 4: that the poet now, as much as any Dante, or Homer (who was a "flower" of the last "polis"—unless you count Bach, who was the purest sign of the local when it was "round") that the POET now is MORE POLITICAL in the root sense than has been true in English at all . . .

Handwritten in the margin of this letter is Olson's note: "the *conception* of the *creation* of a *society* is the art of *politics*, is it not?" (5 January 1960).

    Unfailingly generous, Olson goes on to support this broadened definition of "political" by recommending his friends and students for inclusion in the issue (and giving Ignatow their addresses): Robert Creeley, Ed Dorn, Michael McClure, Philip Whalen, and especially Robert Duncan. And he goes on and on and on with several more numbered lists of points, growing increasingly more abstract (and more concerned with the premises of *Maximus*) as the numbers rise. But he insists that Ignatow lift his gaze from the mainstream "academic" poetry on which he has based his original judgment that political poetry is not being published today. Olson's diatribe is perhaps the most interesting document in the archive, and in the end he suggests to Ignatow that the letter itself might be a suitable contribution for the issue ("In any case, *please keep* letter"). Ignatow ignored the publication suggestion, but it seems clear that this letter, along with a similar-minded but much more coherent letter received later from Creeley, served to explode Ignatow's original concept of the political poem enough so that the final collection could include not only the likes of Wilbur and Hall and Booth and James Wright; not only Ray Durem's trenchant and transparent epigrams ("Since 1619": "Man, it's rough! / Three hundred years / is long enough!"); but also Robert Duncan's "Ingmar Bergman's *Seventh Seal*" and Denise Levertov's "Three Meditations," as well as poems by Paul Blackburn, Jean Garrigue, and Creeley, Corso, Ginsberg, Dorn, and Ferlinghetti. It is clear, at any rate, that he sent a second round of letters once he had received Olson's, in January 1960, and that those letters went to Creeley, Ginsberg, Edward Dahlberg, and Langston Hughes, as well as to Levertov and Duncan, among others. To Dahlberg, in one of these later letters, he wrote: "I write to you because there will be no emphasis on any one style, form, subject matter. I just want the very best" (14 February 1960). Challenged by Dahlberg two weeks later, he wrote with some exasperation,

It should be obvious to any attentive reader that the prophets Jeremiah and the two Isiahs [*sic*] were nothing if not political. . . . I certainly agree that literature in America has had no influence on polity, but it is writers we are writing for mainly here and when I ask for political poems it is a form of protest trying to go to the heart of the matter against the debased writing that passes for literature in America. (4 March 1960)

Ignatow's ultimate collection has the virtues of such inclusiveness. Robert Creeley wrote afterward to say somewhat diplomatically that at least the final volume had "cut through all camps very usefully and happily" (26 December 1960). But Levertov wrote to Duncan calling it "a horrid grab bag" (L 266), and Duncan told her that he wished both their poems had "been elsewhere. . . . What burns me is not only that we got swept into that mound of refuse—but that there was a prize! Fittingly—for it's writ in the predominant aesthetic—given over to that piece of gratuitous

liberal guilt (gilt) of Mr. Wright's, Aie! and I'd thot [sic] he had the possible commitment of a poet!" (L 263).[4] Duncan objects to the presence of
the subtlety and formal innovation of his and Levertov's (and their friend
Ed Dorn's) poems alongside (and subordinate to) the more mainstream
and obvious poetics and politics of the likes of Wright. But the collection
does include poems by Beat poets and Black Mountain poets, as well as
more mainstream "academic" poets. It also includes a good many translations of poems from the Russian, German, and French, though none
from South America. In manuscript, Ignatow's collection was divided into
subject categories: "Political Meditations," "Injustices," "Race," "War &
Bomb," "Political Corruption I," and "Political Corruption II." The fact
that Ignatow abandoned such explicit categories in the end may speak to
the difficulty of grouping the heterodox contributions he ultimately selected, though it is interesting (and commendable) that even initially, he had
divided the manuscript by subject rather than by style or school.

In the manuscript, Levertov's "Three Meditations" closes out the
opening "Political Meditations" section. The poem was apparently written in response to Ignatow's request, and this fact alone lends the *Chelsea*
collection historical significance. Eventually collected in *The Jacob's Ladder*
(1961), the poem shares with many of the others in that volume the feeling (available to us in hindsight, of course) of existing in a kind of aura between the visionary poetics of Levertov's earlier work and the articulated
political commitment of her later poems, fully presented for the first time
perhaps in *The Sorrow Dance* (1967). Audrey Rodgers has seen the poem as
occupying a fertile ground between "her continuing interest in social action and the persistent and haunting remembrance of things past. . . . [It
is] in many ways . . . a transitional sequence" (70). Levertov sent it to Ignatow with a characteristically self-deprecating note: "I have a poem for you,
which came out of thinking about what a 'political poem' might be. Hope
you'll like it—don't worry if you don't, though" (3 April 1960).

Indeed there is some evidence that Ignatow was not altogether com-
fortable with the poem. Sonia Raiziss, one of *Chelsea*'s general editors,
wrote to Ignatow on 16 April 1960 suggesting that he accept the poem, but
added, "omit Part I, but use Olson's epigraph to introduce section III . . .

4. James Wright's "Confession to J. Edgar Hoover" won the fifty-dollar
prize as the "best" poem in the *Chelsea* political poetry issue.

use II as is—poem and epigraph." "If she objects," Raiziss said, "give her the alternatives of sending something more engagé and/or leaving the pres- ent tripartite poem for one of our later issues." In the end, Ignatow printed the poem as Levertov had presented it to him, his definition of "engagé" having been significantly expanded.

In "thinking about what a 'political poem' might be," Levertov is cer- tainly not confronting the immediate political reality she would take on so directly later in the 1960s. But she is considering the possible political roles and responsibilities of the poet. Each of the "Three Meditations" (Levertov considered the group a single poem in sections and would not have toler- ated a cut) opens with an epigraph, culled from the notebooks Levertov had kept for nearly all her writing life. It is clear from later statements and essays that these epigraphs had long represented touchstones for the poet, and each is a cogent statement on the place of the poet in the social and political world; Levertov would meditate on this question, of "the poet in the world," for a long time. The first epigraph is from Olson, and it sug- gests that to be a poet at all is to be a political actor, and to write is suffi- cient political action in itself:

> the only object is
> a man, carved
> out of himself, so wrought he
> fills his given space, makes
> traceries sufficient to
> others' needs
>   (here is
> social action, for the poet,
> anyway, his
> politics, his
> news) (JL 29)

Later, in her 1968 Hopwood Lecture at the University of Michigan, Lever- tov glossed this seminal passage retroactively as consistent with her later practice of a poetry of witness:

Olson is saying . . . that it is *by* being what he is capable of being, *by* living his life so that his identity is "carved," is "wrought," *by* filling his given space, that a man, and in particular a poet as a representative of an activity peculiarly human, *does* make "traceries sufficient to others' needs" (which is, in the most profound sense, a "social" or "political" action). Poems bear witness to the manness of man, which, like the strawness of straw, is an exiled spark. (PW 51)[5]

By 1968, Levertov is able to say confidently that the essential work of the poet is, "in the most profound sense," political.

The first meditation suggests that idea by instructing the poet in HOW to fill "his given space," and implicitly sees a powerful (in that sense, political) poetry emanating from the physical grounding of the poet herself in the world, at dawn, at noon, at evening:

> Breathe deep of the
> freshly gray morning air, mild
> spring of the day.
> Let the night's dream-planting
> bear leaves
> and light up the death-mirrors with
> shining petals.
> Stand fast in thy place:
> remember, Caedmon
> turning from song was met
> in his cow-barn by One who set him
> to sing the beginning.
> Live
> in thy fingertips and in thy
> hair's rising; hunger
> be thine, food
> be thine and what wine
> will not shrivel thee.
> Breathe deep of
> evening, be with the
> rivers of tumult, sharpen
> thy wits to know power and be
> humble.   (JL 29)

The poem's imperatives—"Breathe," "Stand fast in thy place," "Live"—

5. The subject of Levertov's Hopwood Lecture was her 1960 poem "The Necessity," in which Levertov links "Three Meditations" closely with that less explicit meditation on the poet's responsibility.

are expressed in archaic poetic language that Levertov said in the Hopwood Lecture she had gotten from Edward Young's *Night Thoughts*: "'dive deep in thy bosom. . . . let thy genius rise'" (PW 52). The self-consciously poetic diction also suggests that the instruction is timeless, stretching from the founder of Thebes and the poets of ancient Greece to the present audience, all of whom are charged "to sing the beginning" and therefore both to "know power"—the operations of the political world—and to "be / humble."

The second section opens with a quotation from Ibsen, which was clearly a touchstone to Levertov in her thinking about the poet's role. The statement again emphasizes that role as a medium of sorts, for the immediate as well as the eternal, the seen as well as the unseen: "The task of the poet is to make clear to *himself*, and thereby to others, the temporal and eternal questions." Levertov returned to this statement again and again. It is among the quotations tacked to the wall of *The Poet in the World* (1973), and she recalls it in the 1968 Hopwood Lecture as well. Referring directly to the second "Meditation" with reference to its epigraph, she emphasized the "to *himself*," which she also highlights in the epigraph:

My emphasis was on asking oneself the questions, internalizing them, on coming to realize how much the apparently external problems have their parallels within us. . . . This internalization still seems to me what is essential in Ibsen's dictum: what the poet is called on to clarify is not answers but the existence and nature of questions; and his likelihood of so clarifying them for others is made possible only through dialogue with himself. Inner colloquy as a means of communication with others was something I assumed in the poem but had not been at that time overtly concerned with, though in fact I had already translated a Toltec poem that includes the line, "The true artist / maintains dialogue with his heart." (PW 45)

The poem itself acknowledges an oppressive "temporal" reality that both threatens the poet's clarity of vision and sharpens her sense of responsibility, while recognizing that the chaos without is both mirror and in part created by the chaos within. The idea of "inner colloquy" is not yet explicit, except perhaps in the discipline of "meditation" itself.

> Barbarians
> throng the straight roads of
> my empire, converging
> on black Rome.

There is darkness in me.
Silver sunrays
sternly, in tenuous joy
cut through its folds:
mountains
arise from cloud.
Who was it yelled, cracking
the glass of delight?
Who sent the child
sobbing to bed, and woke it
later to comfort it?
I, I, I, I.
I multitude, I tyrant,
I angel, I you, you
world, battlefield, stirring
with unheard litanies, sounds of piercing
green half-smothered by
strewn bones. (JL 30)

The equation of marauding "barbarians" with the mother's impatient scolding of a child suggests a prescient conflation of the personal with the political, if not the poet's urgent conversation with herself. But this Whitmanian assumption of universal experience, which identifies with both the oppressor and the victim, with both the individual and the masses, with both sorrow and joy, is an almost intolerable burden in a world expressed in images of the Holocaust's mass graves, "stirring / with unheard litanies, sounds of piercing / green half-smothered by / strewn bones."

This world of inner and outer turmoil ultimately demands from the poet a response, an "utmost response," as the epigraph to the third section claims, in which D. H. Lawrence insists, "Virtue lies in the heroic response to the creative wonder," and in the poem Levertov works her way through the whole contemporary world of genocide, nuclear threat, space race, and international conflict, all the way back to "song":

Death in the grassblade
a dull
substance, heading blindly
for the bone
and bread preserved without
virtue,

sweet grapes sour to the children's children.

We breathe an ill wind,
nevertheless our kind
in mushroom multitudes
jostles for elbow-room
moonwards

an equalization of
hazards
bringing the poet
back to song
as before

to sing of death
as before
and life, while he
has it, energy

being in him a singing,
a beating of gongs, efficacious
to drive away devils,
response to

the wonder that
as before
shows a double face,

to be
what he is
being his virtue

filling his whole space
so no devil
may enter. (JL 30–31)

The poet's task, even in the terror of contemporary reality, is "as before," is timeless. It is to sing, both in order to drive away threatening devils, and to "fill his given space" "so no devil / may enter." "Wonder . . . / shows a double face," and always has, and the poet must record both views. Later, as we have seen, Levertov would come to distrust even this carefully balanced calibration of the poet's responsibility in a threatening and unjust world, and "song" becomes something more like "testimony."

Robert Duncan hesitated for a few months, then sent Ignatow his "Ingmar Bergman's *Seventh Seal*" in the late spring of 1960. The poem was finished by the time Ignatow asked for it, and was collected immediately into Duncan's volume *The Opening of the Field* (1960). Its starting point resembles Levertov's "Barbarians," who "throng the straight roads of / my empire"; specifically, it is Bergman's brilliant 1957 film, a religious allegory set during a single day in the late Middle Ages, in a Nordic land wracked by crusades, plague, and vindictive witch hunts. Duncan's attraction to the film as the basis for his poem may stem from the imaginary medieval world of his first collection of poems *Medieval Scenes* (1950; reissued in 1959) and his mid-1950s studies of medieval and Renaissance culture at Berkeley with Ernst Kantorowicz (Johnson 48). In Bergman's fable the analogy with Europe in the aftermath of the Second World War is apparent enough (Ignatow included the poem in the "War & Bomb" section of his manuscript), and Duncan's contemplation of the film's desperate imagery further collapses the thirteenth century and the mid-twentieth century; Europe and the United States; the chaos outside and the chaos within the individual.

> This is the way it is. We see
> three ages in one: the child Jesus
> innocent of Jerusalem and Rome
> —magically at home in joy—
> that's the year from which
> our inner persistence has its force.
>
> The second, Bergman shows us,
> carries forward image after image
> of anguish, of the Christ crossd
> and sends us from open sores of the plague
> (shown as wounds upon His corpse)
> from lacerations in the course of love
> (the crown of whose kingdom tears the flesh)
>
> . . . There is so much suffering!

What possibly protects us
from the emptiness, the forsaken cry,
the utter dependence, the vertigo?
Why do so many come to love's edge
only to be stranded there?

The second face of Christ, his
evil, his Other, emaciated, pain and sin.
Christ, what a contagion!
What a stink it spreads round

our age! It's our age,
and the rage of the storm is abroad.
The malignant stupidity of statesmen rules.
the old riders thru the forest race
    shouting: the wind! the wind!
Now the black horror cometh again.

And I'll throw myself down
as the clown does in Bergman's *Seventh Seal*
to cower as if asleep with his wife and child,
hid in the caravan under the storm.
Let the Angel of Wrath pass over.
Let the end come.
War, stupidity and fear are powerful.
We are only children. To bed! to bed!
    To play safe!

To throw ourselves down
helplessly, into happiness,
    into an age of our own, into
    our own days.
There where the Pestilence roars,
where the empty riders of the horror go.   (OF 93–94)

Given the title, we assume that the perspective of this poem lies within the film. "This is the way it is" in thirteenth-century northern Europe,
and the mention of what "Bergman shows us" in the second stanza supports that; the images come directly from the film. But the shift to the first

person singular in the sixth stanza: "I'll throw myself down / as the clown does in Bergman's *Seventh Seal*," introduces the idea that the "age," "our age" of malignantly stupid statesmen and galloping horror, is the era of the filmgoer/poet himself as well as that of the film's protagonist. In that case, the poem's final gesture of withdrawal or escape into clownish or childish "happiness"; "an age of our own" in the midst of the age of pestilence and horror, is all the more striking. Duncan asks the questions of the compelling figure of Antonius Block (Max Von Sydow), whose anxious search for evidence of God's presence in the world is the central action of Bergman's film: "There is so much suffering! / What possibly protects us . . . ?" But he identifies (as Block himself ultimately does) with the visionary fool, Jof (read: Joseph) and his wife Mia (read: Mary), and their joyful, bare-bottomed son, the infant Christ of the first stanza, "from which / our inner persistence has its force."

"We are only children. To bed! to bed!" The contrast between this and Levertov's vision of the poet standing her ground, expanding to fill the whole contemporary space so that "no devil may enter"—surely an active rather than passive response to living in troubled times—may predict the painful rift in friendship that occurred when both poets, a few years later, were presented with the urgent moral and political question of the war in Vietnam.

Works Cited

Anon. Letter to David Ignatow. 29 April 1960. David Ignatow Papers. Mandeville Special Collections Library, University of California, San Diego. Quoted with permission of the Library.

Booth, Philip. Letter to David Ignatow. 23 April 1960. David Ignatow Papers. Mandeville Special Collections Library, University of California, San Diego. Quoted with permission of Philip Booth, and of the Library.

Brunner, Edward. *Cold War Poetry*. Urbana: University of Illinois Press, 2001.

Ciardi, John. Letter to David Ignatow. 27 January 1960. David Ignatow Papers. Mandeville Special Collections Library, University of California, San Diego. Quoted with permission of Myra Ciardi, and of the Library.

Creeley, Robert. Letter to David Ignatow. 26 December 1960. David Ignatow Papers. Mandeville Special Collections Library, University of California, San Diego. Quoted with permission of Will Creeley and Hannah Creeley, and of the Library.

Duncan, Robert. "Ingmar Bergman's *Seventh Seal*." *Chelsea* 8 (October 1960): 53–54. Reprinted in Robert Duncan, OF 93–94. Quoted with permission.

Ignatow, David. Letters to Edward Dahlberg. 14 February 1960 and 4 March 1960. Edward Dahlberg Papers. Harry Ransom Humanities Research Center, University of Texas, Austin. Quoted with permission of Roy Harvey Pearce, and of the Center.

————. Letter to Langston Hughes. 22 January 1960. Langston Hughes Papers. Yale Collection of American Literature, Beinecke Rare Book Library, Yale University. Quoted with permission of Roy Harvey Pearce, and of the Library.

————, ed. "Political Poetry." *Chelsea* 8 (October 1960): 12–71.

Johnson, Mark Andrew. *Robert Duncan*. Boston: Twayne, 1988.

Justice, Donald. Letter to David Ignatow. 22 March 1960. David Ignatow Papers. Mandeville Special Collections Library, University of California, San Diego. Quoted with permission of Jean Justice, and of the Library.

Lebel, Jean Jacques. Letters to David Ignatow. "Friday 1960" and n.d. David Ignatow Papers. Mandeville Special Collections Library, University of California, San Diego. Quoted with permission of the Library.

Levertov, Denise. Letter to David Ignatow. 3 April 1960. David Ignatow Papers. Mandeville Special Collections Library, University of California, San Diego. Quoted with permission of Paul Lacey, and of the Library.

————. "Three Meditations." *Chelsea* 8 (October 1960): 20–22. Reprinted in Denise Levertov, JL 29–31.

Olson, Charles. Letter to David Ignatow. 5 January 1959 [1960]. David Ignatow Papers. Mandeville Special Collections Library, University of California, San Diego. Reprinted as Letter no. 87, in *Selected Letters: Charles Olson*, ed. Ralph Maud, 267–71. Berkeley and Los Angeles: University of California Press, 2000.

Raiziss, Sonia. Letter to David Ignatow. 16 April 1960. David Ignatow Papers. Mandeville Special Collections Library, University of California, San Diego. Quoted with permission of the Library.

Rodgers, Audrey. *Denise Levertov: The Poetry of Engagement*. Rutherford, NJ: Fairleigh Dickinson University Press, 1993.

Starbuck, George. Letter to David Ignatow. 30 March 1960. David Ignatow Papers. Mandeville Special Collections Library, University of California, San Diego. Quoted with permission of Kathryn Starbuck, and of the Library.

CHAPTER 9

Poetic Authority and the Public Sphere of Politics in the Activist 1960s: The Duncan-Levertov Debate

Anne Dewey

Recent analyses of the New American poetry of the early 1960s focus on constructions of voice and authority in relation to projected audience. Libbie Rifkin shows how avant-garde poets bidding for membership in the canon construct "professional" identities. For Terrell Scott Herring, Frank O'Hara's intimate yet impersonal "personal poem" creates a homosexual public sphere within mass culture. Michael Davidson theorizes that poetry of the Cold War period implicitly forges social alliances of homosocial community. The debate in letters between Duncan and Levertov over whether and how to write political poetry during the Vietnam War articulates yet another of the multiple public spheres New American poets address: that of social and political activism.[1] Little magazines like *Origin*, *Evergreen*, and *Yugen* reflected their editors' and contributors' sense of art's role as a force for social change (Dewey, "Idiom"), and political commitments strain friendships. Amiri Baraka and Ed Dorn argued over the

1. I use Habermas's phrase "public sphere" to indicate the official or unofficial social spaces in which individuals debate ideas and form group consciousness. In conceiving of multiple public spheres, I follow Nancy Fraser, who modifies Habermas's theory of a relatively homogeneous bourgeois public sphere to posit the existence of different public spheres based on different subcultures.

significance of race in political poetry (von Hallberg 206–8), Levertov and Rich over feminist allegiances. In theorizing their conflicting conceptions of poetic agency and authority, Duncan and Levertov voice a crisis of political subjectivity valuable for understanding the political origins of the New American poetics in changing conceptions of the public sphere.

The Vietnam War strains the deep friendship between Duncan and Levertov and inspires some of their most troubled poetry, as both direct their writing away from an intimate countercultural audience to a national political culture.[2] Since the mid 1950s, both had adapted Charles Olson's notion of "composition by field," and the Poundian conception of the poet as giver of cultural forms, to see the poet's role as renovator of colloquial language—a role they embrace with increasing intensity and optimism in the growing poetic and political countercultures. Set initially in domestic contexts, Duncan's and Levertov's poems of the 1950s ground renovation of culture in communication between intimates and extend similar familiarity to the reader. *The Opening of the Field*'s liberation from tormented homosexuality into a new language of love emerges through dialogue between the lovers at their shared hearth.[3] Levertov's work of the late 1950s finds beauty in the household, rendering everyday chores epiphanies that bring sacred communion with her family. The poets feel each other's work is most powerful when read in a circle of close friends (L 507, 557). As Duncan writes to Creeley from the perspective of 1979 (4 June), "we are also, you and I, more dedicated, or would be, to the practice of loving, the honor of those we love, the Romance of a Household" (Stanford).

In the early 1960s, Duncan and Levertov become suspicious of collo-

2. Alan Golding's tracing of the discussion between editors and contributors to *Origin* and *Black Mountain Review* shows that editor Cid Corman sought to create a close-knit community of writers whose exchange of ideas and mutual support would inspire their writing (698–700). The change in Duncan's and Levertov's perception of the community for which they write coincides with increasing acceptance and institutionalization of these poets and their communities, a factor whose influence I cannot trace here.

While Habermas distinguishes between the family and the bourgeois public sphere originating in the salon (45–46), Duncan and Levertov elide these two communities in their poetry (although not necessarily in their correspondence) to extend a relation of familiarity to the reader.

3. For fuller description of the importance of domesticity as a realm of safety for Duncan, see Rumaker.

quial immediacy as easily corrupted by a massified public arena. Levertov complains to Duncan of the "Madison Avenue commercialism" (L 234) of many poetry magazines. For her, Ginsberg's popularity reduces his writing to the sensationalism of "a newspaper report of a victim's words at some catastrophe" (L 158). The "hero-worship" Olson has won leads him to cater to the crowd, distorting his idiosyncrasies and rendering him incapable of self-criticism (L 504). Duncan believes that popularity has diluted the creative impetus of much contemporary art, both Beat poetry and action painting (L 245). For him, Abstract Expressionism illustrates the "danger of securing the chic." Initially original and groundbreaking, Clyfford Still's abstract style now appears to Duncan mass-produced, standardized as an easily recognizable style for conspicuous consumption. While he continues to admire Still's work, Duncan condemns much of it as "grandiose, megalomaniac" (L 239), an assertion of personality based on mass demand for spectacle rather than self-searching.

Duncan and Levertov respond to the perceived massification of art by distancing artistic value and creative agency from audience demand and reception. Despite this distance, their constructions of poetic authority are shaped by images of power in the public sphere. Whereas their poetry of the late 1950s located renovation of colloquial language in domestic settings as communication between familiars, they begin in the early 1960s to imagine the relation between reader and writer as more distant and to construct poetic voice in the image of authority in the mass public sphere. Implicitly acknowledging the power of figures that live in the collective imagination, they ground inspiration in an alternate community of literary tradition rather than in political necessity or individual psyche. Individual agency dissolves in a legitimating poetic tradition whose collective identity and authority confront the power of mass stardom on its own terms.

Duncan's "The H.D. Book" traces a spiritual tradition in poetry that preserves a life of the imagination Duncan believes absent in mass culture. A homage to H.D. begun in 1960 (Bertholf viii), "The H.D. Book" imagines a city of "those who are devoted to Beauty," particularly "the beautiful English language," "an invisible city more real than the [historical] city in which they are," with its "squalid commercialism" (Duncan, "Nights" 142). This ideal city preserves a richer range of expression than that tolerated by a modern "mass democratic State," which seeks to control popular consensus through mass communication as well as law and education ("From the H.D. Book" II.5, 343; "H.D. Book" II.4, 44–47), to substitute "the mass-man" for "the individual" ("Two Chapters" 98). For Duncan, H.D. uses the collective "'we' throughout [*The Walls Do Not Fall*] to refer to the community of a mystery within the larger society" ("From the H.D. Book" II.5, 344). His literary community is modeled on that of H.D.'s occult traditions, whose mystical vision evolves within but apart from history. However, Duncan's grounding of poetic authority in a collective consensus borrows public symbols of power with which to distinguish his literary heroes. Punning on the hero worship of movie stars, he creates his own "star cult" of fellow poets, both living and dead, as a projected universe of astral influences who, like the heroes of popular culture, seem to be natural forces shaping individual character ("Nights" 101–2, 115).

In shifting his poetic roots from historical to ideal community, Duncan distances creative agency from the personal, locating it instead in the impersonal exigencies of art. "The H.D. Book" and the contemporaneous *Roots and Branches* (1964) replace the biological family with an artistic one. Poetry is "re-membering the Mother," "the Mother of those who have destroyed their mothers [and] . . . created their own mothers" ("The H.D. Book" I.2, 28). Duncan replaces his parents, who pressure him to follow a practical trade, with ideal progenitors of all poetry, "Father of roots and races, / Father of All, / Father who is King of the dream palace, . . . Father who is architect of the eternal city . . . " and "that other Great Mother / or metre, of the matter" (RB 76). Poetry as kingdom rather than individual creation can become the measure and substance of reality. Although Duncan's "re-membering" implies both passive recall and active creation of his heritage, this identification with an ideal community locates agency in a power and authority independent of the individual and the historical family. To Levertov, he writes of "schizophrenic aspects of the authority the art has over the artist" (L 472), imagining inspiration as an alien force that works through the artist. "The H.D. Book" describes the world of poetry as an "autonomous play" or "melody of events" in which the artist is "cast." The title image of *Roots and Branches* refers to tradition as a world tree with "Authors . . . in eternity" (L 48). "And now the spring of an urgent life / pushes up from the trunk of the idea of me, / from a whole system of ramifications, / so many mortal entrances . . . " (RB 47). The individual is incorporated into a greater organism, the self's boundaries lost as it branches into forms of a larger communal being that shapes or confirms its vision.

Levertov's poetics undergo a similar transformation in the early 1960s, her dialogue with Duncan affirming and influencing changes in her work. Feeling the need to formulate her own poetics, she questions William Carlos Williams's "American Idiom" and Pound's injunction that "the natural object is always the adequate symbol," principles she had followed in training herself to become an "American" poet in the 1950s. In response to a negative comment from Williams concerning her poem "The Jacob's Ladder," she writes that, while his "American Idiom" freed some young poets from unsuitable literary language, she will not "put the idea of American Idiom *first*. For you it has always been a focus, almost a mission" (MacGowan 99–101). In 1964, she writes Duncan of her rediscovery of literary language as she personifies "Grief" in "A Lamentation" and of her return to the Romantic diction of her nineteenth-century British roots (L 445). Like Duncan, she invokes literary tradition to legitimate the development of her own poetry and poetics.

Levertov shares Duncan's admiration for H.D. and responds enthusiastically to his location of poetic authority in a living community of tradition. While not changing her belief that poetry is grounded in the personal, she admits increasingly the influence of forces beyond deliberate craft in poetic composition and praises Duncan's formulation of H.D.'s gift as a transcendence of the personal, "no longer *her* art" but "*The* Art" (L 301). Admiring H.D.'s power to evoke myth in the everyday world, "the interpenetration of past and present, of mundane reality and intangible reality" (PW 182), Levertov distinguishes between historical and literary fields and affirms literary tradition as the ground of a spirit world beyond the mundane.

Like Duncan, Levertov comes to imagine her poetic craft as part of a communal pursuit rather than as private or individual creation. "A Common Ground" articulates her new preference for literary over colloquial language. The poem distinguishes between different kinds of language, contrasting everyday speech, "gritty with pebbles," to literary

> shining pebbles,
> that soil where uncommon men
> have labored in their virtue
> and left a store
>
> of seeds for planting!

Although the poem presents both kinds of language as seeds and later as grain capable of nourishing, it privileges poetic speech, "not 'common speech' / a dead level / but the uncommon speech of paradise" (P60 3–5). The epigraph by Pasternak— " . . . everything in the world must excel to be itself"—renders a voice from tradition rather than the concrete object as the occasion of her image. To Duncan, Levertov quotes Thomas Mann's observation that it is essential "*for [artists] to keep in constant touch with masterpieces, so that the creative spirit may be maintained at its height* & prevented from backsliding" (L 499; my emphasis). Her poetry of the early 1960s uses the language of literature and tradition to frame epiphanic experience of the everyday, shifting inspiration from concrete objects to a community of literary kindred spirits. Allusion provides the basis for a widening visionary scope. By including mythological figures such as Ishtar, elves, and angels as active presences, and by composing allegories of creative forces such as "the Spirit of Poetry," Levertov roots her imagination in a spirit world nourished by poetic tradition.[4]

Increasing concern about the Vietnam War impels both poets to articulate the relation between the literary and political communities more precisely. Although they begin to write poetry about the war with a common goal of making the war real to their readers, their conceptions of how to communicate this reality soon diverge. As the political demands of writing about the war challenge simple distinctions between poetic and political language, Duncan and Levertov develop new poetic forms to enable greater interplay between personal and public history not easily achieved in short lyrics. Duncan's "The Passages Poems" imply sporadic interventions in history, imagined either as architectural connections in the edifice or birth canals in the organism of contemporary culture. Levertov subordinates poetic plot to history in her diary/documentary "Staying Alive." The debate in letters between Duncan and Levertov in which they attempt to justify their diverging poetics reveals the different character and relative authority each attributes to poetic and political voice.[5]

4. See, for example, "A Vision," "Matins," "The Rainwalkers" (P60 223, 59, 13).

For Duncan, Levertov's involvement in the war resistance movement narrows her writing about war. Commenting on Levertov's appearance at a women's peace rally televised in a PBS report in March
1968, Duncan interprets Levertov's frenzied appearance as embodying
the collective energy of the enraged crowd, "the demotic urgency, the
arousal of the group against an enemy." "The person that the *demos*, the
citoyen—mass of an aroused party, awakes is so different from the individual person . . . the *soul* is sacrificed to the demotic persona" (L 607).
Although he agrees with Levertov's opposition to the war, Duncan resists group advocacy as a means of activism, believing that it absorbs the
participating individual into factional group opinion and thus prevents
free thought.

And hardest of all, just here where we might be thought to be in agreement, to
drive thru to the doubts I have in the area of agreement, the resistance to Resistance [the activist organization RESIST urged opposition to the draft and protested the war]. And driving thru I find I go with a free morality, I do not assent to
whatever social covenant nor do I assent to the inner command as authority; but
seek a complex obedience to "What is Happening." (L 612)

Duncan finds both allegiance to political faction and "inner" opinion inadequate. As he seeks to define this "complex obedience to 'What is Happening,'" his criticism and Levertov's response develop into an extended
debate on "Staying Alive," particularly the poem's engagement of group
activism and the language of political advocacy to which Levertov lends
her voice. For Duncan, polarized debate between government and protesters represents the "loss of relation between the individual organism and its
ecological field." Both groups have assumed an identity modeled on a de-
structively competitive ideology of nationalism. Nation is no longer one
force among many shaping a universal "humanity," but an end in itself, its
energy dividing rather than unifying the international totality of "Man" (L
609–10). Throughout their discussion, Duncan insists that the poet must
resist the "commanding conscience" of embattled contemporary perspec-

5. Marjorie Perloff's "Poetry in Time of War" (Perloff 208–11) traces the
early stages of this debate, in which Duncan criticizes Levertov's short early war
lyrics for relinquishing poetic craft to propagandistic moral message. I would like
to focus on the later debate over Levertov's long poem "Staying Alive" and thus
to contextualize the debate in the discussion of the poet's public role that grounds
Duncan's and Levertov's esthetic decisions.

tives (L 611) to "imagine" or reinterpret the war in the larger context of an evolving cosmic drama.

Duncan resists Levertov's embrace of the protest movement's language as a loss of poetic freedom to deadlocked political faction. For him, the slogan "Revolution or Death" expresses the same destructive double-speak of the U.S. major whom Levertov quoted in "Staying Alive" as saying he destroyed a town to save it (L 673). Doubting the ability of the embattled group to effect social change, Duncan also rejects Levertov's representation of People's Park as an idyllic community. For him, the protestors work not to create a political utopia but rather to release their rage against the state's tyranny. Too angry to engage in constructive creation, the protesters mouth "empty and vain slogans" and moralize "war waged under the banner of peace" (L 669, 661).

Levertov resists the view of the crowd as possessed of energy both radically different from that of the individual and destructive of its idealistic goals. To counter the seemingly greater authority of governmental rhetoric, she demystifies public voice, representing it as mere consensus, the product of individual voices. She explains her involvement in and description of the protest movement as an effort to affirm the power of the individual to shape public meaning. Viewing the public arena as a vehicle for direct communication rather than distortion of individual voice, she defends her appearance at the rally not as an incitement to collective violence but as a message of peace. Her letter to Duncan cites her actual words ("Mothers, don't let your sons learn to kill and be killed. Teachers, don't let your students learn to kill and be killed. Wives and sweethearts, don't let your lovers learn to kill and be killed. Aid, abet, and counsel young men to resist the draft!" [L 677]; [I supply repeated words that Levertov indicates with ditto marks]), rather than her appearance on the screen, as the essence of her message. Describing her role at the rally as private citizen rather than poet, she grounds her authority in representative activism, not a special poet's understanding of the war.

Levertov condemns Duncan's resistance to such immediate reporting as "DISGUSTINGLY ELITIST" (L 683). For her, verbatim conversation, correspondence among members of the movement, and the group's political slogans constitute appropriate, authentic poetic language to record this struggle. "In the whole poem I attempted to range in language from that traditional literate that is my heritage to the flippest colloquial that is also part of me and that I use just as much. A long diary kind of poem gave me the opportunity to swing between extremes in diction . . . which short lyrics don't give" (L 683). While leveling the hierarchy (although not abolishing the distinction) between poetic and colloquial diction, Levertov admits both as essential elements of her expression. As one in a continuum of individual utterances that establish consensual public meaning, poetry can engage colloquial idiom directly and transform it. The revolutionaries' activism thus constitutes not rebellious revenge but the effort to realize the community sketched in their rhetoric. For Levertov, the intent of People's Park is inviolable. Her perception that the collaborators *"stayed together and wd not be driven away by intimidation, and we did experience love and community"* (L 686; Levertov's emphasis) affirms that shared rhetoric and ideals can build social harmony. Because collective inspiration radicalizes many to devote themselves to such goals, revolutionary slogans, although imprecise and changing, represent important progress. "This is a movement that can only learn by doing. (And by & large it does.)" (L 682). For Levertov, embrace of group language represents not loss of freedom but a positive, mutual transformation of self and community.

Recent theories of the public sphere enable us to trace Duncan's and Levertov's conflicting poetics to different conceptions of the public sphere and of political subjectivity and agency within it. Whereas Levertov's presentation of the poet as representative citizen and of group language as the product of democratic consensus projects a Habermasian bourgeois public sphere of private individuals engaging in rational debate, Duncan's assertion that the "demotic" persona of the crowd possesses and overpowers individual agency resembles in some aspects Habermas's massified public sphere, in which the individual achieves identity by bonding with the crowd through anonymous collective consumption of a common object, whether commodity or celebrity (Habermas 181 ff.). While Levertov and Duncan clash in their letters over the nature of poetic and political agency, their Vietnam poetry shares location at the crisis-ridden threshold between different images of the public sphere. Both find that public forms of authority subvert imagination in powerfully troubling ways. Their war poetry ends in disorientation and awareness of the painfully intolerable stances into which their commitments have led them. Both poets find themselves in what Wendy Brown calls "politics out of history," the radical confusion concerning identity and historical process that follows loss of faith in such foundational concepts of liberal democracy as "personhood," "right," "free will," and "progress" (Brown 3–5). Reading their poetry in the context of this historical crisis illuminates alternate forms of political subjectivity and public culture that their extreme, troubled poetry struggles to articulate.

Although the collage notebook form of "Staying Alive" implies Levertov's belief in a liberal democratic public form, the development of the poem's narrative and imagery expresses her growing difficulty in embracing such a conception of the public sphere. In setting her own memories, letters, and poetry in dialogue with those of other specifically named protesters and politicians, Levertov represents political advocacy as a debate among autonomous individuals on the model of face-to-face community. Even as the poem records her increasing exhaustion and despair in dedication to long-term activism, it continues to assert the distinction between private and public spheres, "daily life" and "history," and to project their ideal "meshing" in "song" (P68 181–82). By the end of the poem, however, the private realm has shrunk from expansive, sustaining havens of childhood memory and vacation landscapes to a barely accessible "well" in the "grim middle of the tunnel" (P68 188). Threats to the private realm disrupt Levertov's dialogue of individual voices as the principal political agents.

Against the imagery of solid ground and territorial boundaries that distinguish private from public in "Staying Alive," Levertov portrays the private individual as increasingly overwhelmed by history's turbulent floodwaters, which threaten to erode the distinction between public and private. Although Levertov's earlier water imagery also links public and private, it does so in more constructive ways: the reviving force of the sea in childhood memory (P68 130), a flood that becomes a crowd of swimmers capable of creating solid land in their solidarity (P68 155), and social energy that in the right form may become "communion wine" (P68 147). By the end of the poem, however, water has become an unfathomable "roaring silence." Its formless, inhuman power mesmerizes but destroys, as in the suicides of two revolutionaries, Judy and Grandin, whom Levertov views as casualties of history. "Judy ignored the world outside herself, / Grandin was flooded by it. / There is no suicide in our time unrelated to history" (P68 188). Grandin's death by "flooding" signals directly the invasion of the pri-

vate individual by public history. Although less directly public, Judy's so-
lipsism also represents intolerable alienation from self in activism.

Levertov's lament of these deaths focuses on the loss of nurturing
community that might have saved the revolutionaries. Letters and conversation give way to eulogy and address to the dead. In attempting to remember these individuals, "to gather up the fragments of it, fragments of
her [Judy]" (P68 184), Levertov attempts to recompose the integrity of the
private individual "smashed" in political struggle. The vacillation between
"it" and "her" indicates the fragility of the individual person possessed or
transformed into an impersonal historical event. Levertov has trouble focusing her memory. Her imagination gravitates instead to the reason for
the suicides, reflecting her preoccupation with broken community.

> Further away than 17th-century China
> nearer than my hand, you smashed
> the world in the image of yourself, smashed
> the horror of a world lonely Judy,
> silently plunging forever
> into her own eyes' icy green, never even saw;
> you raged bursting with life into death.   (P68 186)

Judy's "mirror" refers most immediately to the pool whose depths she
sought as a child to fathom, but Levertov's water imagery links the pool
to the inhospitable waters of history suggesting Judy's isolation and self-
absorption in the commitment to activism, her entrapment in the foreign
self history reflects back to her. Like the vacillation between "you" and
"her," Levertov's contradictory feeling of unity with Judy yet inability to
reach her reveals the alienating displacements of identity in the revolutionary community. Judy simultaneously looms powerfully as a public figure in
the struggle to which Levertov has dedicated herself and remains unreach-
able, cut off from the personal communication of letters or conversation
by her status as a public figure.

Like Levertov, Duncan portrays history as a chaotic "storm" or
"mêlée," an engulfing substance in which the poet tunnels "passages."
Whereas "Staying Alive" struggles to maintain faith in the individual as a
locus of political agency, *Bending the Bow* abandons the limitations of individual "conscience" to articulate alternate historical agents from a disturbingly distanced, at times amoral perspective that Nathaniel Mackey has

called Duncan's "cosmologizing stance" (Mackey 163). I would like to read the outlines of Duncan's cosmos as a reconfiguration of historical agency in a public sphere no longer structured by the agency of private individuals. In "Passages 2," the war intrudes into the private, domestic world as the distant point on which the pet cat's eyes focus.

> The secret!   the secret!   It's hid
>   in its showing forth.
> The white cat kneads his paws
>   and sheathes his eyes in ecstasy against the light,
>   the light bounding from his fur as from a shield
>   held high in the midst of a battle. (BB 11)

Although entering the poem only in the oblique comparison of simile, the light displaces the ec-static cat and conceals its body behind flashing reflection. At the end of the poem, battle replaces the domestic scene, shifting focus to a public narrative of national identity that distorts the mutual reflection of heroes into that of patriotic hero and enemy-victim: "the heroic Hektor who raised / that reflection of the heroic // in his shield . . ." (BB 13). The private individual disappears in the public sphere's hall of mirrors, which conceals human on human violence behind the nationalistic heroic rhetoric of war. In identifying with the national hero, private citizens bond in "the legion, that the / vow that makes a nation / one body not be broken" (BB 12).

While images of light and reflection throughout *Bending the Bow* develop the displacements and projections of identity created by such mass identification with public figures, Duncan's counterpoint of carnage and physical mutilation registers the accompanying destruction of the private individual. As President Johnson, the "swollen head of the nation" (BB 83), replaces the democratic body politic of autonomous individuals with a hierarchical medieval one, private citizens disappear into "the endless Dark" surrounding the television screen, gaining substance only through consumption of its "goods," both economic and political (BB 115). Duncan's body imagery undercuts such bloodless disembodied triangulation of identity, accentuating the construction of this new community from the dismemberment of private individual and local community. "Passages 30, Stage Directions" exemplifies this violent reconfiguring of history.

He brings the camera in upon the gaping neck
    which now is an eye of bloody meat   glaring
    from the womb of whose pupil   sight

springs to see,   two   children of adversity.

The Mother's baleful glance in romance's
                              head of writhing snakes haird

        freezes the ground.

                    Okeanos   roars,

wild oceanic father,   visage   compounded of fury and of wind

    (the whole poem becoming a storm   in which faces arise)

    Mouths yawn immensely   and hours,
                          as if they were mad brothers,
stare.
            From the body of the poem, all that words create

presses forth to be: [Chrysaor and Pegasos] (BB 128–29)

The poem traces the beheading of Medusa and the generation from her murder of mythic creatures as the main actors in the drama of history. However, we encounter Medusa first as an unidentified decapitated body, in context a war victim. Only under Perseus's sword does her gaze become threatening, that of the mortal individual challenging heroic violence. Replacing the head, site of reason and autonomy, the uncanny wound's "eye of bloody meat" is horrifically animate and inanimate. A new center of vision and agency radically unlike that of the embodied person, the wound becomes an eye only under the objectifying gaze of the camera, whose lack of compassion denies empathetic reciprocity. By destroying the individual's autonomous gaze, Perseus as mythic hero renders the wound a womb bearing a tautologically impersonal "sight" whose "seeing" produces a new family of monstrous agents: the "wild" Okeanos, the "mad brothers" of time, and ultimately Pegasus and Chrysaor, mythic animal and warrior linked for Duncan as figures of poetry. Just as the body representative of individual integrity fragments into discordant parts (eye, womb, pupil, head, face, mouth), each acquiring a life of its own, so the embodied person's vision is replaced by confusedly impersonal, disembodied viewers (camera and unidentified cameraman, wound, Medusa's severed head, staring mouths). Focus on the horrific wound and voraciously "yawning" mouths replaces compassionate, familiar human gaze with dizzying abyss and appetite out of control.

This confusion resolves into the lineage of mythical creatures from Perseus and Medusa to Pegasus and Chrysaor, allying poetry and war. By the end of the poem, the poet's "dying body" merges with "the dying body of America" (BB 132). Medusa's body preserves, however, the destruction of private integrity and the resultant inchoate welter of agency and affect exposed in the absence of conventional political agents. Although this chaos coalesces into the deceptively coherent national drama on an artificial "stage" whose action is focused by the camera's public eye, the passage's twisted syntax denaturalizes these mythic agents, revealing their roots in the violent destruction of the private body and resulting undefined loci of energy that propel history.

Although Levertov and Duncan imagine political agency differently, their political engagement produces intense rage. For both, Judy Collins's "there comes a time when only anger is love" becomes a touchstone for the erosion of utopian domestic community in the public sphere (P68 165; GW 46). This rage seems to come from their awareness of an imbalance of power and the unjust terms of their struggle. For both, the public sphere polarizes into victim and aggressor, a phenomenon Wendy Brown traces as emerging when liberalism's "egalitarian ideal is shattered." For Brown, conceiving one's status as unprivileged victim or dissenter rather than equal citizen produces an "identity rooted in injury" that requires repeated victimization or imaginative identification with other victims to affirm the one's identity as different (Brown 52–53). The marked individual who despairs of inclusion in the universal remains bound to the dominant political order through this need for definition. "But restaging the trauma of suffering reassures us that what we need or love—the social order that originally hurt or failed us but to which we were and remain terribly attached—is still there" (Brown 56).

For Brown, imagining oneself as victim produces political paralysis like that fueling Duncan's and Levertov's doubts concerning activism. Levertov focuses increasingly on the martyrdom of political activists before police aggression. Nancy Sisko's description of Levertov's vacillation at the end of "Staying Alive" between self-hatred for clinging to her private difference from group politics and idealization of the revolutionaries' willing to sacrifice their lives supports this sense of authenticity shifting from private experience to identification with public victims. Likewise, Duncan's agency polarizes around victim and hero-aggressor. That Duncan theorizes his poetic voice during the war alternately as that of the fascist dictator (FC 27) and as a prisoner of the law and order of language (BB v) reflects the interconnection of these subject positions in a postliberal public sphere.

Although the wounds to their friendship never heal completely, Duncan and Levertov recover a space for greater imaginative freedom in the early 1970s, and their engagement of poetic tradition as the source of topoi from which the poet can respond to contemporary culture reveals their deep affinity. Duncan's "Structure of Rime XXVIII, IN MEMORIAM WALLACE STEVENS" praises the imagination's power to erect "a Gate" "beyond the boundaries of all government . . . " (GW 56). "The Museum" reinforces this architectural, sheltering solidity of imaginative constructions, making art's orders stable places for the mind to inhabit (GW 59). The "Dante Études" recover the multiplicity of perspective of the early "Passages Poems" in the autonomy but interdependence of familial, political, literary, and divine orders. Levertov also restores balance among her richly varied idioms. In her political poetry after the mid-1970s, ideal political culture is domestic, formed in the empathetic imagination and communication possible between living beings in a shared ecosystem, whether regional or global (Dewey, "Art"). Duncan and Levertov return to a field poetics that recovers the distinction between and productive interplay of a wide range of environmental forces.

The crisis that political engagement produces in Duncan's and Levertov's poetry and their attempts to theorize this crisis as they justify their poetics reveals the powerful influence of the public sphere of national politics. Characterizing this public sphere as a threshold between either bourgeois and mass culture (Habermas) or liberal and postliberal political culture (Brown) helps to explain not only the extravagances of their Vietnam War poetry but also the fate of field poetics. Duncan's and Levertov's opposed positions, privileging mass and individual agency respectively, reflect the imbalance of power in the public sphere that strains the field's model of productive interplay and foreshadows the next generation's need to develop new poetic strategies. Whereas other New American poets (O'Hara and the Beats, as Herring and Davidson have shown) "work strategically *within*" (Davidson 52) this mass public sphere, Duncan's and Levertov's experience of the transition as crisis reveals the radical, often violent transformation of poetic and political subjectivity this transition requires. The field as a model of poetic agency allows both poets to register the forces in this public sphere with great sensitivity and to articulate an openness/vulnerability of the poetic subject that forms a crucial aspect of their "poetic culture."[6]

Works Cited

Beach, Christopher. *Poetic Culture: Contemporary American Poetry Between Community and Institution*. Evanston, IL: Northwestern University Press, 1999.

Bertholf, Robert J., ed. *A Great Admiration: H.D. and Robert Duncan Correspondence, 1950–1961*. Venice, CA: Lapis Press, 1992.

Brown, Wendy. *Politics out of History*. Princeton, NJ: Princeton University Press, 2001.

Davidson, Michael. *Guys Like Us: Citing Masculinity in Cold War Poetics*. Chicago: University of Chicago Press, 2004.

Dewey, Anne. "'The Art of the Octopus': The Maturation of Denise Levertov's Political Vision." *Renascence: Essays on Values in Literature*. 50.1–2 (Fall 1997–Winter 1998): 65–81.

———. "Public Idiom and Private Voice in John Ashbery's *Three Poems* and Ed Dorn's *Gunslinger*." *Sagetrieb* 11.1–2 (Spring–Fall 1992): 47–66.

Duncan, Robert. "The H.D. Book, Part I: Chapter 2." *Coyote's Journal* 8 (1967): 27–35.

———. "The H.D. Book, Part II: Nights and Days, Chapter 4." *Caterpillar* 7 (April 1969): 27–60.

———. "From the H.D. Book, Part II, Chapter 5 (Section One)." *Stony Brook* 3–4 (1969): 336–47.

———. "Nights and Days." *Sumac* 1.1 (1968): 101–46.

———. Letter to Robert Creeley. 4 June 1979. Robert Creeley Papers. Special Collections, Stanford University Libraries.

6. I borrow this phrase from Christopher Beach.

———. "Two Chapters from H.D." *TriQuarterly* 12 (1968): 67–98.

Fraser, Nancy. "Re-thinking the Public Sphere." In *Habermas and the Public Sphere*, ed. Craig Calhoun, 109–42. Cambridge, MA: MIT Press, 1992.

Golding, Alan. "Little Magazines and Alternative Canons: The Example of *Origin.*" *American Literary History* 2 (1990): 691–724.

Habermas, Jürgen. *The Structural Transformation of the Public Sphere: An Inquiry into a Category of Bourgeois Society.* Trans. Thomas Burger and Frederick Lawrence. Cambridge, MA: MIT Press, 1991.

Herring, Terrell Scott. "Frank O'Hara's Open Closet." PMLA 117 (2002): 414–27.

MacGowan, Christopher, ed. *The Letters of Denise Levertov and William Carlos Williams.* New York: New Directions, 1998.

Mackey, Nathaniel. "From *Gassire's Lute*: Robert Duncan's Vietnam War Poems." Pt. 2. *Talisman* 6 (1991): 141–66.

Perloff, Marjorie. *Poetry On and Off the Page: Essays for Emergent Occasions.* Evanston, IL: Northwestern University Press, 1998.

Rifkin, Libbie. *Career Moves: Olson, Creeley, Zukofsky, Berrigan, and the American Avant-Garde.* Madison: University of Wisconsin Press, 2000.

Rumaker, Michael. *Robert Duncan in San Francisco.* San Francisco: Grey Fox Press, 1996.

Sisko, Nancy. "To Stay Alive: Levertov's Search for a Revolutionary Poetry." *Sagetrieb* 5.2 (1986): 47–60.

von Hallberg, Robert. *American Poetry and Culture, 1945–1980.* Cambridge, MA: Harvard University Press, 1985.

CHAPTER 10

Prophetic Frustrations:
Robert Duncan's *Tribunals*

Peter O'Leary

I CAN'T UNDO THE GRIEVOUS HUMAN SITUATION.

The power of the poet is to translate experience from daily time where the world and ourselves pass away as we go on into the future, from the journalistic record, into a melodic coherence in which words—sounds, meanings, images, voices—do not pass away or exist by themselves but are kept by rime to exist everywhere in the consciousness of the poem. The art of the poem, like the mechanism of the dream or the intent of the tribal myth and dromena, is a cathexis: to keep present and immediate a variety of times and places, persons and events. In the melody we make, the possibility of eternal life is hidden, and experience we thought lost returns to us.

—"RITES OF PARTICIPATION," IN "THE H.D. BOOK"

Later in this essay, first published in 1967 but written earlier in the 1960s, Duncan alludes to the predestined election that endows poets with goggles of a Freudian hermeneutic to allow them "in their vision—to keep the dream of 'everyone, everywhere'. . . . The very heightened sense of the relatedness of everything," continues Duncan, "sets poets apart. The very secret of the impulse in poetry is the troubled awareness the poet has of meanings in the common language everywhere that those about him do not see or do not consider so important" (SP 127–28). These statements from "Rites of Participation" are characteristic of Duncan's prophetic, cathectic vision of poetry—which generates attachments of ideas and language to meanings both hidden and revealed. At the core of his poetry is a prophetic understanding of language and vision whose authority he holds sacrosanct.

His vision of poetry came to its fullest expression in the late 1960s when he composed the "Passages" that belong to the series of poems he named *Tribunals*. Of the *Tribunals*, the broadest, most completed expression of his prophetic powers is the poem "Before the Judgment, Passages 35." *Tribunals* was first published in a deluxe edition by John Martin's Black Sparrow Press in 1970. This was a book that famously infuriated Duncan, contributing to the vow of publication silence he took—not publishing another book of new poetry until 1984, when *Ground Work: Before the War* was issued by New Directions.[1] That these events are sequential is worth attending to. But are they consequential? Did Duncan enter into his silence because he was so frustrated with the way his work was being pub-

1. Though Duncan's reaction to *Tribunals* most certainly informed his decision not to publish, Duncan did not state this intention until he wrote the preface for *Caesar's Gate*, published by Sand Dollar Press in 1972. It's worth noting here that Duncan's sense of this publishing silence is complex, especially in the light of the ongoing publication of his earlier poetry during this period, as well as the small press editions and numerous journal publications he managed during this time, including books such as *The Years as Catches*, *Caesar's Gate* (as already mentioned), and the two Fulcrum editions of his work in the UK. What he intended with this declaration is that he wouldn't publish a "new" book of poetry, one made up of poems written since the time of his decision. Nonetheless, he also published fine editions of some of the poems that would enter into *Ground Work: Before the War*, including an edition of "Achilles' Song" as well as photocopied editions of his work he sent out to friends, for which he collected money. (See, for instance, letter 448 from Denise Levertov to Duncan [L 660], in which Levertov tells Duncan she will be sending him a check for "*ground work*." Duncan responds in the next letter by telling her not to worry about sending any money.) This period would also see the publication of previously unpublished but earlier work, especially *Book of Resemblances*, in a holograph of Duncan's calligraphy and Jess's drawings. This is not so much a criticism—none of these publications was with a major press, some were decidedly ephemeral—as it is a reflection that Duncan's sense of this silence needs to be examined with some readerly care. As with so much else in his creative life, I suspect he made this declaration as much for the tensions it would generate in his writing as for the criticism of publishing and publishers that it implied.

lished, or was this in a sense an inevitable decision on his part, arising from deeper poetic concerns his publication problems merely alluded to?

Three statements by Duncan in letters to Denise Levertov from the late 1960s and early 1970s suggest the tensions at work in Duncan's thought during this period of intense political and creative anxiety for him, tensions that reinforced his consternation about his poetry publications. On August 30, 1966, speaking of the way he perceived U.S. policy in Southeast Asia—a point of significant concern for both him and Levertov, whose son Nik was of draft age—Duncan wrote:

It struck me this morning that what has been impending in "Passages" and I don't know when or how it will emerge at the level of the poem's content is—that the Vietnam war is a stripping away of pretense and hypocrisy from the social order in which we live and a showing forth of the true face. As, in the Bible the joy in the catastrophic rings true because a wish is made evident. (L 552)

The "Passages" Duncan is imagining in this letter are the core, prophetic inclusions in the sequence of *Bending the Bow*: "The Fire, Passages 13," "The Multiversity, Passages 21," "Up Rising, Passages 25," and "The Soldiers, Passages 26." All four of these poems are directly concerned with the war in Vietnam and its consequences in the United States. In intuiting the content of these poems to Levertov, he is beginning to articulate the sense that "Strife"—in a Heraclitean sense—plays in his work, a notion that War is as revelatory a state in the imagination as peace or well-being. In a later statement, written to Levertov on February 26, 1970, Duncan apologizes to her for the way he attacked Hayden Carruth—a friend of Levertov's whom she deemed too psychically fragile to withstand Duncan's vehemence—stating, "I can't undo the grievous human situation," a paraphrase of sorts for "what's done is done," even as he expresses regret for the way he treated Carruth. But he follows his apology with the draft of a statement he intended to appear in the magazine in which he attacked Carruth, writing: "There are times when my own views regarding the nature and meaning of poetic form flash forth with an intolerance that betokens remnants of the Puritan bigot in me, whipping the poor would-be heretic anthologist or critic publicly in the stock or driving him forth from the covenant of the righteous into the wilderness" (L 651).[2] In the third statement, Dun-

2. See Duncan, "A Critical Difference of View," in the appendix at L 729–33. The publication was *Stony Brook*.

can is describing to Levertov the difference he experiences between kinds of witness demanded of him during the stressful time of the war in Vietnam. He had taken to wearing a peace button on a reading tour, so that people would ask him what it meant, giving him the opportunity to profess his antiwar views. But even this kind of witnessing was inadequate to the poetic tasks he felt were at hand. Explaining himself, he wrote: "Even 'Up Rising' is not this kind of witness; for ultimately it belongs to the reality of that poem and a vision of Man. And I do not answer for myself in my work but for Poetry" (L 563).

These three statements, which seem to me utterly characteristic of Duncan, suggest a triangular tension that is articulated—sometimes strenuously—in Duncan's poetic work from this period. This is especially true of *Tribunals*, which can be regarded as a culmination of the forces manifesting themselves in these statements. In one corner of the triangle, there is war, or War as he frequently writes it, which shows to us a true face of our social order. On October 4, 1971, Duncan would write to Levertov: "THERE HAS BEEN NO TIME IN HUMAN HISTORY THAT WAS NOT A TIME OF WAR" (L 661). There is the sense, then, that the Vietnam War was revelatory to Duncan, showing him an irrefutable truth of the nature of reality, not aside from but consonant with the suffering and agony that war wrought on its combatants as well as those, like Duncan and Levertov, who protested the war at home. In the second corner of the triangle, there is Duncan's anger—the flashing forth of intolerance—that is connected directly to the publication of poetry or ideas about that poetry. Duncan's anger toward Carruth is a smaller instance of a larger tendency to respond to what he perceives as poets' betrayals of poetry by attacking them publicly. The two most catastrophic such confrontations Duncan staged were against Robin Blaser for his translations of Gérard de Nerval's *Chimères*, and against Levertov over her use of the Vietnam War in her poetry, which resulted in the dissolution of their friendship.[3] We witness this flashing forth of intolerance by Duncan in his response to John Martin's publication of *Tribu-*

3. The disintegration of Duncan's and Levertov's friendship is spelled out in one of the striking features of their correspondence: of the 720 pages of surviving correspondence, 700 of them are filled with letters prior to their dispute in 1971, covering a period of eighteen years. The last 20 pages cover the same period, eighteen years up to the point of Duncan's death in 1988. I discuss the Duncan-Blaser dispute in some detail in *Gnostic Contagion*, 151–60. See also, Andrew Mossin.

nals with Black Sparrow, as well, a minor squabble that seems a tremor to a more catastrophic quaking of Duncan's poetic self.

The third corner of the triangle, which is related intrinsically to the other two, is the notion that poetry—as an equivalently prophetic mode of discourse—is inviolate and inviolable, such that he can say to Levertov that he does not answer for himself in his work but for Poetry. He is a messenger, a transmitter of Poetry's true face, which is revealed in War and Strife just as it ought to be transparent in its published form. Duncan's attitude reminds me of an analogy from Islam, in which the place of the Quran is similarly inviolate and inviolable. Muslims hold that the principal miracle of Islam is the revelation of the Quran to Muhammad over the course of twenty-one years in the seventh century, C.E. Furthermore, when making analogies to the salvific nature of Christianity, Muslim scholars have proposed that while Muhammad and Christ both represent exemplary types as the foundational figures of their religions, the truer analogy is that as Christ is to Christians, so the Quran is to Muslims—that the Quran is the way through which salvation is attained. In Islam, the Quran's salvation is only available in its Arabic form; translations are invariably understood as interpretations. The inviolability of the Quran extends to its transmission and publication: in order for a new edition of the Quran to be published, it must be checked meticulously by a scribe whose sole purpose is to ensure that none of the Arabic is misplaced, distorted, or misread. Each edition of the Quran in Arabic bears a seal attesting to its lack of blemishes, amounting to a book-by-book imprimatur.[4] Duncan's position toward poetry—or Poetry—is surprisingly consonant with this Muslim view toward the Quran. That he felt violations against poetry as a blasphemy is not, therefore, surprising. The question worth asking is how personally he took these violations. Was Duncan pursuing a grander vision of poetry in

4. See Nasr, especially chapter 1, "One God, Many Prophets," 1–55. It's also worth mentioning here the fatwa issued against Salman Rushdie for invoking the so-called "Satanic Verses," Quranic revelations Muslims believed to have been inspired by Satan, in which Muhammad approves the worship of three idols, verses subsequently rejected by Muhammad himself. Rushdie, then, was believed to be a satanic agent himself, because his use of these verses suggests the human, that is, violable, character of the prophecy itself. For this reason, without ever reading a word of *The Satanic Verses*, it was "permissible" for the Ayatollah Khomeini to issue the fatwa against Rushdie.

his flashings-forth against Blaser, Levertov, or Martin? Or were these evidences of a more deeply entrenched personal anxiety—one that would be expressed (as in "squeezed out under pressure") in his anger over the way his publications were handled?

The publication of *Tribunals* by John Martin's Black Sparrow Press in 1970 serves as a heuristic viewpoint from which to understand this triangular tension—of War, Anger, and Poetry—in Duncan's work. Duncan found himself furious with the way his poems were laid out in this edition. Was it typesetting and orthography that really provoked such ire in Duncan? He felt his burgeoning prophetic powers betrayed by the misrepresentative laying out of his poems in this edition of *Tribunals*. The transparent content of his prophecy is a broadly issued condemnation of the American government and culture in its pursuit of war in Vietnam, treated—as it ever is in Duncan—in the light of a highly allusive mythopoeic reading of the present. George Butterick, in one of the earliest reviews of *Ground Work: Before the War*, wrote, "I am of an age that I cannot read 'Before the Judgment,' for example, and not feel the old surge of righteousness in my veins, my body alive in an all-stage alert, morally armed. . . . [*Tribunals*] were poems that gave focus and legitimacy to our feelings, that gave leadership—when poets could still command audiences of thousands, by authority of their words" (Butterick 273–74). I think we can take such a contemporaneous reaction to this poetry as in kind with Duncan's intentions. Butterick is feeling the force of Duncan's prophecy, responding to its vigilance, and even allowing himself to imagine a blessèd time when poets gathered vast audiences over whom they felt their influence radiate and project. A powerful poetry this was, to say the least. What, then, is the content of this prophecy, and why was its manhandling by a printer so upsetting to the poet?

BAD FAITH: Composing and Printing *Tribunals*

Readers of Duncan's poetry, both fans and detractors, have confronted the difficulties of Duncan's typographic imperative in the New Directions edition of *Ground Work: Before the War*, from 1984, "typeset" almost entirely in the Courier font of his IBM Selectric. Graphic designers feel about Courier the way many of us react to sharp fingernails on a chalk-board. On his Blog and elsewhere, Ron Silliman, for instance, has argued that the physical ugliness of this edition has prevented many a reader from entering the poetry.[5] Duncan's dictates on the typesetting of this book can act as a visual fortress, or as barbed wire the reader needs to crawl under to get to the poetry. For a book with many of my very favorite Duncan po-ems, it's certainly my least-favorite looking of his books. On October 4, 1971, a year or so after the publication of *Tribunals*, Duncan declared to Levertov:

> I've been typing the first volume of the H.D. Book for publication, having decid-ed to issue it at this stage in typescript edition. I have come to dread printed publi-cations—I've had such bad luck with proof-reading and with faulty printers. And now I have it to issue all first editions from my typewriter straight off. Where any errors will be my own. Coercion has always seemed to me the only true evil; and it's a form of coercion to rage against what somebody else does to one's copy when right at hand is the means to do said copy for oneself. (L 660)

Duncan's determination here suggests to me less that he had a command or grasp of what's involved in typesetting than that he understood his rag-ing against his printers and typesetters was misplaced, leading him to co-ercive arguments that themselves were disobedient to Poetry.[6] By appro-priating the means of his poetry's (and prose's) production for himself, he intended to circumvent his tendency to "rage against what somebody else does," a persuasion that defies the prophetic permission he obtains from Poetry in the first place. Typing his poetry and then distributing it allowed Duncan to reassert his priorities.

The decision to mutiny against typesetters and to take over this work himself follows directly from the controversy of the publication of *Tri-bunals: Passages 31–35* by Black Sparrow Press in 1970; these poems are among the first in the chronologically arranged *Ground Work: Before the War*. Those who acquired one of the 250 hardcover editions of *Tribunals* were given a first public glimpse at the trouble brewing in Duncan's imag-

5. E-mail to the author, March 26, 2003.
6. The evidence suggests that while Duncan understood the work involved in typesetting, he so mistrusted his printers that he was never able to accept type-setting as an art in its own right. See, for instance, in "A Narrative of Memos," the letters from Duncan to Fredericks, on January 17 and July 15, 1958, in *Letters* 68–70.

ination. Included in this edition, in a pocket glued onto the back cover, was a stapled booklet, entitled "Robert Duncan, *The Feast: Passages 34*," and subtitled, "Facsimile of the holograph notebook and of final typescript." An introductory note to this pamphlet, dated November 1970, asserts: "The printer's work, where the poet himself is not the printer, is an extension of the author's intension; the typed copy, where the poet works in typing, is the realized statement of those intensions." That Duncan was an adherent to the School of Typing is no surprise, beholden as he was to Olson's notions of projective page space illuminated in "Projective Verse." That Duncan worked for a period as a typist only reaffirms his vocational involvement with the typewriter. In the booklet's introduction, Duncan describes how the typewriter allows him to surpass the handwritten drafts of his poems in his notebooks, such that the machine virtually collaborates in the composition of the new draft, creating new developments in the poems, due to the special "spacings and relationships" generated on the page. The typescript, then, per Olson's idea, becomes the "score" of the poem, as close as a reader can get to its essence, barring a performance of the score by a skilled reader. One of the interesting revelations in his letters to Levertov is the way both poets shared their work with each other, almost always in typed manuscript. They traded them back and forth, creating copies with carbons (much of their sharing occurred before the advent of the photocopier), frequently typing out the work of others they received (especially Creeley's work). They both seem frequently disaffected by seeing each others' poems in book form, preferring to read the work in typescript.

The development from typescript to typography in Duncan's mind represents not an advance but a regression through refinement, thus a problem. In the pamphlet included with *Tribunals*, he writes, "The printed version . . . subject to close-space conventions of modern printing, in striving for a homogenized density of type on the page against open spaces, rides over decisions that appear in the typed version as notations of the music of the poem, minute silences in the space after a comma or a period." A serious, if idiosyncratic concern, but one that betrays Duncan's problematic understanding of the relationship between analphabetic characters (periods, commas, and dashes, for instance) and text. Similarly confusing is Duncan's dismissal of the development of typography over several hundreds of years in the West, a tradition, owing to its origins in Western religious and Renaissance culture, toward which you would imagine Duncan would be very sympathetic. The subtlest, most nuanced evolutions in type are among the analphabetic characters, which give print and aesthetic eras so much of their character. As poet and typesetter Robert Bringhurst, in *The Elements of Typographic Style*, asserts: "Punctuation is cold notation; it is not frustrated speech; it is typographic code" (84). Duncan's critique of the printed version of his poems in Black Sparrow's *Tribunals* voices above all his frustration at not seeing his prophetic "speech" reproduced in the typesetting of his book.

In the printed text of the introductory note for the inserted booklet to *Tribunals*, publisher John Martin had the parenthetic phrase "(though not this printed version)" inserted in Duncan's phrase "the printed version . . . subject to close-space conventions of modern printing," further infuriating the poet (Duncan calls it an "unauthorized amendment of my text" [*maps* 1]).[7] The booklet itself is a holograph of Duncan's notebook, in which "The Feast" arises out of his handwritten improvising of phrases and sentences, followed by a carefully typewritten version of the poem that translates the notebook into typescript before our eyes.[8] As a readerly artifact, this booklet is as astonishing as it is pleasing: a chance for the reader to track a poem from handwritten origin to typeset fruition. The dissonance the booklet emits, however, is something belatedly attended to: only upon the publication of *Ground Work: Before the War*, with its own typewritten version of "The Feast," do we have the chance to compare the version typeset by Saul Marks for Black Sparrow, and then to realize that not only is Marks's typesetting fastidious to the intentions of Duncan's poem, it attains the ideal goal of all typesetting; namely, in Bringhurst's words, that "typography . . . is idealized writing," and that the satisfactions of its craft come from "elucidating, and perhaps even ennobling, the text" (19, 18). In his typesetting not only of "The Feast," but the rest of *Tribu-*

7. Duncan didn't always feel bellicose toward Martin. In a letter of July 17, 1967, Duncan urges Levertov to contribute to a Black Sparrow series Martin was planning, praising him as a "true *amateur*: i.e., one who has the care that comes from the love of what he works in or studies" (L 580).

8. It's worth noting that this typescripted version is not the same one that appears in *Ground Work: Before the War*, and that, indeed, there are some few slight differences between these typescripts.

nals, Marks honors Duncan's lines with generously wide pages, good margins, and an abiding sense of the pace of Duncan's poetry visible in the use of leading between lines and stanzas, as well as the ample caesuras found throughout the volume.

Against this act, Duncan nonetheless railed, focusing his rage on what he believed to be the too-small spacing between letters and the commas or periods following them. (In typesetting, this spacing falls in the category of proportional letter spacing and "kerning," which is the taking into account of letters' slopes to generate a harmonious-looking page). In his preface to *maps* 6, the journal John Taggart edited in the 1970s, beginning an issue devoted entirely to his work, Duncan inveighs against both Martin and Marks:

Nor was I wrong in my sense of [their] bad faith. When all was done, as the reader turning to *Tribunals* can verify, on the first page we find the copy unchanged from that earliest galley proof sent in August, some four months before. Correction, and pointed out especially, and corrected and argued again, there, unrepentant, are the printer's stubborn settings of the lines:

> a severd *distinct* thing; and the stars also

and

> in the influences of the stars, as it pleaseth.

The all-important articulations between movements of *Passages 33* are to the last sacrificed to Saul Mark's [*sic*] dislike of the look of blank spaces marring his page and to the publisher's contempt for what he takes to be the author's fussy discriminations. (5)

Duncan proceeds then to vent his spleen in this preface against the issue of *maps* Taggart was preparing for the poet. Taggart, owing to budget constraints, was unable to provide Duncan with proofs for correction; nor for the same reason could he agree to allow Duncan to provide typescripts that would be reproduced in the magazine. Duncan only reluctantly agreed to allow his poems and notes to be typeset in the issue after Taggart phoned him to assure him that everything would be as carefully proofread as humanly possible. Even so, Duncan was dissatisfied enough to devote his entire preface to the justification of the use of his typewriter.

Duncan's prolusion of frustration with typesetting, in his "Preface, prepared for *maps #6*," published in 1974, authorized his new book silence. A decade later, he published *Ground Work: Before the War* with New Directions. I submit that the physical appearance of that volume is visual evidence of Duncan's frustration. The history of self-published or self-designed poetry in English is long and complicated; Duncan's contribution to this lineage offers nothing surprising (even at the level of using the typewriter), at least not in comparison to, say, Blake's illuminated prophetic books, to Whitman's 1855 *Leaves of Grass*, to William Morris's Kelmscott designs, nor even, more recently, to Ronald Johnson's Xero Ox editions of the *Ramparts* of ARK, which he typed and illuminated with illustrations, then mailed to friends during the 1980s.[9] What it does however indicate—in visual relation to the rest of Duncan's printed poetry—is that something about the content and the materiality of the poems in this volume is so important that Duncan felt only his own publication of the work would satisfy its message. The material force of this prophecy is felt first and fullest in this volume in the soaring, difficult lines of its most ambitious poem, "Before the Judgment, Passages 35."

LURKING IN THE HEART: Duncan's Prophetic Mantle

In "The Concert," *Passages* 31, Duncan uses a definition of prophecy as a point of departure:

"Prophecy,

which uncovers the mystery of future events
but which also reveals what lurks in the heart
—prayers . . . song and especially ecstatic
speaking in tongues"

They shout,   leaping upon the tables,
outpouring vitalities,   stammering—   (GW 12–13)

Prophecy in poetry is not a telling of the future; rather, it is an expression of present necessities free of mediation. As Duncan indicates, historically

9. Johnson was inspired, perhaps, by Duncan's own circulation of his work through the 1970s in photocopied typescript; Johnson felt a frustration with his publishers similar to Duncan's, marked by a sense that since no publisher could "get" what he was doing, he needed to make the work available to those who could.

and culturally, prophecy has been perceived as a kind of ecstasy, uttered by prophets from altered states of consciousness. (Muhammad, for instance, is understood by some scholars—and critics of Islam—to have been epileptic.) To speak of Duncan as a prophet is to try to understand what is prophetic in poetry, as well as to determine the nature of prophecy itself. For Duncan, prophecy is what arises from a conscientious, vigilant answering for Poetry. He takes this in part to be a visionary state, but more importantly it is an incantational rising up through the levels of poetic insight into an aural and lexical Platonic realm, one that is ever present but invisible and inaudible to most of us because we lack in our consciousness the melodic coherence in which words do not pass away. The prophet in poetry is one who keeps the poem present.

This is as difficult to fathom as it is grand in scope. There's an enclaved, hieratic sense to Duncan's understanding of poetry as prophecy that a skeptical reader might well dismiss as esoteric cultishness. How do we place a prophetic sense of poetry in the context of Duncan's aggravations, making his position clearer to us? Poet Lew Daly, in conceiving of a belated prophetic tradition in American poetry, proposes the necessity of "a combative poetics of decision before the tribunal of spiritual force" (56).[10] Daly speaks of the recovery, through a prophetic poetry, of "news of a power beyond the reach of mediators, and, unlike politics, unmanipulatable at the level of language, like dictation in the Prophets is" (37). Daly regards the unmediated, untampered quality of such poetry as proof of its covenantal, consecrated nature—not that it defies published speech or politics, but in its catastrophic austerity, it rectifies these things:

With the incursion, in public, of a specifically auditory character of revelation and therefore of divinity, as manifested among the classical prophets of the Bible, coincided a kind of dehiscence in the meeting-point of history and the infinite, which is the point at which the very principle of public prophecy indeed re-covenanted, as historicity itself, the word of God in absolutizing ethics and the sacrifice of self. (61)

In other words, the biblical prophets, in bursting open the word of God, transformed the act of listening into one of covenant, binding the eternal promise of God to the time in which this truth is first heard (perpetuat-

10. In speaking of Howe's and Taggart's work, Daly places them as direct descendants of a Duncanian prophetic tradition in poetry.

ing it eternally). Thus, a bursting-forth of prophetic speech has the power of commanding subservience. It is into such a sense of time and word that Duncan utters his poems.

To Daly's sense of a prophetic poetry, I am inclined to add a hermeneutical sense of prophecy as imagined by Moshe Idel in *Absorbing Perfections*, his vast analysis of language and its arcanization in Kabbalah. In that work, Idel makes a telling distinction between prophetic experience and the prophetic intellect, suggesting that while experience must necessarily always have authority in matters of spiritual authenticity, it is the imagination (which he calls the "emanated intellect") that allows for the insights that permit experience to thrive:

Knowledge of the inner aspects of the Torah is conditioned on the attainment of the highest intellectual faculty, the prophetic intellect, which is seen as tantamount to prophetic experience. Understanding the secrets is a function of blurring the gap between God as intellect and the human intellect; the latter acquires a divine, holy intellect, which is the sine qua non for fathoming the secrets of the Torah. The Pentateuch, a text thought to have been written under divine inspiration, can only be properly understood by re-creating an appropriate state of consciousness. (187)

In this light, I suggest, Duncan's poems of this period of the late 1960s are best understood as vehicles for re-creating an appropriate state of consciousness, one in which the truth of Poetry is made clear. (I believe it is the poetry's regeneration of this state in the reader to which Butterick was responding in his review of *Ground Work: Before the War.*) For Duncan, the poem at its core is both inviolable and unmanipulable. The ambiguity that this position inspires in the poet, however, is one of utmost anxiety. Indeed, for Duncan, poetry is the vocalization of Poetry's sacral, prophetic truth and his simultaneous anxiety that his truth is being compromised in the poetry itself, or even by poets (as with Blaser and Levertov). And into this snare, Duncan's publishers regularly stumbled.

That the prophetic frustration driving Duncan's poetry is fixated in Duncan on the *made* quality of poetry, its very wroughtness, is perhaps Duncan's novel contribution to a definition of prophecy, one apprehended even as he was beginning to envision the project of *Passages*. "Before the Judgment, Passages 35" marks out a deliberately juridical setting, but one not fixated on condemnation so much as asserting our belatedness, in standing, always as we do, both *after* and *behind* the Judgment we witness. Duncan's poem constructs its vision of the present out of four distinct literary references meshed into the backdrop of the Vietnam War. Passages from Dante's Malebolge cantos of the *Inferno*, in both Italian and English, mark our progress through the Hell of war. Similarly, Pound's invective "Hell" (Cantos 14 and 15) provide invective vocabulary, allowing him to invoke as well the Hydra of Usura, a hybrid figure of the apocalyptic Book of Revelation and Pound's rage. But perhaps the most striking, because most mythologically strange, inclusion in the poem is Duncan's frequent references to passages from Hesiod's *Works and Days* that describe the beings who lived during a Golden Age now lost to us, referred to throughout "Before the Judgment, Passages 35" as "Golden Ones." In one of the most vivid moments in the poem, Duncan writes:

For they go about everywhere over the earth,

   attendant, daimons not only of men but of earth's plenitudes,
   ancestral spirits of whatever good we know,

      wherever judgment is made   they gather round watching,
      what the heart secretly knows   they know,

clothed in mist, golden, ever existing,   the host that comes in to conscience,

      deathless   they swarm in Memory and feed at the honeycomb. (GW 29)

Duncan proceeds to refer to these daimonic beings by their Hesiodic epithet: *epichthonoi*, or "spirits of the earth," later in the poem calling them "the Golden Ones," hearkening to the "Age of Gold" in which they emerged, and the "Ancestral Design" that forged them. Duncan's "Golden Ones" serve as emblems of the lost covenant, of the speech vanished with their assumption into a ghostlier existence. They exist on the one hand as proof of the certainty of his prophecy but on the other as reproof of its inherent failure, because they are mute to the world which cannot hear them or understand their wisdom. Their swarming in the honeycomb of memory is as vital as it is entombed, only faint buzzings in our unconscious.

    Hesiod's reference to the "Age of Gold," as well as that of the Heroic Age, the Age of Silver, and down through a line of metallic degenerations, results, in part, from his desire to situate himself and the divinities populating his imagination properly, especially in relation to the Homeric epics. The idea of an idyllic past corrupted is as central to the biblical tradition as it is the Greek mythological tradition. The difference is that in the biblical tradition, we are given two stories of failure: the disobedience of Eve and Adam, followed by the miscegenation of angels and human women, resulting in the propagation of the *nephilim*, the grasshopper-legged race of giants whom God felt the need to eradicate from creation.[11] In the Hesiodic tradition, these *epichthonoi* are indeed Golden, a brief shining moment in divine-human relations. But Gold is a color of loss in this poetry. Hesiod, in *Works and Days*, describes:

> In the beginning, the immortals
>   who have their homes on Olympos
>   created the golden generation of mortal people.
>
> . . .
>
> They lived as if they were gods,
>   their hearts free from all sorrow.
>
> . . .
>
> When they died, it was as if they fell asleep.
>
> . . .
>
>   Now that the earth has gathered over this generation,
> these are called pure and blessed spirits;
>   they live upon earth;
> and are good. They watch over mortal men
>   and defend them from evil.   (ll. 109–10; 112; 116; 121–23)

Following the Golden Ones come the people of the Silver Age. Hesiod's poem is a chronicle, then, not so much of generations and creative mistakes, as in Genesis, but rather of a record of degeneration, of the fall from Olympian communion and perfection to the war and strife of the Iron Age in which Hesiod found himself. Like Hesiod, Duncan looks from war and strife back to a golden time, not to persuade himself of an Edenic past, but rather, to assert his conviction that only through war and strife is the revelation of a Golden Age visible, that "the catastrophic rings true because a wish is made evident," as he wrote to Levertov in 1966.

---

11. See Genesis 6:1–6.

Duncan surrounds this mythos of the Golden Ones in his poem with pointed references to Dante's progress through Malebolge, quoting passages in both Italian and English, to register his profound discomfort with the evil he feels encroaching into him through Vietnam and the political actions and protests in the Bay Area in the late 1960s. "Before the Judgment, Passages 35" begins, memorably:

> Discontent with that first draft.   Where one's own
>   hatred enters   Hell   gets out of hand.
>
> Again and again   Virgil   ever standing by Dante
>   must caution him.   In Malebolge
>
> where the deep violation begins,
>
> *Mentr' io laggiu fissamente mirava,*
> *lo duca mio, dicendo   "Guarda, guarda"* (GW 28)

The first lines are crucial toward understanding the anxiety and chaos this poem generates for Duncan. "Discontent" is malcontent, thus an informing evil (and a nod to Dis, who reigns in the underworld). His sense of failure in the first draft (with its pun on military conscription) is an admission to or an intuition of an evil, a chaos—through whose opening, his own hatred has entered—a mean-spirited coerciveness. It has gotten out of hand because the writing hand—instrument of a prophetic consciousness—has let it—was obliged to let it—slip through. Thus Virgil's warning to Dante in the "evil pockets" (Malebolge) reverberates in Duncan's ear: *Guarda, guarda.* These last lines translate: "Where I stared fixedly upon the seething pitch, / my leader cried: 'Look out, look out!'" (*Inf.* 21.22–23). This caution leads Duncan into a visionary catalogue of the horrors of the deep violation: the immolation of fields, forests, and villages with Agent Orange in Vietnam, to the greed of oil barons whose "smoking tankers crawl toward Asia," leading him to quote again from Dante:

> men with fossil minds,   with oily tongues
>   "to lick the mirror of Narkissos" (GW 28)

In *Inferno* 30, Master Adam the counterfeiter suffering dropsy chides Sinon the fevered perjurer, who is so thirsty he desires to lick the mirror of

Narcissus, which Robert Hollander informs us "would thus reflect Sinon's true hideous self, one he would destroy in the thirst of his fever" (562).

Similarly, Duncan punctures his prophecy with harangues and insults against figures in the Bay Area political scrums of Vietnam protest movements, including Mayor Joseph Alioto, who oversaw the city during the students strikes of 1968, and who officially nominated Hubert Humphrey as presidential candidate at the infamous 1968 Democratic National Convention in Chicago; Samuel I. Hayakawa, a professor of education who was brought in as president to manage the rapidly deteriorating student strike at San Francisco State in 1968 after president John Summerskill was forced to resign in the wake of the strike and the creation of a Black Student Union; Yippie cofounder Jerry Rubin; as well as Nixon and Reagan. Much as in "Up Rising," these figures are represented as archons, emblematic of a "deep violation," the evil from which we need protection in the care of the Golden Ones. Duncan says of these figures, "as we go upwards the stupidity thickens, // reflections in the oil slick multiplied" (GW 32). One can understand Duncan's loathing of Nixon and Reagan, as well perhaps of Alioto, or even Hayakawa. But Jerry Rubin's presence deserves some analysis. Rubin and his fellow prankster Abbie Hoffman belong less to a political action group than to an artistic tradition of the absurd. The stunts of Rubin and the Yippies—like running a pig for office—had much more in common with Dada, Surrealism, and actionism than with Sacco and Vanzetti or the Haymarket. Their quest was the exposure of meaninglessness in public settings. To this type of "art"—let alone demagogic politics—Duncan was extremely antipathetic, as his letters to Levertov make clear. He frequently chides Allen Ginsberg and his fellow Beats for the poetic stunts they regularly pulled. And there's a sense that his disappointment in Levertov stemmed from his perception that she too was pulling a stunt in an effort to avoid inspecting her feelings toward the War. Thus he has Kali—the Hindu goddess of war and chaos—stand for Levertov in his "Santa Cruz Propositions" (GW 45–46).

Speaking of Thoreau, Lewis Hyde suggests that the purpose of prophecy is to "induce in us that second sight by which we see the workings of an invisible world" (ix). This accords with Duncan's argument that through prophetic poetry, "in the melody we make, the possibility of eternal life is hidden, and experience we thought lost returns to us." Duncan's hostility is increased by what he perceives to be the blindness of the participants in the world affairs that so anger him, events he strives to reconceive through a vast project of interiorizing his vision. Duncan's process of understanding such events, then, is analogous to what happens to a person in mourning, in terms of Freud's formulation, who desperately tries to connect to the ideas—or "golden" ghosts—of lost "objects": people, places, ideas. The failure of our vision infuriates him, inspiring his affection for the hidden, Golden Ones mournfully watching over himself and the world. To these Golden Ones, he commends both our care and his prophecy, for only they have eyes to see truly what Duncan witnesses. Like the Hidden Imam of Shi'i Islam, Duncan's Golden Ones slumber in a spiritual reality simultaneous with our own, into which they emit pulsations of knowledge, frequencies of judgment, which we might only dimly perceive in our unattuned reception. The reality of his time—the late 1960s—is so thoroughly saturated with evil, even dreams seep with visions of horror, whether for president, soldier, poet, or *epichthonoi*:

The president turns in his sleep and into his stupidity seep the images of burning peoples.
The poet turns in his sleep,   the cries of the tortured and of those whose pain survives after the burning   survive with him,   for continually
he returns to early dreams of just retributions and reprisals inflicted for his injuries.
The soldier gloating over and blighted by the burning bodies of children, women and old men, turns in his sleep of Viet Nam or,
dreamless, inert, having done only his duty, hangs at the edge of such a conscience to sleep.
The protestant turns in his sleep, setting fire to hated images,
entering a deeper war against the war. A deeper stupidity gathers.

The Golden Ones, the ancestors of the Good, cloak themselves in Sleep's depth,

eternally watching.   (GW 33–34)

Duncan includes one curious dreamer in his list: the protestant. Presumably, because the word isn't capitalized, Duncan is referring here to war protestors, rather than Protestant Christians; such protestors increasingly earned his scorn through the years of the war. Yet it's this "deeper war against the war" that Duncan feels he is seeing in his wakeful, prophetic state, transmitted to him from the sleep of the Golden Ones. He initiates this catalogue of sleepers with an oracle from the Golden messenger: "*In this mirror . . . our Councils darken*" (GW 33). These darkening deliberations are as inevitable as sleep, but as difficult to interpret as dreams. The art of the poem, as we have seen, is like the mechanism of the dream: to keep present a variety of times and places. "Keeping present" is the work of the prophetic intellect—a recreation of an imaginative state the inviolable truth of the poem can thrive in. By invoking a dream state, however, Duncan brings us into his most personal-prophetic sanctum of poetic force, the apocalyptic dream at the center of his work.

"Before the Judgment, Passages 35" concludes with a sweeping apocalypse, intriguing—in this light—for its near lack of any kind of Judgment:

> As if from the depths of Hell, the sleepers seek rest in what they are,
> so that again   the Wish of Death lifts them
> and passes over them.
> This pain you take
> is the pain in which Truth turns like a key.
>
> . . .
>
> but the Golden Ones meet in the Solar Councils
> and their alphabet is hidden in the evolution of chemical codes.
>
> In this place the airy spirit
> catching fire in its fall from flight
> has started a burning of conscience
> in the depths of earth and the primal waters,
> and all of Creation rises to meet him,
>
> as if to answer a call,   as if to call   into Being,
> forth from a raging Absence, even among men,
> the Body of "Man" cries out   toward Him.
>
> Children of Kronos,   of the Dream beyond death,
>
> secret of a Life   beyond our lives,
>
> having their perfection   as we have,

their bodies a like grace, a music,   their minds   a joy, abundant,

foliate,   fanciful in its flowering,

come into these orders as they have ever come,   stand,

as ever,   where they are acknowledged,

against the works of unworthy men, unfeeling judgments, and cruel deeds.
(GW 34–35)

Two striking elements stand out for me in these passages. The first is the metaphor of truth turning in the poet like a key in a lock—this movement he analogizes to pain, which I take to be an internal, prophetic pain of coming to terms with Poetry's difficult verity. He is speaking of the mute Golden Ones, who find themselves as if in the depths of Hell, wishing for Death but passed over, preserved in preternatural half-life, condemned to their Aeonic, Gnostic Solar Councils, from which their disembodied knowledge radiates into the slumbering world. The other element is the subtle but unmistakable evocation of what I take to be the myth central to Duncan's creative enterprise, his so-called Atlantis dream, a recurring dream from Duncan's childhood spelled out obsessively in his mature poetic work. In this dream, Duncan finds himself in a meadow where children dance in a ring. The grasses sway, then bend toward him in deference, as do the children, because he is clearly "It." The dream shifts and Duncan finds himself in an underground cavern, which is a throne room. The throne is empty. He recognizes that he is King, and with this understanding comes the panicking revelation that he has failed, at which point the dream darkens and the cavern bursts with flood. Duncan's theosophist family interpreted this dream for him as an oneiric memory of Atlantis, where his soul had last been incarnated. Duncan feeds off this dream incessantly in his poetry, from direct expressions of it in master poems such as "Often I Am Permitted to Return to a Meadow" and "A Poem Beginning with a Line by Pindar," to more embedded interpretations of the dream in poems such as "Apprehensions," "My Mother Would Be a Falconress" and "Achilles' Song."

That Duncan's apocalyptic conclusion to "Before the Judgment, Passages 35" revisits the themes of this dream—the depths of the earth and the primal waters, the willowy bodies of the Golden Ones like a grace, dancing with an abundant joy—is not surprising. What strikes me here, however, is the inversion of the narrative Duncan envisions here: first comes the catastrophe, the catching fire and the burning of conscience, which bears Christ into life (whom I take to be the Body of "Man")—a figure of redemption. Then comes the vision of the Golden Ones fanciful in their flowering, coming into their orders, for me, intuitively making a motion like the children in the grasses of Duncan's dream. Before the judgment, then, there is a holy order of life, one Duncan absorbs through the over-layered destruction of the world of strife he lives in and perceives through his own catastrophic dreams.

Duncan's Atlantis dream is the inexhaustibly interpretable, prophetic source of his poetry. As such, it is as unmanipulatable as it is mysterious and foreboding of a doom of meaning. Toward this source, Duncan is unwaveringly curious and protective. The dream authorizes and confounds his poetry, in its insistence that the teleology of meaning is catastrophe. I take this dream to be as generative an individual creative myth as Blake's childhood conversations with Ezekiel or Dante's adolescent enchantment with Beatrice. It seems to inform the whole of his art. What is difficult and troubling about "Before the Judgment, Passages 35," then, is not that it rearticulates the myth central to Duncan's creative life, but that he concludes a poem about Vietnam with a vision of his Atlantis dream, such that one not so much anticipates the other, but that Vietnam verifies for him the sacral, inviolable prophecy out of which his poetic effort springs. His prophetic frustration, in this light, is an admission of coercion on the one hand—the sense that he has been lured into an obsession with the Vietnam War—and a fearsome protectiveness on the other, the feeling that his dream is Poetry itself, and that his work as a poet is to speak for this dream.

And so Duncan's prophetic frustrations come fully into the light. The Golden Ones—compassionate, Platonic beings—are powerless, except as witnesses and transmitters of a truth turning in him painfully like a key in a lock. Unlocking is opening, thus seeing. Duncan seeks to transform the witness of the Golden Ones into an active, articulate vision, one of a feeling judgment he finds absent in unworthy men and their cruel deeds.

Only Duncan himself—as a poet turning in his prophetic sleep—can sufficiently act as intermediary to this insight. His pen and his typewriter are extensions of his own being. Typography, however, represents a reversion to blindness, to an inability to "see" the poem as he sees it, written in a golden alphabet hidden in the chemical codes of his vivid dreaming. For Duncan, politics—a kind of derogated prophecy—is only redeemed in poetry. In this light, his own war protest was not a physical marching in the streets, but a publishing silence. Here, following Duncan's own lead, we misread him, because his protest of silence was never a mutedness (he was too outspoken for that) but instead a blindness, or a blinding to any publication of his prophecy but his own.

Works Cited

Bringhurst, Robert. *Elements of Typographic Style*. Version 2.4. Point Roberts, WA: Hartley and Marks, 2001.

Butterick, George. "Seraphic Predator: A First Reading of Robert Duncan's *Ground Work*." *Sagetrieb* 4.2–3 (Fall–Winter 1985): 273–84.

Daly, Lew. *Swallowing the Scroll: Late in the Prophetic Tradition with the Poetry of Susan Howe and John Taggart*. Buffalo, NY: M Press, 1994.

Dante Alighieri. *The Inferno*. Trans. Robert Hollander and Jean Hollander. Notes by Robert Hollander. New York: Anchor, 2000.

Duncan, Robert. "A Preface Prepared for *maps* #6: THE ISSUE." *maps* 6 (1974): 1–16.

———. *Tribunals: Passages 31–35*. Santa Barbara, CA: Black Sparrow Press, 1970. Including "The Feast, *Passages* 34" booklet.

Hesiod. *Works and Days*. Trans. Richmond Lattimore. Ann Arbor: University of Michigan Press, 1959.

Hyde, Lewis. "Prophetic Excursions." *The Essays of Henry D. Thoreau*. New York: North Point Press, 2002.

Idel, Moshe. *Absorbing Perfections: Kabbalah and Interpretation*. New Haven, CT: Yale University Press, 2002.

Mossin, Andrew. "In the Shadow of Nerval: Robert Duncan, Robin Blaser, and the Poetics of (Mis)Translation." *Contemporary Literature* 38.4 (1997): 673–704.

Nasr, Sayyed Hossein. *The Heart of Islam*. San Francisco: HarperSanFrancisco, 2002.

Silliman, Ron. E-mail to the author, 26 March 2003.

CHAPTER II

Revolution or Death: Levertov's Poetry in Time of War

Jose Rodriguez Herrera

> When I can pull it together, I work in solitude surrounded by community, solitude in dialogue with community, solitude that alternates with collective work. The poetry and the actions of friends and strangers pass through the membranes of that solitude. This kind of worklife means vigilance, for the old definitions of "inner" and "outer" still lurk in me and I still feel the pull of false choices wrenching me sometimes this way, sometimes that. But if we hope to mend the fragmentation of poetry from life, and for the sake of poetry itself, it's not enough to lie awake, in Lillian Smith's words, listening only to the sound of our own heartbeat in the dark.
>
> —ADRIENNE RICH, *What Is Found There: Notebooks on Poetry and Politics*, 53

"Wittgenstein's war experience," as Marjorie Perloff says in *Wittgenstein's Ladder*, "became one of the mainsprings of his philosophy" (27). While stationed as an ordinary soldier in Galicia on the Romanian frontier, Wittgenstein formulated many of the logical propositions that would later form an integral part of his *Tractatus*, among them his famous aphorism "the limits of my language *mean* the limits of my world" (no. 5.6). Amid war experience, some decades later, Denise Levertov was forced to reflect on the truth of Wittgenstein's insight. What some of Levertov's antiwar poems ("Relearning the Alphabet" being one of the most salient cases) try to do is explore the limits of her language in time of war in order to see whether those limits could be stretched farther, whether it was possible to imagine other boundaries, other worlds. Moreover, Wittgenstein's maxim can be useful in comprehending the series of misunderstandings that would eventually provoke her final rupture with Robert Duncan. As I shall argue, their diverging interpretations of the meaning of the word "revolution" lie at the heart of the dispute ongoing in their letters.

Commentary on Levertov's political poetry has focused, mostly negatively, on polemical matters that are common to antiwar poetry: slogans, moralizing tone, venting of personal anger, radical diction, vivid images of suffering and death. Yet those critiques neglect how much she strives, however failed some of her attempts might have been, to project personal and social revolution into poetic language. Levertov's decision to write social poetry cost her very dearly in the critical appraisal of her work; her first incursions in political poetry marked a turning point in the reception of her work. Until then, each publication of a new volume of her poems had been received with great enthusiasm on the part of critics and readers alike. But the appearance of her first lines against Vietnam turned that enthusiasm first into skepticism and then into outright dismissal.

As an example of one line of argument, Roberta Berke's *Bounds out of Bounds*, dismisses Levertov's Vietnam poetry on the grounds of an alleged failure to persuade prospective readers: "The reader who comes to her Vietnam verses already repelled by the sheer horror of that war," Berke asserts, "will not have his or her conviction changed or widened by them; the reader who may have felt the war was justified will turn the page when faced with the familiar propaganda, which is less vivid than the gory news films that flickered over millions of supper tables in those years" (39). Is Berke implying that in order to be more effective poets must imitate the "gory news" flashing on TV screens? Besides, there is ample testimony from readers that Levertov's political poems brought them to a new level of political and ethical consciousness. A different line of argument criticises Levertov for "picking out," as she herself quoted from another poet in part 2 of "Staying Alive," "[her] own song from the uproar," with the result that she is misusing and tainting the high purpose of "Art." But in the essay "Blood, Bread, and Poetry," Adrienne Rich lashes out against this "mystical" overrating of "the song over the struggle":

There is the falsely mystical view of art that assumes a kind of supernatural inspiration, a possession by universal forces unrelated to questions of power and privilege or the artist's relation to bread and blood. In this view, the channel of art can

only become clogged and misdirected by the artist's concern with merely tempo-
rary and local disturbances. The song is higher than the struggle, and the artist
must choose between politics—here defined as earth-bound factionalism, corrupt
power struggles—and art, which exists on some transcendent plane. . . . In the fif-
ties and early sixties, there was much shaking of heads if an artist was found "meddling in politics"; art was mystical and universal, but the artist was also, apparently, irresponsible and emotional and politically naïve." (246)

As Levertov's case also shows, that shaking of heads was even more
severe if the artist found "meddling into politics" happened to be a woman. Surprisingly enough, George Oppen was one of the first male poets to
declare his antipathy to Levertov's antiwar poetry, in "The Mind's Own
Place," an essay "almost written *at* her" (1990, 57), as he recognized in a
1962 letter to his sister June Oppen. His letter discloses the true nature of
his objections: "she is very determined to be (or become?) a good mother, to enter political (anti bomb, at least) activity, etc etc——The essay very
nearly tells her to stop writing for a while——if she must, just now, arrive
at edifying conclusions, or comforting conclusions." There can be little
doubt about Burton Hatlen's conclusion that Oppen's animus stems from
"the fact that she was a woman" (9). Hatlen contends that in "Who Is at
My Window?" Levertov had Oppen in mind as "the blind cuckoo, mull-
ing / the old song over," whose counsel she rejects because "I want to move
deeper into today; / he keeps me from that work" (P60 122).

In fact, it was in her Jewish-Christian household that Levertov
learned early the redemption of man through his actions and the poet's
prophetic role and moral obligation to call "'Sleepers Awake!'" as she put it
in her poem "Candles in Babylon." Her activist conscience, inherited from
her parents, was put into practice at an early age and in later years committed her as a poet to political involvement.[1] In her essay "Some Duncan Letters: A Memoir and a Critical Tribute" she argued that Duncan's anarchism
and his mistrust of any group action didn't allow him to "see that there
was nothing I was engaged in that was not 'volunteered from the heart'"

1. Barely twelve years old, Levertov told her sister Olga that she wanted to
join the Communist Party. Informed that she was too young to join the Communist League, she volunteered to sell the *Daily Worker* every Sunday on Barker
Street. "In knee socks and a reefer coat, with two long braids," she would go from
house to house, urging "Read *The Daily Worker*, the worker's own paper, written
by workers *for* workers" (TMS 67).

(NES 226). All this, coupled with her understanding of life and poetry as entwined, made her perceive poetry as an agent of social transformation, a site for calling to revolution, both social and personal. Finally she was influenced by some feminist efforts in the 1960s to connect the civil rights movement with women's resistance to oppression in their lives.

Duncan was quick to find in some antiwar poems a "deep underlying consciousness of the woman as a victim in war with the Man" (L 667). The moment when pacifism was no longer a personal option was, she said, when she intuitively saw "a connection between the Vietnamese people struggling for self-preservation and between people's struggling for self-determination in all places, and with racism" (1998, 91). But in a speech for a rally at the University of Massachusetts she committed herself further: "the days of mere protest are over, and the days of separating war, and racism and pollution of natural resources, and social injustice, and *male chauvinism* [my emphasis], into neat little compartments are over" (1973, 122). Fighting against war could not be compartmentalized from fighting against racism, or fighting for the preservation of one's identity; resistance on all fronts required political decisions and not simply opting out. Moreover, her willingness to "move deeper into today" extended beyond active participation in sit-ins, teach-ins, rallies, and readings to engage and inform her writing itself. In fact, she says explicitly in the preface of *To Stay Alive* that she intends the poems to be "a record of one person's inner/outer experience in America during the '60's and the beginning of the '70's" (SA ix). Its diary-like form is to be a fusion of the personal and the public.

Thus it was during those years of sociopolitical convulsion, that Levertov developed a keen awareness of herself as a woman poet fully committed to her time, her community, and her true vocation as a poet. Instead of viewing her political poems as a detriment of her development as a poet, I would suggest that in those very poems many aspects of her new poetics began to crystallize. I would like to show how some of her antiwar poems try to articulate issues related to the aesthetics and the ethics of writing in order to forge a reinvigorated language capable of merging the song and the struggle.

"Relearning the Alphabet," the long title poem of her 1970 collection, is a showcase of Levertov's attempt to revise and reimagine the language of our common usage and understanding. She chooses the alphabetical focus to demonstrate how the roots of our language determine our modes of thinking. By questioning the letters of the alphabet, and the words they originate, she destabilizes the reader's most deep-rooted judgments concerning language. As Rachel Blau DuPlessis points out, "what is more basic than the alphabet, what more ubiquitous, or more taken for granted?" (226). Each letter of the alphabet enacts a "monolithic block of consciousness" (DuPlessis's phrase) that ultimately informs our ways of perceiving reality. Deconstructing each letter into its various aspects revises and reinvents language and world, making the alphabet, in Charles Altieri's words, "a syntax of moral values and their possible relations with one another" (145). For example, though letter *B* immediately gives rise to "being," Levertov inflects the word by linking "being" with "love," and with accepting the other's right to be: "To be. To love an other only for being" (RA 111).

"Most original in this long poem," as Audrey Rodgers observes in *Denise Levertov: The Poetry of Engagement*, "are Levertov's tonal effects as each 'letter' encompasses a poem made up of alliteration, assonance, and consonance" (100). Thus letter *A* yields a whole register of a-sounds: "ardor," "Anguish," (swept up "as with a wing-tip") and "ashes" (brushed "back to the fire's core"). In a similar fashion, letter *E* in various sounds and combinations records the emotional experience of "endless / revolution":

> Endless
> returning, endless
> revolution of dream to ember, ember to anguish,
> anguish to flame, flame to delight,
> delight to dark and dream, dream to ember   (RA 111)

Duncan immediately noted the sound quality of the poem. In a letter to Levertov just after he read the manuscript she had sent him, he praised the sound of the poem as one of its strongest assets: "The 'Alphabet' reads richer and stronger with the full mixture of magic and moralizing, exclamation and expression—the letters and the sounds of letters giving a subtle shadow-warp on which to weave" (L 650).

But through its melopoeic qualities, "Relearning the Alphabet" substantiates itself as a work of personal rediscovery, a crucible of words in which the poet hopes to alchemize a new self, "to beget, self-out-of-self / selfless, / that pearl-of-great-price," as H.D. announced in her war epic *Trilogy* (9). As letter *E* shows, the poet self-reflectively revises her different emotional phases so as to reach a final emotional balance. As she voyages through the letters of the alphabet, "letter to letter as though each were a signpost on her journey and her own return to language" (Rodgers 100), she tries to chart the whole alphabetical map, recording not only the new places, but also the absences, the erasures, and the wrong turnings. Yet, in the middle of her journey, the poet cannot avoid losing herself amid the intricate web of the letters, and decides to ally herself with the world of transformation to find her new self: "Into the world of continuance, to find / I-who-I-am again" (RA 112).

The loss of the self among the letters of the alphabet is compounded by yet another absence: the lack of love, projected in the letter *B*. Thus, by the time the poet reaches *L*, the twelfth letter of the alphabet, she can only document its absence, at the same time that she confesses her incapacity to utter the word "(love)," now enclosed in parentheses. Together with the word "presence," it is separated from the rest of the words—yet still posited in their absence in the left margin:

> Absence has not become
> a presence.
> > Lost in the alphabet
> > I was looking for
> > the word I can't now say
> (love)
> > and am called forth
> > unto the twelfth letter
> > by the love in a question.   (RA 114)

Does Levertov want to suggest here that she has reached one of the dangerous turning points of her language? It seems so, for the absence of the word love coincides with her incapacity to imagine the other as presence. "Love in a question" suggests that love itself needs rediscovery; it marks the turning point at the middle of the sequence. For recovery at a personal level begins in the very next letter, *M*, associated with her husband Mitchell Goodman, whose revolutionary activities against the war had brought him, during the months in which "Relearning the Alphabet" was written, to trial and conviction and a subsequent overturning of the verdict:

> your mouth
>   has found
> my mouth once more
> —I'm home.   (RA 115)

That personal connection allows her to begin to relearn the world with revolutionary love in the second half of the alphabet.

Wittgenstein warned that "language sets everyone the same traps; it is an immense network of easily accessible wrong turnings. . . . What I have to do then is erect signposts at all the junctions where there are wrong turnings so as to help people past the danger points" (1980, 18). "Philosophy ought really to be written only as a *form of poetry*" (1980, 24), he also once said, and Levertov seems to be writing her own poetry as a kind of philosophy of language. Through the alphabet Levertov erects her own signposts in her poem, and at the midpoint of the poem it is precisely the absence of the word love, in its meaning of compassion and respect for the other and for the other's right to be, that seems to forestall the recognition of the self. But just as H.D. invoked in war-torn *Trilogy* "the need for a new kind of spiritual approach to existence" (Graham 175), when she confessed, "we are at the crossroads, / . . . let us light a new fire" (26), so Levertov, facing a similar crossroads amid the blurring chaos caused by war, also seeks for new forms of light, new forms of vision. As the poem advances to the last letters of the alphabet, this new approach to existence translates into a personal commitment to the spirit of quest, at once personal and political.

By the letter *U*, near the end of her journey through the alphabet, she affirms the injunction to relearn the alphabet and the world through acting in the world.

> *U*
> Relearn the alphabet,
> relearn the world, the world
> understood anew only in doing, under-
> stood only as
> looked-up-into out of earth,
> the heart an eye looking,
> the heart a root
> planted in earth.
> Transmutation is not
> under the will's rule. (RA 119)

The last two lines of the poem can be read as a response to Duncan's words in a letter in which he rejects submitting the will to conscience or any other authority: "I draw back from commanding conscience, as I wld avoid whatever tyranny of the will" (611).

It is within the ideological framework of relearning the alphabet and world through allegiance to change, I would argue, that Levertov's slogan "Revolution or Death" can be best interpreted. For when the last stanzas of "Relearning the Alphabet" announce her commitment to revolution and her will to move toward "continuance: into / that life beyond the dead-end" (RA 118), she is affirming revolution as an evolution into a new life beyond dead ends. Yet diverging views about the meaning of the slogan and about how revolution could be of import to the poem soon began to tear apart the fabric of the friendship that Duncan and Levertov had woven through years of intense correspondence.

As Albert Gelpi aptly argues in his introduction to the published letters, their different theological origins serve to account for their conflicting views of the aesthetic ethics of the poem. Duncan's anarchist individualism ("And my spirit leaps up at Whitman's each man his own law" [L 632]) made him suspect any group action as a coercive infringement of the absolute freedom of the individual to create and realize himself. In his view, Levertov's strong moral convictions and her commitment to antiwar movements could result in a self-coercion of the imaginative faculties that it was her responsibility as a poet to preserve intact. In an outright dismissal of *To Stay Alive*, Duncan reminded Levertov that "the question is the poetry and not the revolution—the book clearly isn't 'revolutionary' in the sense of the poem." Moreover, the theme of the poem seemed to him something other than revolution: "the theme may be *anguish*" (L 660). After seeing a televised image of Levertov giving a speech before a peace rally in Washington, Duncan became convinced that she was being savagely possessed by "the demonic spirit of the mass" (L 663). In his eyes she became Kali, the Hindu goddess of rage. "Kali," wrote Duncan in one of his letters to Levertov, "belongs to the Wheel of Inexorable Revolution. Her wrath destroys good and evil alike, consumes us in an age of conflicts" (L 689).

Duncan read "Revolution or Death" as a kind of ultimatum or threat: "Brecht's '*Alles oder Nichts*' is, like your '*Revolution or Death*'" (L 673). Levertov, however, was echoing Rilke's "*Unlived life / of which one can die*" (SA 29; Levertov's emphasis), lines which she cites in the poem as a gloss on "Revolution or Death." Rilke is crucial not only in order to set "Revolution or Death" in its proper frame in order to understand what kind of death and so what kind of revolution she meant. Levertov understood "*Unlived life*" as a form of "drowsy numbness" (SA 30; Levertov's emphasis) self-induced by willful evasions of what is actually happening. The only way out of that impasse was the active engagement with life in and through language in order to "pick out / [her] own song from the uproar" (SA 42). Thus making the poem became its own vivid testimony to the need to revitalize the world in which she lives. As Anne Little states, "she finally realizes that poetry ('song') is not just a way to ease the pain or celebrate victory after the struggle; it can, in fact, be a source of transforming energy" (38).

Duncan staunchly denied that the song could be distilled from the uproar ("partisan feelings and resolutions act as censors of the imagination" [L 670]), or that the poem could be made a vehicle to express any form of conviction exterior to itself: "we do not say something by means of the poem but the poem is itself the immediacy of saying" (L 668). In Gelpi's words, Duncan saw that the only resolution was "imaginative and poetic, not political and social; ethics were aesthetic" (L xxii). Levertov, in opposition, was fully convinced that the resolution could be both political and imaginative, revolutionary and poetic. The poem was the place *in* and *through* which revolutionary convictions could be tested and fully realized. As she confessed in her essay "Poetry and Revolution: Neruda Is Dead— Neruda Lives," "the altered structure of the inevitable revolution must be *in* the poem, in it. Made of it. It must shine in the structural body of it . . . " (1995, 127). The only way in which this can be made possible is through "conjunctions" of song with "patient courage." As she stated in part 4 of "Staying Alive":

> only conjunctions
>   of song's
>   raging magic
>   with patient courage
>   will make   a new life: (SA 82)

By connecting the new song with the new life, Levertov posited the necessity of revolution to poetry and living. At one point, as we have seen, Duncan accused *To Stay Alive* of not being really revolutionary. But his deeper and contrary objection was that revolution and poetry were themselves opposed and at odds:

Revolutions have all been profoundly opposed to the artist, for revolutions have had their power only by the rule that power not be *defined*. And as workers in words, it *is* our business to keep alive in the language definitions as well as forces, to create crises in meaning, yes—but this is to create meanings in which we are the more aware of the crisis involved, of what is at issue. In posing "revolution or death" you seem to feel that evolution—which as far as we know is the way in which life actually meets its test and creates its self—does not come into the picture. As if, i.e., Man got to "overthrow" reptiles. (L 661)

As Marjorie Perloff states in her essay "Poetry in Time of War: The Duncan-Levertov Controversy," "to go so far as to declare that revolution is the enemy of art because revolution must, to succeed, betray the poet's *language*, that revolution belongs to the old Ptolemaic Universe and should be supplanted by evolution—this is to give avant-garde theory a curious spin" (1998, 212). We know historically that in fact the desire for sociopolitical revolution has often been a catalyzing force behind many European avant-garde movements. But Duncan's radical anarchism made him see revolution as opposed to individual freedom—for the poet, destructive of the exercise of his creative, imaginative faculties. As he wrote in one of his letters, "the poet's role is not to oppose evil but to imagine evil" (L 669). In order to imagine evil the poet had to practice a discipline of voluntary self-detachment from the surrounding tumult.

Both Levertov and Duncan subscribed to Coleridge's definition of the imagination as "living Power prime Agent of human perception." Levertov, however, found that the only way in which she could perceive other people's sufferings as real to her mind was through immersion in the here and now of the conflict. In a poem titled "Snail," from *Relearning the Alphabet*, she puts into allegorical language her major differences with Duncan on this matter. Though she admits in the poem she envies the worm's capacity for subterranean evasion, "the worm's / lowly freedom that can go // under earth," she prefers to go on as a snail, dragging the brittle shell on her back yet with eyes "adept to witness / air and harsh light // and look all ways" (RA 77).

As a result of these deeply held differences, where Levertov saw revolution as a rolling wheel of advancing progress, Duncan figured revolution as a wheel that endlessly revolves on a stationary axis. The image of revolution as a wheel mirrors his understanding of the Vietnam War as a repetition of "America's unacknowledged, unrepented crimes," as he claimed in "Up Rising." Such a recognition, in Duncan's view, would free the poet from the futilely revolving wheel of war and equally blind opposition to war, and thus be able to assimilate war and evil into the larger imaginative creation of his poems. Duncan could only see Levertov's allegiance to revolution as binding her to a wheel of self-consuming anger and moralizing which thwarted vision and imaginative creation. To the self-destructive anger of revolution, Duncan could only propose the "slow and long durations of evolutionary change as without moral justification" (L 691).

In part 2 of "Staying Alive," Levertov goes finally to the crux of the matter and points to their different understandings, though, she goes on to admit, the problem might lie again in the limits of our language:

> Robert reminds me *revolution*
> implies the circular: an exchange
> of position, the high
> brought low, the low
> ascending, a revolving,
> an endless rolling of the wheel. The wrong word.
> We use the wrong word. A new life
> isn't the old life in reverse, negative of the same photo.
> But it's the only
> word we have . . .   (SA 41)

In a biting response, Duncan derides Levertov as a poet for admitting she might lack the right word: "Do you really, a poet, take the charge of *words* as of so little account that the 'wrong' word can be 'the only word we have'?" And then he magisterially supplies it himself: what she wants is *rebellion*: "We have the word 'rebellion'—to start the war once more, that belongs to your 'Alle oder Nichts' proposition. The old war between good and evil, to the end. . . . *Rebellion* is the word for your resolve 'to pull down this obscene system before it destroys all life on earth.' The hatred that backs that word "obscene" is apocalyptic; and apocalyptic fervor charges the righteousness that accuses" (L 688).

In this standoff between the two poets we are faced again with Wittgenstein's observation that "the limits of my language *mean* the limits of my world." However, I would like to suggest in conclusion that the word *(r)-evolution*—not *rebellion*—expresses more accurately Levertov's understanding of her commitment: first, (r)-evolution as the opposite of "unlived life," that is, as a personal commitment to confront challenges in life as a woman poet by involving herself in the cause she writes about; secondly, (r)-evolution as a way to make people aware, through poetic imagination, of the crisis in meaning and of the need to relearn alphabet and world; and finally, (r)-evolution as a proof that the song is not "higher than the struggle," for the song, if combined with the rhythms of (r)-evolution, always constitutes the struggle to regain and renew life.

Works Cited

Altieri, Charles. "Denise Levertov and the Limits of the Aesthetics of Presence." In *Denise Levertov: Selected Criticism*, ed. Albert Gelpi. Ann Arbor: University of Michigan Press, 1993, 126–47.

Berke, Roberta. *Bounds out of Bounds: A Compass for Recent American Poetry*. New York: Oxford University Press, 1981.

Block, Ed, ed. *Spirit in the Poetry of Denise Levertov*. Special issue. *Renascence* 1–2 (Fall 1997–Winter 1998).

Doolittle, Hilda [H.D.]. *Trilogy*. New York: New Directions, 1973.

DuPlessis, Rachel Blau. "The Critique of Consciousness and Myth in Levertov, Rich, and Rukeyser." In *Denise Levertov: Selected Criticism*, ed. Albert Gelpi, 218–42. Ann Arbor: University of Michigan Press, 1993.

———, ed. *Denise Levertov: Selected Criticism*. Ann Arbor: University Press of Michigan, 1993.

Graham, Sarah H. S. "We Have a Secret. We Are Alive": H.D.'s *Trilogy* as a Response to War." *Texas Studies in Literature and Language*. 44. 2 (2002): 161–210.

Hatlen, Burton. "'Feminine Technologies': George Oppen Talks at Denise Levertov." *American Poetry Review* (May–June 1993): 9–14.

Levertov, Denise. *Candles in Babylon*. New York: New Directions, 1982.

———. *Conversations with Denise Levertov*. Ed. Jewel Spears Brooker. Jackson: University Press of Mississippi, 1998.

———. *Poems, 1960–1967*. New York: New Directions, 1966.

Little, Anne Colclough. "Old Impulses, New Expressions: Duality and Unity in the Poetry of Denise Levertov." In *Spirit in the Poetry of Denise Levertov*, ed. Ed Block, special issue, *Renascence* 1–2 (Fall 1997–Winter 1998): 33–48.

Oppen, George. "The Mind's Own Place." *Kulchur* 10 (1963): 2–8.

———. *The Selected Letters of George Oppen*. Ed. Rachel Blau DuPlessis. Durham, NC: Duke University Press, 1990.

Perloff, Marjorie. *Poetry on and off the Page*. Evanston, IL: Northwestern University Press, 1998.

Rich, Adrienne. *Adrienne Rich's Poetry and Prose*. Ed. Barbara Charlesworth Gelpi and Albert Gelpi. New York: Norton, 1993.

————.*What Is Found There: Notebooks on Poetry and Politics*. New York: Norton, 1993.

Rodgers, Audrey T. *Denise Levertov: The Poetry of Engagement*. Toronto: Associated University Presses, 1992.

Wittgenstein, Ludwig. *Culture and Value*. Ed. G. H. von Wright. Trans. Peter Winch. Chicago: University of Chicago Press, 1980.

————. *Tractatus Logico-Philosophicus*. Trans. G. K. Ogden. New York: Routledge, 1988.

CHAPTER 12

The Vision of the Burning Babe:
Southwell, Levertov, and Duncan

Paul A. Lacey

Whenever one poem takes its start from another, we ask what added resonances, what conversations between texts, emerge. What mirroring—reversing, enlarging, distorting—do we see? Thus we may approach Denise Levertov's "Advent 1966," a thirty-line poem that builds on her reading of Robert Southwell's Christmas poem of 1595, "The Burning Babe." The resonances become more complex when we look at how Robert Duncan later uses the same Southwell poem in his poem sequence "A Seventeenth Century Suite," for now we not only have two modern poets exploring the trope of the burning babe, we also know that Duncan's poem is inflected by hers and in some sections directly grows out of unfinished business with Levertov. In his letter of January 25, 1972, which immediately follows their agreement to leave off any further discussion, for a year and a day, of her book *To Stay Alive*, which had been at the center of their heated arguments, Duncan writes: "There will follow, as soon as I have got the two remaining parts, the 'Metaphysical' suite that the Christmas retake on Southwell's 'Burning Babe' after your Advent 1966 poem, belongs to" (L 700).

The first clear cracks in the sad shattering of their friendship, recorded in their letters from 1965–72, become visible when Levertov sends Duncan "Advent 1966" in early December and he replies on December 16, 1966. Albert Gelpi's careful, detailed, and compassionate discussion of their "political/ideological/philosophical/aesthetic differences" in his introduction to *The Letters of Robert Duncan and Denise Levertov* is and will remain the indispensable balanced overview of the subject. With the complete Duncan-Levertov correspondence now available to us, we can discern the shape of their argument and reflect on how each of them converses with Southwell. This essay cannot fully explicate the scores of letters which record their many and complex disagreements and ultimate disaffection, but it will begin, in Henry James's phrase, by "harking back to make up," examining what leads up to this exchange over "Advent 1966" and then, by looking closely at the letters of 1968–72, identifying what elements of their conflict get into and help shape Duncan's "Seventeenth Century Suite."

Here is what Duncan says:

Denny, the last poem brings with it an agonizing sense of how the monstrosity of this nation's War is taking over your life, and I wish that I could advance some— not consolation, there is none—wisdom of how we are to at once bear constant (faithful and ever present) testimony to our grief for those suffering in the War and our knowledge that the government of the United States is so immediately the agency of death and destruction of human and natural goods, and at the same time continue as constantly in our work (which must face and contain somehow this appalling and would-be spiritually destroying evidence of what human kind will do—for it has to do with the imagination of what is going on in Man) now, more than ever, to keep alive the immediacy of the ideal and of the eternal. (L 563)

It is important to recognize what is happening here. Levertov sends a *poem* to a friend and reader she trusts, expecting it to be read *as* a poem, but Duncan responds to it only as *a psychological document* recording a danger to her poetry. He sympathizes with her pain and urges her to continue in "our" work "to keep alive the immediacy of the ideal and of the eternal." To understand Duncan's treatment of "Advent 1966" this way, it is useful to consider what he says half a year earlier, in a letter of May 18, 1965, where he describes hearing LeRoi Jones read what Duncan considers racist work:

But poetry often has to include the dementia of the poet, the thing was that what he read was blatantly demagogic. Written for its effect on the audience and I suspect swept up in the sense of its opportunity. *Insincere* in the only meaning of that word that seems important to me. There have been poems of LeRoi's in the past where the hate was most really communicated—but now the hate is being put across or put over—it does not take long in that direction for the writer himself to be taken in by his own opportunity. (L 492–93)

Duncan's assertion that "our work . . . has to do with the imagination of what is going on in Man," suggests, as in similar passages elsewhere in the letters, modes of detaching from the immediate outer-world facts by turning inward, taking those facts and transforming or "alchemizing" them through images, symbols, archetypes. Though he identifies himself as primarily Freudian in his theoretical orientation, Duncan seems here to be working from the kind of distinction Carl Jung makes in *Two Essays on Analytical Psychology* between a personal unconscious and "an impersonal or transpersonal unconscious." The personal unconscious contains our memories, fantasies, repressed materials, the "personal infantile form of transference," everything—for example, "the dementia of the poet"— which may have traces of personal pathology in us. For Jung, the collective unconscious contains all the sleeping primordial, universal images, to which the libido gains access by following "its own gradient down into the depths of the unconscious, and there activates what has lain slumbering from the beginning" (75–77). Drawing the appropriate archetypes up out of this deep storehouse enables the artist, as it might enable someone undergoing therapy, to connect, clarify, and finally transform personally unhealthy materials into greater knowledge, or into a work of art. This process seems closely analogous to Duncan's layering or "collaging" of materials in his poetry.

From the perspective of their whole correspondence, Duncan's response to "Advent 1966" appears as both a danger sign and a logical outgrowth of the previous year's letters in which, largely driven by how both are dealing with the Vietnam War in their poetry, Levertov and Duncan each engage in a lot of amateur psychoanalysis of what the other has written. Levertov's letter of January 25, 1966, twelve months earlier, begins, "I've been absolutely paralyzed by unwritten poems. But have at last come out of it, with one absolutely direct anti-war poem" (L 519). She isn't sure it is a good poem, but "it is even so a tremendous relief to have at least opened my mouth." She then turns to critique Duncan's "Xmas Poem," "Earth's Winter Song," about which she expresses "considerable reservations," based on the violence of its language and imagery and "the reduction to a willed 2-dimensional state, of a living person." She is worried that the poem's judging Hubert Humphrey and Lyndon Johnson derives from self-righteousness, "whereas the more fitting attitude is to *grieve, deplore, agonize*, without judging, because anguish doesn't separate itself from compassion. . . . It's so *easy* to think one is feeling for the burned child but so hard to remember the human soul, capable of doing good, of the murderer" (L 519–20). Duncan had written earlier, December 3, 1965, that he was still having trouble with "'Passages 26—The Soldiers'. . . . It's not to be an anti-war passage, but another vision: of those who have only the war to take their lives in. The vision appalls me but impels me, and I do not want to see it perhaps . . . " (L 517). It is worth pausing to note that conjunction of "appalls/impells" as foreshadowing of his later feelings about Levertov's poetry. In "Up Rising, Passages 25" he describes

> . . . the all-American boy in the cockpit
> loosing his flow of napalm, below in the jungles
> "any life at all or sign of life" his target, drawing now
> not with crayons in his secret room
> the burning of homes and the torture of mothers and fathers and
> children,
> their hair aflame, screaming in agony, but
> in the line of duty . . .   (BB 81)

This sexualized evocation of the effects of napalm is far more graphic than anything Levertov attempts in "Advent 1966." On July 13, 1966, Duncan says he is still waiting for "Passages 25" to "undergo its sea change or alchemical phase towards rendering up its purely poetic identity, where the figures do not *refer* to contemporary history only but are happenings of the poem itself" (L 528). "The Soldiers," he says, "delivers up its images of my own mounting blood pressure." His medication keeps his blood pressure within range but leaves him feeling subdued and "lowerd," so two days before writing on the poem he deliberately suspends taking his medicine, returning to it only "when the symptoms of pressure become troublesome" four days later:

> tho we fight underground
> from the body's volition, the body's inward sun
> the blood's natural
> up rising . . .   (L 528)

Later in this same letter, talking about Levertov's "What Were They Like?" and "Life at War," he says: "We are not reacting to the war, but mining images here the war arouses in us." His image of the "all-American boy in the cockpit" he believes has behind it James Dickey's actual war experience, which Duncan knows through Dickey's poems and which in turn connects with Duncan's childhood fantasies of burning houses and people, alchemized through Boehme "to reach the redemption of the real, to be 'containd'" (L 530). From this self-reflection, Duncan turns to a passage in "Life at War," which will become a major crux in the disagreements and ultimately the break in his friendship with Levertov:

> what is going on in your
> still turns without surprise, with mere regret
> to the scheduled breaking open of breasts whose milk
> runs out over the entrails of still-alive babies
> transformation of witnessing eyes to pulp-fragments,
> implosions of skinned penises in carcass gulleys

The words in their lines are the clotted mass of some operation . . . having what root in you I wonder? Striving to find place in a story beyond the immediate. (L 530)

Duncan's questions reflect the mind-set from which he criticized LeRoi Jones's "dementia of the poet," turned into writing for effect on its audience, and from which he analyzed "Advent 1966." In effect, he asks, what personal pathology, unmediated or transformed by art, accounts for these lines? And on July 18, 1966, Levertov tries to reply forthrightly to what could easily have felt like a personal attack:

. . . yr question seems to mean, what affinity in you (in me) makes you capable of imagining those words? . . . yr question makes me requestion myself & ask in what way the horror *at* violence (that makes one need to make oneself face it by writing it down in images that one makes oneself see,) is related to, first my own violent temper which in the last few years seems to have been converted into other energies, & second my anxieties, my "imagination of disaster," which so often presents the most horrid possibilities to me in graphic terms? (L 532–33)

Duncan and Levertov are each circling around what it means to experience a vision that impels *and* appalls, a vision that neither wishes to see. Is one somehow personally to blame for being able to conceive of brutal, violent acts? In her response, Levertov acknowledges the possible unhealthy origins of some of this content, but she also asserts that her violence has been "converted into other energies." Near the end of this very long, self-reflective letter, Levertov sounds a theme which will reverberate tragically in her poems, letters, essays, and notebooks for the rest of her life: "Dear Robert, do you think we are coming to the end of the world? . . . sometimes I am very fearful. Of the end of all things" (L 537).

On August 17, 1966, Duncan says: "the question of poetry is *not* whether one feels outrage at the war or feels whatever—other than the imperative of the poem. It's the force of word-work (I mean in the sense I always use the word 'work,' the recognition of the process of language as a spiritual process) that I miss" (L 543). Levertov answers by return mail, August 19–20, 1966:

About the new letter, which came this morning, there is one thing I feel I must mention, & that is, that in repeating, here and elsewhere, that you feel *outraged* by the war you seem perhaps, just a little, to assume that others—Mitch & I for example?—*don't*, but only "deplore" etc. Maybe I am wrong but that is the way you, in several allusions or rather in these allusions taken together, seem to me to make it sound & if it is true it is something I cannot let pass. (L 546)

She claims that his attitude is based on two things, first, that she criticized his words about Humphrey in "Earth's Winter Song," which were, in her judgment not artistically strong enough: "they sounded like the screams of a temper tantrum." Second, *"That my own poems that object to the war are elegiac in tone, and don't express outrage"* (L 546; Levertov's emphasis). Acknowledging that they are elegiac, she argues that this does not mean they do not express outrage.

II

To summarize the issues of this year of poems and letters, 1965–66, which culminate in Levertov's sending "Advent 1966" and Duncan's reply: Duncan and Levertov are both concerned with rendering the war, and the poet's responses to it, in language that is artistically strong enough. They struggle with what emotions are appropriate to the war—outrage, grief, anguish, agony, compassion, forgiveness—what the proper balance is between sympathy for the victim, the napalmed child, and remembering the human soul of the murderer. Each, dwelling on graphic descriptions of napalm's effects on human flesh, makes napalm stand for many other things. They also contend over where the violence comes from in a poem, and what can give it the artistic form Duncan wants always to call *vision.* While Duncan seems almost accusatory in asking from what root in Levertov the clotted mass of images of imploded penises emerges—as though imagination's alchemizing power can have no effect here, the images must have been merely dredged out of Levertov's personal desires—he is forthright in seeking for the origins of his own imagery of napalm setting houses and people aflame. To get the energy to write "The Soldiers," he gives up blood pressure medication, literally feeling on his pulse, as John Keats urged, the pounding pressure that he wants to get into the poetry. Duncan wants first to open himself to the body's out-of-control agony and then to "alchemize" the too-personal, the untransformed rage, into "word-work" that will "contain" feelings and images into "the redemption of the real." One senses that Levertov and Duncan agree almost entirely on the nature of the poetic project but come to grief over their assessment of each other's success in specific poems, or later, in Levertov's book *To Stay Alive*, in the artistic arrangement of poems.

From early 1967 until March 26, 1972, when Duncan describes how he is using "Advent 1966" in his "Metaphysical Suite" (L 701–2), Levertov's letters record her intense political activity, the pressures resulting from Mitch Goodman's trial for conspiracy to counsel draft resistance, and her frequent sense of exhaustion and despair. She speaks of being "as near a sort of crack up as I have ever been" (L 566), of being "down, way down" and of realizing "how much I have lost of you" (L 622–23), and of Mitch's eagerness "to get back to some sort of normal life" (L 613). In 1967–69, she sends Duncan poems in progress, sections from "From a Notebook," *Relearning the Alphabet*, and *To Stay Alive*. She writes unguardedly about herself, as one does with a trusted friend. Duncan responds sympathetically, though obliquely, lamenting of the RESIST movement, "It is the sacrifice of your human individual lives that you make in your convictions that so appalls me. It is like the carnage and destruction of lives in Viet Nam—the breaking up of ways of life" (L 610). He calls this being "conscripted" into antiwar activity (L 568). Two years later, quarrelling with Levertov's "Revolution or Death" theme in *To Stay Alive*, he says to be "conscripted into a *Movement* is as horrible" (L 629).

In what will become a crux of their argument, Duncan comments on seeing "the sudden apparition of Denny in full ardor" in a video of a rally of the Jeannette Rankin Brigade in Washington. "The person that the *demos*, the *citoyen*-mass of an aroused parry, awakes is so different from the individual person." He argues that taking on the demotic role or persona requires withdrawing commitment "from the wholeness of the individual life," the erotic and social life, to focus it into arousing the group against an enemy. "In the PBL view of you, Denny, you are splendid but it is a force that, coming on *strong*, sweeps away all the vital weakness of the living identity; the *soul* is sacrificed to the demotic persona that fires itself from spirit" (L 607).

This is a prose draft of the "Santa Cruz Propositions." In section 3, dated 7:30 A.M., 28 October, Duncan writes "But it is Denise I am thinking of—":

SHE appears, Kālī dancing, whirling her necklace of skulls,
trampling the despoiling armies and the exploiters of natural resources
under her feet.   Revolution or Death!
. . .

She has put on her dress of murderous red.
She has put on her mini-skirt   and the trampling begins.
She has put on her make-up of the Mother of Hell,
        the blue lips of Kore,   the glowering
        pale of the flower that is black to us.
. . .

        to put down the rage of revolt with *Love, Sweet Love*, she cries

                from the center of terror
                that is the still eye of the storm in her:

"*There comes a time when only Anger is Love.*"   (GW 45–46)

Levertov responds on January 9, 1971, "In what I'm now working on (part IV of "Notebook" poem) I talk about how in fact I'm *not* Kali at all—cannot (even if I wd.) sustain that anger—but this is not an *objection* to being mythologized, only a personal disclaimer" (L 658). In fact, however, Duncan's *projection*—a word he uses often, derived initially from Charles Olson's "Projective Verse" manifesto but accruing many other meanings from analytical psychology as well—of her as Kali concentrates the many aspects of their disagreement into the final devastating quarrel. His letters rush headlong into urgent, broad attack on individual poems, on the fact that *To Stay Alive* reassembles poems from two of her volumes and therefore has destroyed the aesthetic unity of their "field," and on the political meaning of such events as the People's Park violence. "All this 'issue' stands between me and thee. I feel guilty or tired of my disappointment in what is clearly so important to you. And project on you some opposition to the issue of art. The art of the poem—which has fallen into disrepair—the art of long persisting and careful work" (L 661). Duncan is genuinely concerned for Levertov's personal and psychological well-being as well as for what might be called her poetic soul. He presents himself as mentor, but though he has been that to Levertov in the past, mentors are always chosen, they do not appoint themselves.

In October 1971, Levertov asks for clarification of Duncan's objections to *To Stay Alive*, whether he objects because the poetry is not revolutionary in form, or that he feels her political commitments have caused the quality of her poetry to fall off, or that the argument is all ideological. If it is the last, she hopes to show

where I think you are setting me up as an adversary without due reason. Because you *do* have that habit of projection, of setting people up in rôles—of mythologizing, as you did for instance when you identified me with Kali. There are in all of us flickering moments when we are representative of this or that archetypal role—but it is wrong I am certain to *fix* on these moments, . . . to build a system out of them. That leads to the deadly abstract, the inhuman, the false. (L 662)

Duncan acknowledges that he has "more than a *habit* of projection," but argues that he wishes "to go beyond passive to active [i.e., creative, one that makes something up] projection" (L 663).

In the "Santa Cruz Propositions" I am projecting, not a picture of you but . . . a latent up-rising out-raging spirit in the mass. Of course *you* are not Kali: one of the troubles you have as a poet is that even the flickering moments in which the grand vision of apocalypse might arise and some outpouring of the *content* of world-anger come, you cannot give it free imaginative expression, cannot "identify" with the anger, but must moralize and humanize. (L 663)

It is hard to imagine any response better calculated to offend Levertov: she is Kali-like when "possessed by the demonic spirit of the mass, seeking to awaken that power in the assemblage," but at a more important level fails to be Kali because her poetry moralizes and humanizes instead of giving imaginative expression to the grand vision of apocalypse. In short, Duncan accuses her of being Kali, blames her for not being Kali, and instructs her in how Kali should behave. He attacks the shaping principle of *To Stay Alive*, what he sees as the moralizing and political stances of "Life at War," "What Were They Like?" "Tenebrae," and "Enquiry." He attacks both her poems and her public witness against the war in the psychoanalytical language of "projection." Returning to that passage in "Life at War" whose origin he had once asked about—"The words in their lines are the clotted mass of some operation . . . having what root in you I wonder?" (L 530)—he now pronounces his answer. The poem is not about the war in Vietnam "but in relation to the deep underlying consciousness of the woman as a victim in the war with the Man" (L 667). The images he objects to are "an explosion or 'implosion' of the poet's sadistic imaginings to illustrate a text for women's liberation." Disputing Levertov's characterization of her sister Olga as "a worker for human rights," he asks, "What language but the language of dreams with its displacement and reversal of values can be at work? It is as if women would give their assurance that altho they are filled with rage, they will be good helpmates in the politics of the revolution. 'In the etiquette of the revolution, I have no desire that isn't at your service'" (L 667).

By the end of this very long letter, Duncan has adopted an authoritarian tone and method guaranteed to infuriate its victims because it imposes upon opponents the role of analysand and thus asserts power over them. (And anyone even slightly bloodied in this method, where the critical tools become weapons, knows that the only response is, "You're another.") He has appropriated Levertov's words, imposed on them the Freudian framework of dream analysis. He has superimposed on her "the spider's most intricate web," his associations of "the cruel machinations of Louis

XI," "the spider King," and will insist later that his associations are more valid and deeper than hers. He has pretended to take literally her image of Lyndon Johnson's "coprophiliac thumbs": "Since I know of no story of Johnson's being a coprophiliac, I can only imagine that your projection alone supplies this as an image of evil." He has lectured her on "the true poetic message of *The People's Park*." He has accused her verse of becoming "habituated to commenting and personalizing," accused her of calling up personal details in her life in order to derail the imagination from the work he believes it should do, and of invoking her political stance "to forestall any imagination of what that system is." "These, Denny, are empty and vain slogans because those who use them are destitute of any imagination of or feeling for what such greed, racism or imperialism is like. The poet's role is not to oppose evil, but to imagine it" (L 669–73).

Levertov's reply, written between October 25 and November 3, 1971, covers twelve printed pages. In it she lists what she sees as Duncan's "wilful misapprehensions" based on "prejudices, opinionated preconceptions, a need to make things fit with your projections"; his coercive ways, his setting himself up as "the Authority, stating your opinions as unquestionable dogmas de haut en bas." She objects to his criticism, which "insists people are saying what they do not mean. To interpret art as a series of Freudian slips (which is essentially what you do when that perversity takes you) is as tiresome and compulsive and reductive as, for the instance, 'the method of St Beuve' which Proust railed against" (L 682). She challenges his reading of her poems, tells him he has no basis to judge the meaning of the People's Park since he was not there and she was, furiously rejects his comments on Olga's character, and defends her speaking at the Washington rally. Perhaps most notably, she denounces his claim that her poems are about women's war with men as "unmitigated bullshit, Robert. . . . I call that kind of criticism doubletalk and evasion." Elsewhere she calls him disgustingly elitist, insulting, arrogant, quibbling, and offensively patronizing. She rejects some of his most doctrinaire assertions about the source and nature of art. "I have always had a strong preference for works of art in which the artist was driven by a need to speak (in whatever medium) of what deeply stirred him—whether in blame or praise. I'd sooner read *Dubliners* than *Finnegans Wake*. Beckett bores me. Most of Gertrude Stein bores me—she's nice for tea but I wouldn't want her for my dinner. I love George Eliot. I prefer Rouault to Juan Gris, or Mondrian. . . . I prefer, then works where need to speak (in whatever medium was theirs) arose from experiences not of a technical nature but of a kind which people unconnected with that medium also shared (potentially anyway)" (L 678–80).

Duncan cannot stop. Three more letters, November 8, November 9, and November 11, 1971 (letter numbers 454, 455, 457), pour out, returning to the same battles. He cannot let the Kali image rest. Levertov writes on November 9 to ask that they

> not go on with this whole thing until it becomes more rancorous and destroys our long and deep regard for one another: Let's try to just be friends again in a new way. . . . From the day you receive this letter . . . put aside my book and your notes thereon for a year and a day; and then if you want to look at it all anew at that time, do what you must, and I shall say nothing. . . . Call a truce, in all courtesy and good faith. (L 693)

Duncan agrees, and the few letters of the next year avoid anything controversial, though the friendship is "shaky." Writing on January 25, 1972, Duncan reflects that he has been seeing his quarrels with Levertov as

> contention with my own *anima*—as Jung proposes such an archetype of a woman and I would read it to be an idea of womanly virtues or powers created in the matrix of collective imagination [the cultural self] and of personalized imagination [the individualization]. For much of what I suspect you of, or accuse you of, I suspect as some womanish possibility in myself. (L 699)

At the close of this letter he announces, "There will follow, as soon as I have got the two remaining parts, the "Metaphysical" suite that the Christmas retake on Southwell's 'Burning Babe' after your Advent 1966 poem belongs to. I think this sequence will lead into, *does* lead into, the emerging 'Juliet' theme that my conversion to the anima concept belongs to" (L 700). His next letter, March 26, 1972, reports that sections 4 and 5 of his "Metaphysical Suite" are drawn from "Advent 1966's" "reference points: a) Southwell's poem and b) photographs of napalm victims." In section 8 " . . . the matter of my controversy with you comes forward as present in the content of 'the end of an old friendship'—tho the 'her' is you only in passing and soon is 'very like' my mother. It is, I believe, what Jung would call my *anima* and, perhaps, the Anima." The Suite is, at the end of section 8, "in something like the same place as the 'Santa Cruz Propositions' found themselves at the end of part 2 confronting the Imago of Kali, via again some idea of you" (L 700–701).

Now we may consider the poems directly. "Advent 1966" is thirty lines long; the "Metaphysical Suite" covers twenty-three printed pages. As Southwell's poem provides an armature on which Levertov builds her poem, Levertov's is one armature for Duncan's. Each of the three poems speaks in the first person, each ostensibly draws on the immediate events in the poet's life, and each tries to negotiate the personal and the symbolic or archetypal through some degree of poetic artifice, to make the poem.

"Advent 1966" is a poem of two irreconcilable visions and of cause and effect. It points us back, first of all, to the martyred Robert Southwell's vision of Christ, the unique Holy Infant who is both the victim of burning and the furnace in which humanity will be redeemed. Prefiguring the Passion upon Christmas, his trope gathers into itself the image of the burning bush which is never consumed and Christ's descent into hell before the resurrection. The elaborate art of Southwell's allegory, in which the Babe's breast is a furnace, wounding thorns are the fuel, love is the fire, sighs are the smoke, and shames and scorns are the ashes, distances us from the horror. The poet stands shivering in a cold winter's night until he is warmed by the sudden heat which makes his heart glow. As the Babe is transfigured, the searing flames transform into soothing water, and the poet remembers it is Christmas Day. Southwell's vision is briefly horrific in order to become triumphant. To the extent that we are conscious of and admire its artifice, the poem protects us from its horror, though perhaps what makes its "metaphysical" intensity especially resonant for a modern reader is our extrapoetic knowledge that Southwell himself was tortured and martyred for his faith. His life, like the poem, is horrific but ultimately triumphant.

Levertov's poem is not a meditation on Southwell's so much as a variation on a theme. She uses his poem as an index of her hopelessness and a touchstone of a belief system which is not hers. Her vision is only horrified. Though her poem ostensibly commemorates Advent, the period of hope and anticipation before the Savior comes into the world, its tone is Lenten, reflecting the mood of grief and penance so poignantly expressed in Ignazio Silone's comment that in the history of the world it is still Good Friday. The word *because*, repeated twice, brackets Southwell's image of the

Burning Babe, and the poem grows out of the oppositions of unity and multiplicity, the redeemed and unredeemed. Nothing in its art protects the reader from the literal meaning of its images. Here is the cause and effect: "Because in Vietnam the vision of a Burning Babe / is multiplied, multiplied . . . ," the poet's sight is not single but multiple, not clear but blurred, not strong and caressive but invaded as though by a monstrous insect entering her head, out of whose eye she sees burning infants, "as off a beltline, more, more senseless figures aflame" (SA 16).

Despite the poem's multiplicities, in fact the poet's vision *is* single, clear, and relentless in recording what napalm does to human bodies. What she cannot see, because there is none, is any redemptive power to these multiplied, industrialized, assembly-line deaths. The cataract filming over the eye is like the gray filth that coats "the mucous membrane of our dreams" and films the imagination, in "Life at War," a poem that Duncan attacks aggressively in several letters. A concrete knowledge, she says in that poem, "jostles for space / in our bodies along with all we / go on knowing of joy, of love"; "Nothing we say has not the husky phlegm of it in the saying, / nothing we do has the quickness, the sureness, / the deep intelligence living at peace would have" (SA 16).

Duncan's "Seventeenth Century Suite," subtitled "Being Imitations, Derivations & Variations upon Certain Conceits and Findings Made Among Strong Lines," and consisting of ten parts of varying lengths and a coda, appears in *Ground Work: Before the War* (1984). Editorial copy on the back cover says it is his first book in over fifteen years, containing work written from 1968 to 1984. It continues:

The silence was intentional, to permit the book to come into its own, at its own appointed time, and to allow new themes in his worldview to advance. . . . But while this latest volume is a continuation of his capacious mythopoeic vision, Duncan now turns directly to the political issues of our sad history: love, death, and the mask worn by war and "development," behind which industrial-military power hides its contempt for nature and indeed all living things.

Freud says all works of art are "overdetermined," multiply caused and sourced, and Duncan allows all the materials which rise up in him to find their way into his poetry, lets it be overdetermined and thus beyond his conscious control. In the "Suite" Duncan employs all his typical strategies to gain the aesthetic distance he needs to "alchemize" his most deeply felt personal material. Through "word-work," he draws up psychically dangerous material from the unconscious and from memory, and diffuses it through archetypal language, the elaborate artifice of the Court of Love, the playhouse, masque, dream work, alchemical myth, and the symbolism of sun and moon, fire and water, heat and cold, quotations and paraphrases of other writers, the familiar stateliness of the Lord's Prayer. His intent is to collage the painfully personal with all the materials of High Art in order to universalize it.

Parts 4 and 5, the center of the Suite, are devoted to reflections on "The Burning Babe." The simplest—though far from simple—first path through the Suite is to follow the images of fire and burning in parts 4, 5, and 8. In part 4, Duncan begins his first meditation on Southwell's poem: "The vision of a burning babe I see / doubled in my sight." It is not a baby on fire, a napalm victim, but an archetypal Christ Child,

> . . . burning with its own flame,   not toward death
>   but alive with flame,   suffering its *self*
> the heat of the heart the rose was hearth of;

> so there *was* a rose,   there was a flame,
> consubstantial with the heart,

> long burning me through and through . . .   (GW 73)

By word association, the kind of punning that Duncan loved in the metaphysical poets (and which it irritated Levertov to have him read into her lines), he takes us from heat to heart to hearth—the fireplace—from flame to rose, thus reminding us of both Dante and T. S. Eliot in *Four Quartets*, where the purgative fires become the crowned rose of fire, and the rose and the fire are finally reconciled. Internalizing Southwell's imagery, he confirms "the bitter core of me, / the clinker soul, the stubborn residue / that needed the fire and refused to burn" (GW 74). In Levertov's poem, the vision alters the poet's view of the outer world; in Duncan's, the fire penetrates the whole self, forces him to *insight*.

> Envy of the living was its name,   black jealousy
>   of what I loved it was,   and
> the pain was not living,   it was the ashes of the wood;
> the burning was not living,   it was
>   without Truth's heat,
> a cold of utter Winter that refused the Sun. . . .   (GW 74)

The invocation that follows—"O Infant Joy that in Desire burns bright! / Bright Promise that I might in Him burn free!" (GW 74)—echoes William Blake, to subsume Southwell's Christ Child into an archetypal Infant, an image of Innocence and Joy, in preparation for a later association in part 5 with the Christ of Art. Then the poem appropriates Southwell's allegory for the poet's inner turmoil, suddenly breaks the pattern with the surprising interjection, "—it is no more than an Image in Poetry—" and then drives rapidly to an ecstatic-seeming reconciliation of opposites into unity.

> . . . until

> tears breeding flames, flames breeding tears,
> I am undone from what I am,   and in Imagination's alchemy
>   the watery Moon and the fiery Sun   are wed.

> The Burning Babe,   the Rose,
> the Wedding of the Moon and Sun,
> wherever in the World I read
> such Mysteries come to haunt the Mind,
> the Language of What Is   and I

> are one.   (GW 74–75)

Whether this reconciliation on the verbal level is earned in and through the poetry remains open to question. It is certainly typical of Duncan's poetic strategy to establish binary oppositions and then reconcile them "alchemically."

In part 5 Duncan calls the Burning Babe "Art's epiphany of Art new born, / a Christ of Poetry" (GW 75). In an abrupt shift, the poem now turns to the napalm victims.

> I am looking upon burnd faces
> that have known catastrophe incommensurate
>   with meaning, beyond hate or loss or
> Christian martyrdom, unredeemd.   My heart
>   caves into a space it seems
> to have long feard.

> I cannot imagine, gazing upon photographs
>   of these young girls,   the mind
> transcending what's been done to them.   (GW 75)

Employing Christian ritual ironically, he describes the girls as baptized not in water but in napalm, as monstrously baptized in a new name, sees their eyes accusing, mirroring our faces in their eyes, "their very lives / burnd into us. . . . the knowledge in the sight of those eyes / goes deep into the heart's fatalities" (GW 76). It is inescapable that a poem linking Southwell with napalm will also conjoin sight with guilty, crippling knowledge. Whereas Levertov says a monstrous multiple insect eye inhabiting her head has become her only way of seeing, in Duncan's poem, the napalmed girls' eyes, seen in a photograph, engage his sight, accuse him. What is the knowledge in the sight of those eyes?—we note the ambiguity in the wordplay here. Is it the knowledge that resides in my seeing of those eyes? Is it the knowledge that emanates from them, even though they may now be sightless, which we take into our heart's fatalities? Seeing, knowing lead to the question,

> What can I feel of it . . .
>
> . . .
>
> . . . What can I feel of what was done?
> All hatred cringes from the sight of it
> and would contract into self-loathing
> to ease the knowledge of what no man
> can compensate.   I think I could bear it. (GW 76)

The concluding line of this section of the poem gives us another powerful ambiguity: "I cannot think I could bear it." In that contracting, cringing, shrinking from what one sees and thus knows, there is a different knowledge-question: "Can I bear it?" The reader takes note of the self-reflexive answer—"I think I could"—followed by a revulsion, "I cannot think . . . " (GW 76). Here is a thought that is demeaning even to consider. It is unthinkable, as a proposition, as a means of distancing the shock, that I could bear such pain.

Elsewhere in the Suite, other images of fire and burning occur. In "From George Herbert's *Jordan* (II)," where he meditates on Herbert's wish to give up artifice for plainness, in talking of divine love, Duncan tries to incorporate the flame into the body itself.

> As flames do work and wind when they ascend
> So do I work my *self* into the sense
>   as if the only light there'll be
>   is in the fire that tortures the green wood. (GW 79)

Under the gentle tutelage of George Herbert, in the lines that follow he gives up the vehement and passionate dogmatism of his letters to affirm his faith in the restorative power of art itself.

> If we but trust the song   I know
>   its course is free
> and straight and steady goes to work for its good;
>   it needs but trust   unquestioning,
>   a burning without smoke,
>   a heat transparent in its constancy.   (GW 79)

Perhaps the most poignant return to earlier themes appears in "Passages 36" (lines which composed themselves early on December 16, 1971), just after the devastating letters exchanged with Levertov and the agreed year-and-a-day truce.

> *Let it go.   Let it go.*
> *Grief's its proper mode.*
>
> *But O,   How deep it's got to reach,*
>   *How high and wide*
>   *it's got to grow,*
> *Before it come to sufficient grief . . .*   (GW 80)

The emerging poem entangles myths of creation, rituals of mutilation and despoliation of the earth, catastrophes including Vietnam and Bangladesh, burning and laying waste with the elements of communion, bread and water, the love and home the poet shares with his life-partner:

> this room where we are,   this house,
> this garden,   this home
>   our art would make
> in what is threatend from within.   (GW 81)

This section of the poem closes by repeating its opening lines, then shifts:

> It was about the end of an old friendship,
>   the admission of neglect rancoring,
> mine of her, hers of what I am,
>   and festering flesh was there.
> It was very like that coming to know

> my mother was at war with what I was to be;
> and in the Courts of Love I raged that year
> in every plea declared arrogant
> and in contempt of Love.   (GW 82–83)

Here we see Duncan working out the archetypal fusing of Levertov and his mother, expressing grief for what has happened but, recurring to the trope of Court of Love which appears very early in the "Suite," he internalizes his fierce judgments of Levertov into the Court's verdict against him. We see in this passage a regretful acceptance of his loss of Levertov's friendship. This thread in the fabric of the Suite, perhaps barely visible before, traces back to parts 4 and 5, where he assimilates the horror rhetorically, through the patterning of gnostic alchemy—fire and water, sun and moon. But gnosticism always asserts a higher knowledge above daily experience as a way to transcend its suffering. Whether Duncan convinces his readers of the transcendence caught in Art and Song is a live question. As we look at Levertov's strategy in "Advent 1966," and even in her later overtly Christian poetry, she seems determined not to escape into the transcendent, if such transcendence means repairing to a realm of knowledge from which we will assent to the brutalities of war. For Duncan, the Fire and the Rose become one, leading perhaps to Eliot's affirmation from Julian of Norwich that all shall be well. Levertov does not even hope to achieve that affirmation.

Work Cited

Jung, Carl. *Two Essays on Analytical Psychology*. Cleveland: World Publishing, 1965.

CHAPTER 13

Poetic Language and Language Poetry:
Levertov, Duncan, Creeley

Albert Gelpi

I

In the introduction to *The Letters of Robert Duncan and Denise Lever-tov*, I argue that the political differences that ruptured their extraordinarily close friendship after years of mutual trust and dependence were rooted in their different religious sensibilities and theological stances toward reality. I do not want to rehearse the argument here but rather to use its conclusion as a point of departure to reflect further on the two poets' finally different sense of language and how it makes meaning. Duncan's adopted parents and their extended family were theosophical, and through them he assimilated an eclectic gnosticism from a heady mix of Rosicrucianism, alchemy, astrology, and Madame Blavatsky's spiritualism. The gnosticism at the heart of these occult traditions is radically dualistic, based on a conviction of the irreconcilable opposition between light and dark, spirit and matter, good and evil. As a consequence, even though as an adult he did not subscribe to any theosophical group or set of doctrines, Duncan's gnostic inclination led him, in a harsh world of conflicts and contradictions, to rely on the hermetic imagination as his single and supreme source and guide.

By contrast, Levertov's family mingled both Hasidic and Christian spirituality. Her father was a Russian Hasidic Jew who converted to Christianity, married a Welsh woman whose family included a number of visionaries, and became an Anglican priest and a scholar of Jewish-Christian dialogue in Britain between the world wars. As a consequence, Levertov saw spirit in body, light in material creation, and her sense of the world was incarnational and outer-directed, even though she was not a practicing Jew or Christian during the years of her association with Duncan. These different orientations in their basically religious sense of experience had their political expression in Duncan's radical individualism and even anarchism and in Levertov's socialist communitarianism. And these different religious and political orientations also and inevitably informed their different understandings of the nature and function of language as the medium of poetry. In summing up my point in the introduction, I claimed in passing that these differences made Duncan's sense of language self-reflexive and Levertov's sense of language referential (L xxv). I want now both to substantiate that assertion by exploring just how Levertov's and Duncan's conception of poetic language and poetic meaning converged and diverged.

They not only wrote poetry but wrote about it with insight and unflagging, almost obsessive concern. What's more, they wrote poetry and wrote about it to and for each other. The monumental correspondence between Duncan and Levertov regularly contains poems sent to each other—sometimes inspired by and addressed to the other, almost always commented on and even revised by the other. Moreover, the exchange of letters record at length their ongoing dialogue about the character and functioning of the imagination as it constellates language into poetic form. They both recognized that they were soul mates, anima and animus, and their relationship in all its loving intensity, conducted almost completely through letters but confirmed by their too infrequent personal meetings, derives from and rests on their conviction of a shared understanding of the visionary imagination as the agent through which perception takes linguistic shape as poem.

In Donald Allen's pioneering anthology *The New American Poetry* (1960), Levertov and Duncan appeared with the other principal figures in the Black Mountain group, Charles Olson and Robert Creeley. In the contention of the poetry wars of the 1950s between open versus closed form, the Black Mountain poets had coalesced in the pages of *Origin* and *The Black Mountain Review*, and the manifesto of the loose and varied group was Olson's 1950 essay "Projective Verse," which opposed the New Critical notion of closed form with a dynamic sense of form emergent from the experience of the poem. The defining concept of "Projective Verse" was "composition by field," and the poets' individual inflection of that constellating notion—that is to say, of the way in which the field of experience and the field of language coalesce as poem—came to mark the increasingly distinctive and separate courses that their work took in the 1960s and 1970s.

What particularly distinguished and bonded Levertov and Duncan within the Black Mountain group was the religious character of their sensibility and their consequent conviction that the engagement between the experiential field and the linguistic field proceeded from a metaphysical grounding to visionary expression. In Duncan's words their particular relationship rested in "the special view we have . . . of why and what the poem is" (L 189). When Levertov's "Some Notes on Organic Form" appeared in *Poetry* magazine in September 1965, Duncan praised the essay as "more succinct than any I've tried to make" in articulating their common assumptions: namely, her "working consciousness of the field of experience," her "whole account of the process of the poem," and her consequent commitment to what she called "organic form" (L 510).

Levertov's essay posits a correspondence between the poetic organism and the forms of things in the world outside the mind and extrinsic to language. The "conception of 'content' or 'reality' is functionally more important" than the language of the poem because the generative experience projects the language act and thus informs the form: "For me, back of the idea of organic form is the concept that there is a form in all things (and in our experience) which the poet can discover and reveal" (PW 7). The organic poet is therefore not inclined to established and "prescribed forms," which assume that "content, reality, experience, is essentially fluid and must be given form"; instead, the organic poet seeks out "inherent, though not immediately apparent, form," which is therefore fully "discoverable only in the work, not before it" (PW 7, 9).

Levertov is explicit about her Romantic allegiances, citing Hopkins, Coleridge, and Emerson ("Ask the fact for the form"), and she invokes ety-

mological roots to establish in words themselves the contemplative and religious character of the language act:

> To contemplate comes from "*templum,* temple, a place, a space for observation,
> marked out by an augur." It means, not simply to observe, to regard, but to do
> these things in the presence of a god. And to meditate is "to keep the mind in a
> state of contemplation"; its synonym is "to muse," and to muse comes from a
> word meaning "to stand with open mouth"—not so comical if we think of "inspi-
> ration"—to breathe in. (PW 8)

From these premises the essay proceeds to conduct a nuts-and-bolts discussion of how the elements of the poetic organism—rhythm, rhyme,
repetitions and variations, line-breaks, spaces, harmonies and dissonanc-
es—constitute and fulfill the kind of so-called open form she considers organic.

    Early on, Duncan and Levertov acknowledged complementary dif-
ferences within their shared aesthetic: Duncan's imagination was "conceptual" while hers was "perceptual" (L 268). In the reciprocity of their
exchange, they felt, his intellectual and philosophical bent expanded her
perspective, and her vision of the material world had a graphic concision
and vividly sensed precision that grounded his abstractions. These differences, however, ran deeper than they could or at any rate chose to recognize at the time, and there are adumbrations of the difficulties and contentions that would break the surface a few years later. Even in his initial
and positive response to Levertov's essay in October 1965, Duncan notes
that his experience of form is more fluid and unstable than hers and projects not a "constellation" around "a central focus or axis," as she sees it, but
rather "a complex of origins of force that set all matters into a need for a
particular equilibration—not a mandala or wheel but a mobile" (L 510).

    Twice in the letter Duncan quotes her phrase "a method of recog-
nizing what we perceive," but elides the large metaphysical claim of the
statement in which it appears in her essay: "A partial definition, then, of
organic poetry might be that it is a method of apperception, i.e., of recognizing what we perceive, and is based on an intuition of an order, a form
beyond forms, in which forms partake, and of which man's creative works
are analogies, resemblances, natural allegories. Such poetry is exploratory"
(PW 7). While Duncan's letter seems to assume that he is agreeing with
her about "a method of recognizing what we perceive," he goes on to ap-

propriate the term to indicate not the poem's correspondence to forms in nature but, instead, the poem's hermetic self-creation. "Organic form," he contends, cannot mean that it "seeks to imitate the growth forms of shell, tree, or human body" but rather must mean that "the poem itself is an organism growing (living) into its own life as a form" (L 510). Levertov's reply does not take him up on his reductive literalization of her notion of organic form or his realignment of it.

What both poets always agreed upon was that organic form did not mean formlessness. The polemical purpose of "Some Notes" is not just to distinguish organic form from "prescribed forms," since that distinction was clear enough, but also, and just as importantly, to distinguish organic form from free verse. The Beats emerged at the same time as the Black Mountain poets, and the two groups were sometimes lumped together as experimenters in open form. Indeed, the Beats were declaiming their Whitmanian free verse to noisy crowds, becoming a cultural and social phenomenon that aroused a widespread notice in the popular press that Black Mountain poets never received. Though both Levertov and Duncan met Ginsberg and Kerouac and Corso, and acknowledged the energy of some of the work, they quickly came to conclude that its performative aspect meant that its slack language and loose versification lacked sufficient concentration of energies and cohesion of parts to constitute an organic aesthetic entity. Black Mountain looked back not to Whitman but to Pound and Williams and, to a lesser extent, Zukofsky. Duncan was the most Poundian poet of his generation, more so even than Olson; and Williams himself, after his early encouragement to Ginsberg, expressed serious doubts about "Howl's" long, loose lines, and designated Levertov and Creeley as heirs of the Williams short lyric.

So by 1960 Levertov was taking her friend Creeley to task for his association with the Beats and specifically for his participation in LeRoi Jones's magazine *Yugen*, which led him, in her view, to compromise his "sense of craftsmanship" by accepting "so much that is slipshod" (L 234, 237). Duncan, like Creeley more responsive to Whitman than Levertov was, could see why Creeley was energized by the Beats and suggested to Levertov that perhaps the Beats were having the salutary effect on Creeley of opening up the tight minimalism of his early manner (L 236). But in the end Duncan joined Levertov in wanting to distinguish the kind of poetry they stood for from the dissipating looseness of the Beats—much as Pound and Williams had been intent on distinguishing their earlier formal experimentation from Whitman's free verse.

Levertov therefore compressed the "Organic Form" essay into "A Further Definition," with a typology of three distinct categories of poetry: conventional poetry that imposes "pre-existing, re-usable metric molds"; organic poetry that through "the utmost *attentiveness*" discovers and expresses the "immanence of form" "peculiar to" and "inherent in content"; and free verse whose unmeasured flow accepts and reproduces the "formlessness" of experience (PW 14–15). That typology had already been formulated in a lecture that Levertov gave at Wabash College on December 6, 1962, titled with the Emersonian maxim "Ask the Fact for the Form." When she sent Duncan a typescript of the Wabash lecture in May 1963, two years before the appearance of "Some Notes on Organic Form," he found what he said was an "admirable" lecture but revised her poetic categories—"the conventional poet," "the free-verse poet," and "the organic poet"—to include a fourth (L 405). He agrees that most free verse, wrongly assuming that "form = restriction," seeks formlessness; however, in outlining the types of poetry that do "find or make" form, Duncan's fourth category, especially in hindsight, foreshadows the poetic differences that will set these old friends at odds in the late 1960s and bring their relationship to the point of rupture in 1971. To "convention as 'form'" and "organism as 'form'" Duncan adds "'linguistic' form" (L 408).

Whereas conventional poetry fits disordered experience into "made" forms and organic poetry "finds" its form in experience, with "'linguistic' poetry" language itself constitutes the experience of the poem (L 407–8). So much so that the poem itself is the experience; the verbal form finds and makes its autotelic content:

the artist uses language to make forms, and in this he [is] in a creature/creator relation to a god who is also creature/creator of the whole. Where "organic" poetry refers to personal emotions and impressions—the concourse between organism and his world; the linguistic follows emotions and images that appear in the language itself as a third "world"; true to what is happening in the syntax as another man might be true to what he sees or feels. (L 408)

The theological overtones are of course deliberate to suggest a different theology from that of organic poetry: the "god" here is not the "god" who inspires Levertov's musing on the world but is language itself, or Poetry with a capital P. In "The H.D. Book," for example, Duncan links "Poetry" with the gnostic power of the individual consciousness to imagine and thereby realize a linguistic world: "Poems are not objects but events of Poetry, of our consciousness of making a universe of feeling in language" ("The H.D. Book" II.2). Through this gnostic power the poet lives in language as an alternate world, total and transpersonal and so in that sense quasi-divine. Poet and language create and are created by each other; he divines himself by "finding" limitless possibilities, implications, realizations in the play and counterplay of words, the connections and disconnections of syntax in the "made" poem.

At first Duncan sets his stance against Levertov's organic position: "I think of my own [poetry] as linguistic—is different from organic"; but almost immediately and more accurately he reestablishes the connection: "so here I am organic as well as linguistic" (L 407, 408). And on her part Levertov did not at this point yet take in the full implications of this strain of linguistic gnosticism in Duncan: language as the source and means, the substance and end of the poet's special knowing. She acknowledges his correction of her schema and includes him in it:

The word linguistic was particularly meaningful to me as it suddenly showed me what it was I'd dimly felt I left out of that lecture . . . & especially in reference to much that in your work didn't really fit in the scheme of things I'd posited there, even though it was a loved, fascinating part of your work—i.e., my description of poetic activity really doesn't leave much place if any for puns & multiple meanings, does it. (L 413)

It is worth recalling that their correspondence got off to a nearly disastrous start when Levertov misread and misunderstand Duncan's linguistic playfulness. During the early 1950s Duncan was immersed in Gertrude Stein's language experiments and writing the Stein imitations that went into *Writing Writing, Play Time Pseudo Stein*, and *A Book of Resemblances*. However, awestruck by Levertov's poem "The Shifting" in *Origin*, he sent her, in June 1953, "Letters for Denise Levertov: An A Muse Ment" (later the lead poem of his 1958 volume *Letters* under a slightly different title). Levertov had read and admired the Romantic, even Pre-Raphaelite verse of Duncan's earlier *Heavenly City Earthly City*, but was so put off by the "puns & multiple meanings" of the Steinesque word play that she mistook

Duncan's homage for a slyly hostile attack on the manner of her poems. He quickly explained his purpose (while also presciently noting "my own aesthetic is I see *not yours*"), and she abjectly apologized in turn, "abashed at my stupidity—blundering into yr. poem with my defensive misconceptions" (L 5, 6).

Both sought to patch the matter up quickly and buried it in mutual embarrassment and professions of admiration. Duncan's Stein period had receded by the time that their correspondence took off after their first face-to-face meeting early in 1955. And so strong was their sense of complementarity that when Levertov expanded her Wabash lecture into "Some Notes on Organic Form," she unquestioningly included Duncan's notion of "the poetry of linguistic impulse," though at this point she preferred to see it (and Duncan's affinity for it) as "perhaps a variety of organic poetry." For the moment she could reconcile the organic and the linguistic in her own mind: "It seems to me that the absorption in language itself, the awareness of the world of multiple meaning revealed in sound, word, syntax, and the entering of this world in the poem, is as much an experience or constellation of perceptions as the instress of nonverbal sensations and psychic events." Linguistic poetry might seem at odds with the organic because "the demands of his [i.e., the poet's] realization may seem in opposition to truth as we think of it; that is, in terms of a sensual logic"; however, "the apparent distortion of experience in such a poem for the sake of verbal effects is actually a precise adherence to truth, since the experience itself was a verbal one" (PW 12–13). If "*the material of a poem must need to be a poem,*" the poet must need (like Stein or Duncan at times) "to handle the material, play with it, explore its possibilities" (PW 18, 19; Levertov's emphasis).

Nonetheless, for all her attempt to accommodate Duncan, Levertov saw language, much more clearly and consistently than he did, as the medium of poetry, not its source and end. The poet is "*brought to speech,*" and if the exacting process of composition works to constellate sense perceptions, thoughts, and feelings, then, as Wordsworth claimed, "language is not the *dress* but the *incarnation* of thoughts" (PW 18, 16). Near the end of "Some Notes on Organic Form" Levertov encapsulated her position into a one-sentence paragraph in which a single italicized word quietly but effectively revises the founding dictum of Black Mountain poetics: "Form is never more than a *revelation* of content," with italics to mark her revision

(PW 13). In the "Projective Verse" manifesto Olson attributed to Creeley the capitalized injunction: "FORM IS NEVER MORE THAN AN EXTENSION
OF CONTENT" (Allen 387). But at the Vancouver Poetry Festival in August
1963, where Levertov presented a version of the "Organic Form" essay, she
proposed to Creeley, "the originator of this now famous formula," that it
should more accurately read "*revelation* of content—(to which he agreed)"
(PW 60). She does not explain the terms of Creeley's agreement, but her
own terms are clear.

If form as extension of content meant that content informed form,
Levertov would agree, for "thought and feeling remain unexpressed until
they become Word, become Flesh (i.e., there is no *prior paraphrase*)" (PW
17). However, if form as extension of content were construed to signify
that the co-instantiation of form and content is so absolute that content is
only the extension of form, then language loosens (or loses) its source and
reference point and end outside the poem and becomes the hermetic "third
'world'" of Duncan's linguistic poetry. Against that slippery slide she af-
firmed Emerson's dictum that had titled the Wabash lecture: "Ask the fact
for the form." She resolutely maintained Emerson's distinction (in his essay on "The Poet") between the creative process and the resulting poem:
"the thought and the form are equal in the order of time, but in the order
of genesis the thought is prior to the form" (Emerson 450).

In "Testament," written in 1959 for Donald Allen's *The New American Poetry*, Levertov declared, "I think of Robert Duncan and Robert Creeley as the chief poets among my contemporaries" (Allen 412; PW 3). Within the context of their friendship, neither Duncan nor, apparently, Creeley
noted the enormous implications that Levertov's one-word substitution of
"revelation" for "extension" had for the poetics of "composition by field."
Not at least until Duncan and Levertov found themselves, to their pain
and dismay, facing increasingly sharp differences about how poetry should
and could address the Vietnam War.

II

Neither of them addressed political matters overtly in their poetry till
the mid-1960s. What bonded them was their different but complementary
explorations of the visionary imagination, but it was their appalled revul-

sion from the Vietnam War that challenged their visionary poetry in principle and practice. Levertov's first political poem was "During the Eichmann Trial," in 1963. Then the death of her sister Olga in 1964 not only brought personal grief but also roused the social conscience that had been her sister's passion and their parents' legacy in word and example—and focused her political conscience on outrage at the imperialistic violence of the Vietnam War. *The Sorrow Dance* (1967) marked the shift in focus with "A Lamentation," "Olga Poems," and a section called, after one of the poems therein, "Life at War." Moreover, by that same year Duncan had himself written enough antiwar sections of his ongoing sequence the "Passages Poems" to constitute a separate little book, *Of the War.*

Still, they were uncertain about this new turn that their poetry had taken. Duncan found her Eichmann poems lacking in the cogency and concentration of Levertov's celebration of epiphanic moments and tried to show her what he felt were its weaknesses. Nevertheless, in July 1964, Levertov reported working on the "Olga Poems" and praised "The Fire, Passages 13," one of Duncan's anti-war "Passages," as "poetry of tremendous power" (L 462). But when in early 1966 she received Duncan's Christmas poem "Earth's Winter Song," its second half caricaturing shrilly and scatalogically the treacheries of President Johnson and Vice-President Humphrey, she warned against the dehumanizing distortions of self-righteous judgment. Yet at the same time and in the same letter she tells him that she has written her first "absolutely direct antiwar poem" but worries that "exactly what I am saying about 'Earth's Winter Song' may be true of 'Life at War,' the poem I just finished" (L 519, 520). And indeed, through deepening disagreements mounting to the devastating confrontation in the fall of 1971, her antiwar poems—"Life at War," "Advent 1966," "Tenebrae," and the book-length journal poem "Staying Alive"—became contested ground in which they fought out their differences. Convinced that her feelings were falling prey to the violence she was denouncing, Duncan determined to make her see that her futile effort to oppose the war through poetry was not only doomed but was corrupting the visionary imagination that was her special and gnostic trust. Not surprisingly, however, his increasingly brutal attack had the opposite effect of making her define her own position with growing clarity and conviction.

Duncan's poems in *Of the War* are as vehement and virulent as hers, but his very susceptibility to uncontrolled rage and outrage in those poems made him recoil from engaging the war in poems. Since war is, in his gnostic view, a function of the inescapable dualism of mortal existence, only the imagination offers a private and hermetic transcendence. The evil of America's imperial violence, once acknowledged, had to be sublimated into the transfiguring harmonies of the whole poem; *Of the War*, he told Levertov, had to assume its proper and subordinate place within the larger and higher vision of the whole sequence of "Passages." Lines from those very war poems acknowledge the necessity of distance and sublimation: "in the slaughter of man's hope / distil the divine potion"; "In the War now I make / a celestial cave" (BB 112, 120). The imagination's alchemy required anarchist disengagement from political action.

Duncan's position is summed up in this accusatory admonition to Levertov: "The poet's role is not to oppose evil, but to imagine it" (L 669). All Levertov's training and temperament and previous experience in poetry made her vulnerable to Duncan's increasingly personal attacks. She committed herself to writing political poems fearful that she might indeed be sacrificing her capacity for wonder and vision. Nevertheless, if, as she believed, language has grounding and agency in the social world, then the poetic act is inescapably a political act. Fidelity to her own deepest convictions required her to oppose the war by imagining it, and to imagine the war by opposing it with a new polity of faith and love nascent, she felt, in the protest movement. Against Duncan's dualistic gnosticism, she drew on her Christian roots to assert an incarnational ethic and an incarnational vision: "The concept of the Incarnation is the concept of Man's redeemability, however fallen into corruption, for man was made in God's image" (L 684).

The brutal battery of long letters in October and November 1971 left these old friends feeling like wounded but unyielding casualties of their own contention. Religious and political differences underlay their argument about the relation of form and content in the poem's meaning. To make Levertov acknowledge what he felt was the false and manipulative instrumentality of her protest poems, Duncan mounted his strongest and most extreme argument for the hermetic and "linguistic" character of the poem, a "third 'world'" distinct and disjunct from subjective consciousness and objective reference, its meaning self-created and self-contained.

The showdown came when he wrote of "form as the direct vehicle and medium of content. Which means and still means for me that we do not say something by means of the poem but the poem is itself the immediacy of saying—it has its own meaning" (L 668). Her unyielding response, like his pronouncement, left little room for further discussion:

To me it *does* mean that "one says something by means of the poem"—but not in the sense of "using" (exploiting) the poem: rather that the writer only fully experiences his "content" (that which he is impelled to say by means of the poem) through the process of writing it. . . . Which is to say that the poem reveals the content, which is apprehended only dimly (in varying degrees) till the revelation takes place. If it (the poem) "has its own meaning" it is only that the revelation is not only the realization, concretization, clarification, affirmation, of what one knows one knows but also of what one didn't know one knew. I do not believe, as you seem to, in the *contradictory* (& autonomous) "meaning" of a poem, and I think your insistence on that leads you wildly astray often. . . . (L 682)

In refutation of "autonomous" meaning, she cites Emerson against Duncan: once again, "Ask the fact for the form" (from "Poetry and Imagination"); and "it is not metres but a metre-making argument that makes a poem" (from "The Poet"). And then immediately she reiterates her inflection of the Olson-Creeley formula with the key word now in caps: "Form is never more than the REVELATION (not extension) of content" (L 680).

Critics usually divide Levertov's career into three phases: the early poems of visionary wonder, the political poems of the 1960s and 1970s, and the explicitly Christian poems of the 1980s and 1990s. But, reviewing her own course in several late prose pieces—"A Poet's View" (1984), "An Autobiographical Sketch" (1984), and "Some Affinities of Content" (1991)—Levertov could only see the continuity of a pilgrimage. She never stopped writing poems of visionary wonder even during the years of her heaviest political activity, and she found in Christian incarnational theology the grounding and reconciliation of her personal epiphanies and her political hope for a community of love and justice. As a consequence, from the perspective of 1991, she saw her younger self as "drawn primarily" to poems by matters of technique and form (as she remade herself, through Williams and Black Mountain, into an American poet), yet also saw that her older self, while still convinced that "content cannot be fully apprehended without a fusion with form equal to its task," was increasingly "concerned with content, and drawn towards poems that articulate some of my own interests" (NES 2). The two volumes of her own work that she assembled shortly before her death in 1997 indicate two defining centers of interest: *The Life Around Us: Selected Poems on Nature* and *The Stream and the Sapphire: Selected Poems on Religious Themes.*

Levertov was more consistently Romantic in theory and practice than Duncan; for all that she learned from Williams, she is perhaps the leading Neoromantic of the second half of the twentieth century. To her, "no ideas but in things" means that "poetry appears when meaning is embodied in the figure" and thus Williams's famous Modernist adage is thoroughly compatible with Emerson's "Ask the fact for the form." Reading much of Duncan's work makes it easy to see why he could also claim with accuracy and conviction "I read Modernism as Romanticism" (Faas 82). At the same time, it is also equally easy to see that Duncan's notion of "'linguistic' form" makes his Modernist adhesions deeper and stronger than hers. In fact, Duncan's Stein period and his continuing interest in Stein (who never interested Levertov) indicates his attraction to a language-oriented strain of Modernist experimentation that Stein explored more radically than any of her contemporaries but that, with the exception of Stein, became submerged during the heyday of Modernism until it emerged after the Second World War as Postmodernism. As for Duncan, the tension (or coexistence) between his organic and linguistic inclinations makes him a pivotal figure in the dialectic between Neoromanticism and Postmodernism in the second half of the century.

Duncan saw the world double both literally (because of his crossed eyes) and imaginatively. Levertov was aware of dualisms and polarities (her first book is *The Double Image*), but her sense of double vision, inner and outer (*With Eyes at the Back of Our Heads* is her fourth book) resolved the two in the incarnational moment (*Here and Now* is her second book). Duncan was, therefore, making an important differentiation when he told her back in 1965: "my most excited sense of constellation comes not from centrality [as hers did] but from a complex of origins of force that set all matters into a need for a particular equilibration—not a mandala or wheel but a mobile" (L 510). It is precisely the mobile's shifting and decentered equilibration of disparate and often contradictory elements that gives Duncan's poetry a Postmodernist dimension that hers never had or sought.

It is the Postmodernist Duncan who in the late 1960s stopped numbering the poems of "The Passages Poems" so that they could be read in any sequence; who, in essays like "Towards an Open Universe" and "Man's Fulfillment in Order and Strife," proposed a cosmology of order in disorder; who in his 1971 showdown with Levertov told her: "The idea of the multiphasic character of *language* and of the poem as a vehicle of the multiplicity of phases is more and more central to my thought" (L 670). The centrality of decenteredness, the disorder of order: as he put it in "The Self in Postmodern Poetry," "what I would point out in my work as one of its underlying currents is the weaving of a figure unweaving, an art of unsaying what it says, of saying what it would not say. I want to catch myself out" (FC 231). Consequently, when the linguistic experimentation begun by Stein and extended by Zukofsky and Oppen reemerged in the 1970s as Language poetry, it was these aspects of Duncan that made some of those poets, filled with the poststructural theory of semiotics and deconstruction, claim him—and also Creeley—as forebears.

Predictably, Levertov opposed Language poetry, the group designation for poets like Charles Bernstein and Susan Howe, Lyn Hejinian and Fanny Howe, Michael Palmer and Robert Grenier. It becomes increasingly clear how various these poets are, but when the often strident polemics that initially defined their group identity (in *L=A=N=G=U=A=G=E* and other journals) proclaimed the self-deception of lyric subjectivity and the indeterminacy of a closed system of signifiers with indeterminate signifieds, Levertov saw Language poetry as the aesthetic and moral contradiction of everything that she stood for. In a letter of March 1984, addressed to her colleagues in the Stanford English department, she denounced "the arrogantly self-named 'Language' (or L-A-N-G-U-A-G-E) poets" as "sterile and elitist manifestations of creative bankruptcy"; while she could see that Stein was "a great original" who "a long time ago" performed "the necessary service" of fracturing syntax to renew it, the Language poets offered only "rehashed Gertrude Stein veneered with 70's semantics" (unpublished letter in my possession).

For Levertov, the deconstructive thrust of Language poetics subverted language as a means of making meaning and community. Duncan would have seen her denunciations as reductive over-simplifications. Nevertheless, it is an indication that Duncan had assimilated *his* Stein into a quite different aesthetic mix that he felt somewhat uncomfortable in being linked with the Language poets, despite the fact that many of them were students and friends of his in the San Francisco poetry scene. In "The Self in Postmodern Poetry" he inverts the expectation of the title and notes cagily that "'postmodern' is a term used, I understand to discuss even my work, but it is not a term of my own proposition"; after all, "the weaving of a figure unweaving" in his poetry is, as he pointedly remarks, only "one of its underlying currents. . . . If I mistrust 'my' trust, I am yet thruout even simple, whole-hearted and trusting in my mistrust" (FC 219, 231).

With good reason, then, many commentators on recent poetry have pegged Duncan for the Postmodernist camp. It was this aspect of Duncan, from the Stein imitations of the early 1950s, that set him off poetically from the deeply held Romanticism of Levertov, just as his gnosticism set him off theologically from Levertov's incarnationalism and his anarchism set him off politically from her communitarianism. However, the situation is more complicated than that simple opposition, as Duncan's resistance to being the Postmodernist label indicates. Marjorie Perloff, the keen-sighted critic and advocate of Language poetry, sees Duncan as an incurable Romantic, and his correspondence with Levertov, taken in its entirety, demonstrates his Romantic affinities as clearly as it demonstrates his Postmodernist affinities. Having declared himself a linguistic poet to differentiate himself from Levertov, he almost immediately assures her: "so here I am organic as well as linguistic" (L 408).

Creeley reported a conversation with Duncan (undated but probably in the late 1970s or 1980s) that is revealing about the effort to assimilate them both into Language poetry and about their resistance to that effort:

I was talking to Robert Duncan, who'd come to a talk about Emily Dickinson I'd given. . . . I was saying I had very specific commitments and loyalties to friends who were, quote, "language poets." And I was saying, Robert, what do you think? And he said, "I can't—I'm moved by this or that person, but I can't finally buy it. I can't accept it, because they have no story." Well, he didn't actually say all that. He just said, "They have no story." And I knew what he meant. (Clark 104)

For Language poets, the deconstruction of lyric subjectivity, narrative continuity, syntactic connection, verbal signification was a necessary recognition of the postmodern condition and, for some, a necessary political strategy for dismantling the language of capitalist hegemony. Duncan and Creeley could understand and even sympathize with Language poetry in a way that Levertov could not; for her the language of poetry was never Language poetry. Yet both Duncan and Creeley worried that having no story left poetry impaired and in pieces, with nothing coherent or significant to tell. And it was precisely what they saw as the dissociative, even nihilistic tendency in deconstruction that made them, against the claims of the Language poets who looked back to them, pull in the opposite direction.

Two of Creeley's early books are called *Words* and *Pieces*, and his poetry had from the beginning been instrumental in the transition from Modernism to Postmodernism in postwar poetry, providing a link between Oppen and Zukofsky and the Language poets. Creeley repeatedly described himself in terms of his New England roots as a secular, agnostic puritan; and his poetic conscience was one-eyed and puritan in its his scrupulous scrutiny of a wounded and wounding self in a wounded and wounding world. Dickinson might have recognized that in his own dissenting way Creeley saw New Englandly. But there was nothing hermetic about his sensibility, and he made none of the metaphysical claims that Duncan's and Levertov's poetry made. In 1960 he wrote: "I believe in a poetry determined by the language of which it is made. . . . I look to words, and nothing else, for my own redemption as man or poet. . . . I mean then *words*—as opposed to content. I care what the poem says, only as a poem—I am no longer interested in the exterior attitude to which the poem may point, as signboard" (Creeley 477). And that line runs from there to his enthusiastic review of *In the American Tree*, Ron Silliman's 1986 anthology of Language poets (Creeley 346–48).

At the same time, as Creeley's exchange with Duncan about Language poetry suggests, the trajectory of his own painful development out of ironic, self-dissecting introversion led him over the years to see the "words" as more than mere signboards and poetry as more than "pieces." As a result, his poems more and more insistently came to seek "a common place of our own experience" so that a "common language" can tell "the common story" and create a human "company": "It could be the hierarchic, mythic story of a tribe's collective experience, thus, or it could be the imagination of significant values within the social group. It could be many things, but it's the common story" (Clark 88, 97–98, 104). Without losing its painful intimacy and intensity Creeley's later poetry opens out and out to include loved ones of his "company," in "the imagination of a common need, a common place, a common world, a common person" (Clark 98). Creeley's title for a late volume of poems sums the common story up as nothing more nor less than *Life and Death*.

Creeley's sense of the "common" avoided the sacramental word "communion," but on at least one remarkable occasion Duncan invoked that very word to subscribe to a theological poetics that Levertov would have embraced and that takes specific issue with the poststructural basis of Language poetry. On February 7, 1982, Duncan gave a sermon, published under the title "Crisis of Spirit in the Word," at the Westminster Presbyterian Church in Buffalo, New York, after giving a poetry reading and a lecture titled "The Continuity of Christian Myth in Poetry" ("Crisis" 63). Duncan took as the text for his sermon the opening of John's Gospel: "In the beginning was the Word, and the Word was with God, and the Word was God." While maintaining that he was "not a member of church at all" and had "no credo," "the deep ground of my poetry" has always been the "encounter in language" with "the human word," "the human community." But now Duncan says something momentously more: "This is the first time when I am able to say with some passion why I find myself a Christian poet. . . . I read the Gnostics with great fascination but with no total feeling because the body is the spiritual body" in "the Gnostic picture of rescuing spirit and soul from its flesh and matter." But when the word becomes flesh in the Christian context, "the moment of incarnation was a moment of the revelation of the nature of the whole poem—what it meant to tell you" ("Crisis" 63, 64, 67).

At other moments and in other contexts Duncan could maintain that language speaks to itself through the vehicle of the poem, that the poet does not write language but language writes the poem. Here, however, he connects words with things, language with nature in a sentence that could have been written by Levertov: "I believe deeply that we make out of the sound of our mouth a speech to answer the speech, the profound depth with which the mountains speak to us, the sky speaks to us. I see the whole world as creation and revelation" ("Crisis" 65). And with poststructuralist language theory obviously in mind, Duncan went on:

I have none of the trouble that semiotics seem to have of how could a word refer to something. No word refers. Every word is the presence of. Tree is the very presence of the tree, and I have no way of being in the presence in the word alone or in my will that I saw a tree, but in this communion, this communication in which the revelation flows through and through. ("Crisis" 65)

In 1982 Levertov and Duncan had been out of touch for some years, and there was no way for him to know that during those years her "pilgrimage" was bringing her back to the Church. But their years of discussion and particularly the confrontation in 1971 and the terms on which she had rejected his position must have been present in some way in his capacious and acutely aware consciousness when he invoked again and again in his sermon the crucial word in her redaction of Black Mountain poetics: "revelation." "I love to play with words," but "cannot merely play." (64).

The shifting mobile of Duncan's mind made different equilibrations and assumed different configurations in response to different currents of contention. His no-holds-barred argument with Levertov over the public responsibilities of poetry led him to take an extreme gnostic position: in a pluralistic world of "Heraclitean opposites" (L 674), the only private gnosis is the genesis of the autonomous poem in the hermetic mind. But, "in the context of a Christian Church" ("Crisis" 67), his dissatisfaction with the poststructuralist semiotics of a closed but indeterminate linguistic code drew from him his most incarnational assertion of an organic poetics.

The personal friendship between Levertov and Duncan did not survive the confrontation over Vietnam, but, as Levertov recognized in the essay she wrote about Duncan after the rupture (NES 194–230), the affinities that constituted the "deep ground" of their association survived their differences. Their exploration of shared assumptions and underlying differences in poems, letters, and essays is of great historical as well as personal significance because they engaged issues still vital to and contested in contemporary poetry. Their exchange constitutes perhaps the most searching and powerful instance of the dialectic between Neoromanticism and Postmodernism that gave American poetry during the second half of the twentieth century its creative friction and determining character.

Works Cited

Allen, Donald M., ed. *The New American Poetry*. New York: Grove Press, 1960.

Clark, Tom. *Robert Creeley and the Genius of the American Common Place*. New York: New Directions, 1993.

Creeley, Robert. *Collected Essays*. Berkeley and Los Angeles: University of California Press, 1989.

Duncan, Robert. "Crisis of Spirit in the Word." *Credences: A Journal of Twentieth Century Poetry and Poetics*, n.s., 1.1 (Summer 1983): 63–68.

———. "The H.D. Book, Part II: Nights and Days, Chapter 2." *Caterpillar* 6 (January 1969): 16–38.

———. *Of the War: Passages 22–27*. Berkeley, CA: Oyez, 1966.

Emerson, Ralph Waldo. *Essays and Lectures*. New York: Library of America, 1983.

Faas, Ekbert. *Towards a New American Poetic: Essays and Interviews*. Santa Barbara, CA: Black Sparrow Press, 1978.

Levertov, Denise. *The Life Around Us: Selected Poems on Nature*. New York: New Directions, 1997.

———. *The Stream and the Sapphire: Selected Poems on Religious Themes*. New York: New Directions, 1997.

Contributors

Robert J. Bertholf is the Charles D. Abbott Scholar of Poetry and the Arts in The Poetry Collection, University Libraries, State University of New York at Buffalo. He is the author of *Robert Duncan: A Descriptive Bibliography* (1986); editor of *Robert Duncan, Selected Poems* (1997) and *Robert Duncan, A Selected Prose* (1995); and he is co-editor (with Albert Gelpi) of *The Letters of Robert Duncan and Denise Levertov* (2004). He is now at work editing *The Collected Work of Robert Duncan*.

Graça Caphina is Assistant Professor at the Department of Anglo-American Studies, School of Arts and Humanities, University of Coimbra, Portugal, teaching contemporary poetry and poetics, and a member of the interdisciplinary Research Centre for Social Sciences there. She has published extensively on American poetry and poetics and on the relation between poetics and politics. She edits the poetry magazine *Oficina de Poesia. Revista da Palavra e da Imagem*. Her latest publication is "The Three Marxes and the Four Williamses: A Poetics of Immigration," in Isabel Caldeira et al., *Novas Histórias Literárias*. New Literary Histories (Coimbra: Minerva Coimbra, 2004).

Devin Johnston is the author of *Precipitations: Contemporary American Poetry as Occult Practice* (2002) as well as two volumes of poetry, *Telepathy* (2001) and *Aversions* (2004). With Michael O'Leary, he publishes Flood Editions, an independent and nonprofit press. He teaches in the English Department at St. Louis University in St. Louis, Missouri.

Donna Krolik Hollenberg, Professor of English at the University of Connecticut, has published three books about H.D., most recently the edited collection, *H.D. and Poets After* (2000), as well as many essays about other twentieth-century writers. These essays include "'History as I desired it': Ekphrasis as Postmodern Witness in Denise Levertov's Late Poetry," in *Modernism/Modernity* 10:3 (2003) and "'Obscure Directions': Interpreting Denise Levertov's Ambivalence about Ezra Pound," in *Biography* 27:4 (fall 2004). She is writing a biography of Denise Levertov.

Ellen Tallman, long-time friend of Robert Duncan, Robin Blaser, and Jack Spicer, taught for fifteen years in the English Department at the University of British Columbia. She and Warren Tallman brought many poets and much poetry to Vancouver, British Columbia, from the 1960s through the 1980s, and organized the Vancouver Poetry Conference in 1963. She has been a therapist in private practice for thirty-five years, as well as a guest lecturer and supervisor of graduate students in the Clinical Psychology Program at Simon Fraser University.

Aaron Shurin's books include *The Paradise of Forms: Selected Poems* (1999), *A Door* (2000), and *Involuntary Lyrics* (2005). His awards include fellowships from the National Endowment for the Arts, the California Arts Council, and the San Francisco Arts Commission, among others. Since 1999 he has codirected the MFA in Writing Program at the University of San Francisco.

John Felstiner is a Professor of English at Stanford University, teaching in English and Jewish Studies, and has published *The Lies of Art: Max Beerbohm's Parody and Caricature* (1972), *Translating Neruda: The Way to Macchu Picchu* (1980), *Paul Celan: Poet, Survivor, Jew* (1995), *Selected Poems and Prose of Paul Celan* (2001), and coedited *Jewish American Literature: A Norton Anthology* (2000). He is currently working on a book entitled *So Much Depends: Poetry and Environmental Urgency.*

Brett Millier is the Reginald L. Cook Professor of American Literature at Middlebury College in Vermont. She is the author of *Elizabeth Bishop: Life and the Memory of It* (1993), and the associate editor of *The Columbia History of American Poetry* (1993). She is currently at work on both a study of female poets and alcohol, and a critical biography of the American poet Jean Garrigue (1912–1972).

Anne Dewey is Associate Professor of English at St. Louis University's Madrid Campus. Her articles on Denise Levertov, John Ashbery, Ed Dorn, and other twentieth-century American poets have appeared in *Sagetrieb* and *Renascence*. She is also translator of *Memory of the West: The Contemporaneity of Forgotten Jewish Thinkers* (2004).

Peter O'Leary is the author of *Gnostic Contagion: Robert Duncan and the Poetry of Illness* (2002) as well as two collections of poetry, *Watchfulness* (2005) and *Depth Theology* (2006). As Ronald Johnson's literary executor, he has published *Radios* (2005) and *The Shrubberies* (2001), and *To Do As Adam Did: Selected Poems* (2000). He lives in Berwyn, on Chicago's West Side, and teaches religion and literature at the School of the Art Institute of Chicago.

Jose Rodriguez Herrera is an Associate Professor of English at the University of Las Palmas in the Canary Islands and teaches twentieth-century American literature and literary translation there. He is currently also Vice-Dean of the philology faculty. He has published several articles on Denise Levertov, including "Reappropriating Mirror Appropriations: Female Sexuality and the Body in Denise Levertov" (*Denise Levertov: New Perspectives*), "Musing on Nature: The Mysteries of Contemplation and the Sources of Myth in Denise Levertov's Poetry" (an issue of *Renascence* on *Spirit in the Poetry of Denise Levertov*), and "Linguistic Versus Organic, Sfumato Versus Chiaroscuro: Some Aesthetic Differences Between Denise Levertov and Robert Duncan" (published in another Levertov issue of *Renascence*). His translation of Levertov's *Sands of the Well*, the first Spanish translation of Levertov's work, will be published in a bilingual edition.

Paul A. Lacey is an emeritus Professor of English at Earlham College, where he taught from 1960 until his retirement in 2001. He has written on contemporary American poetry, particularly the work of Denise Levertov, and on a range of issues in Quakerism, particularly Quaker education. He is the author of *The Inner War: Forms and Themes in Recent American Poetry* (1972) and *Growing Into Goodness: Essays on Quaker Education* (1998). As Denise Levertov's literary executor, he edited *This Great Unknowing: Last Poems* (1999) and her *Selected Poems* (2003), both from New Directions. At present he is Chair of the National Board of the American Friends Service Committee.

Albert Gelpi is the William Robertson Coe Professor of American Literature, emeritus, at Stanford University, where he taught in the Department of English from 1968 until 2002. He has written *Emily Dickinson: The Mind of the Poet* (1965), *The Tenth Muse: The Psyche of the American Poet* (1976), *A Coherent Splendor: The American Poetic Renaissance 1910–1950* (1987), and *Living in Time: The Poetry of C. Day Lewis* (1993). He was editor of *Wallace Stevens: The Poetics of Modernism* (1987), *Adrienne Rich's Poetry and Prose* (with Barbara Charlesworth Gelpi, 1992), *Denise Levertov: Selected Criticism* (1993), *Dark God of Eros: A William Everson Reader* (2003), and *The Letters of Robert Duncan and Denise Levertov* (2004).

Index

Adam, Helen, 33
Admiral, Virginia, 6, 8
Alioto, Joseph, 142
Allen, Donald, 67; *The New American Poetry*, vii, 44, 45, 181, 188
Altieri, Charles, 152
Altoon, John, 50
Aquinas, Thomas, 9, 25, 28, 29
Artaud, Antonin, 39
Ashbery, John, vii
Augustine, 23, 25

Bach, Johann Sebastian, 97
Bachelard, Gaston, 19
Baraka, Amiri (LeRoi Jones), 109, 162–63, 165; *Yugen*, 109, 184
Beach, Christopher, 44n1, 124n6
Beckett, Samuel, 171
Berke, Roberta, *Bounds out of Bounds*, 149
Berkson, Bill, 49
Bernstein, Charles, 19, 193
Bertholf, Robert J., *The Letters of Robert Duncan and Denise Levertov*, viii, ix, x, xi, 2–3, 13, 67, 72, 110n2, 129n3, 155, 162, 163, 180, 181, 194; *Robert Duncan: Scales of the Marvelous*, 64, 68
Blackburn, Paul, 98
Blake, William, 136, 146, 176
Blaser, Robin, vii, 13, 21, 63, 64, 65–66, 129, 129n3, 131, 138
Blavatsky, H. P., 65, 180
Boehme, Jakob, 165

Boland, Eavan, ix
Bonnard, Pierre, 49
Booth, Philip, 94, 98
Borregaard, Ebbe, 48
Brautigan, Richard, 74
Bringhurst, Robert, *The Elements of Typographic Style*, 134
Brooks, Cleanth, vii
Broughton, James, 33
Brown, Norman O., 46
Brown, Tom, *Trade Unionism or Syndicalism*, 8–9
Brown, Wendy, 118, 122–23
Brunner, Edward, *Cold War Poetry*, 95, 96
Buber, Martin, *Tales of the Hasidim*, 81
Burton, David, 67
Burton, Hilde, 67
Butterick, George, 131, 138
Button, John, 43, 47–54, 48n5, 50n6, 56–57; *Yellow Sunset*, 50, 51fig1

Caedmon, 52
Calhoun, Arthur W., "Can Democracy Be Socialized," 8n4
Calhoun, Don, "The Political Relevance of Conscientious Objection," 2n1
Cantine, Holley, 8, 10; *Retort*, 8
Carruth, Hayden, 1–2, 6, 13, 128, 129
Celan, Paul, "Near, in the Aorta's Arch," 82
Chagall, Marc, 81
Ciardi, John, 95
Ciliga, Ante (Anton), *The Russian Enigma*, 8, 8n4, 9, 9n5, 11

Coleridge, Samual Taylor, 82, 157, 182; *Biographia Literaria*, 5
Colette, 76
Collins, Judy, 122
Comfort, Alex, "Pacifism and the War: A Controversy," 2n1
Conte, Joseph, 52n8
Cooney, Blanche, 6, 11; *In My Own Sweet Time: An Autobiography*, 6n2
Cooney, James Peter, 6, 6n2, 10, 11; *The Phoenix*, 6
Copley, Al, 50
Corman, Cid, 50, 110n2; *Origin*, vii, viii, x, 33, 34, 38, 109, 110n2, 182, 186
Corso, Gregory, vii, 98, 184
Creeley, Bobbie, 67
Creeley, Robert, vii, viii, ix, xi, 12, 33, 45, 66, 67, 76, 97, 98, 110, 133, 181, 184, 188, 191, 193, 194–96; *The Black Mountain Review*, vii, 110n2, 182; *Life and Death*, 196; *Pieces*, 195; *Words*, 195

Dahlberg, Edward, 98
Daly, Lew, 137–38, 137n10
Damásio, António, 27
Dante, 3, 21, 23–27, 29, 97, 141, 146, 175; *Divine Comedy*, 24; *Inferno*, 139, 141; *Monarchia*, 24, 25
Darwin, Charles, 64; *The Origin of Species*, 9
Davidson, Michael, ix, 109, 124
Davie, Donald, 83
Deleuze, Gilles, 19
Descartes, René, 27
Dewey, Anne, 44n1
Dewey, John, *Freedom and Culture*, 8n4
Dickey, James, 165
Dickinson, Emily, 76, 194, 195
Dorn, Ed, 97, 98, 99, 109
Duncan, Robert, "Achilles' Song," 127n1, 145; "Apprehensions," 145; *Bending the Bow*, 29, 32, 119, 120, 128; *A Book of Resemblances*, 36, 127n1, 186; *Caesar's Gate*, 127n1; "Changing Perspectives in Reading Whitman,"

21, 25; "Crisis of Spirit in the Word," 196; "A Critical Difference of View," 1, 12, 128n2; "Dante Études," 123; "Earth's Winter Song," 164, 166, 189; "An Essay at War," 2, 35–36; "The Gestation," 6; *Ground Work: Before the War*, 2, 32, 127, 127n1, 131, 132, 134, 134n8, 136, 138, 174; *Ground Work II: In the Dark*, 2; "The H.D. Book," 45, 46, 111–12, 126, 132, 186; *Heavenly City Earthly City*, viii, 186; "The Homosexual in Society," 8, 10–11, 13, 53; "Ideas of the Meaning of Form," 45, 51; "Ingmar Bergman's *Seventh Seal*," 98, 105–7; "The Law I Love Is Major Mover," 28, 29; *Letters*, x, 32–34, 37–39, 41–42, 132n6, 186; *The Letters of Robert Duncan and Denise Levertov*, viii, ix, x, xi, 2–3, 13, 67, 72, 110n2, 129n3, 155, 162, 163, 180, 181, 194; "Man's Fulfillment in Order and Strife," 13, 193; *Medieval Scenes*, 195; "Medieval Scenes," 64; "An A Muse Ment" ("For A Muse Meant") x, 34–35, 37, 38, 186; "The Museum," 123; "A Narrative of Memos," 132n6; "A Natural Doctrine," 77; "Notes on Poetics Regarding Olson's *Maximus*," 18; *Of the War: Passages 22–27*, 189–90; "Often I Am Permitted to Return to a Meadow," 12, 46–47, 50, 145; "My Mother Would Be a Falconress," 145; *The Opening of the Field*, 1, 7, 35, 46, 77, 105, 110; "Pages from a Notebook," 32, 35; "Passages 2," 120; "Passages 13, The Fire," 128, 189; "Passages 21, The Multiversity," 128; "Passages 25, Up Rising" 2, 128, 129, 142, 157, 164; "Passages 26, The Soldiers," 128, 164, 167; "Passages 30, Stage Directions," 120–22; "Passages 31, The Concert," 136–37; "Passages 33," 135; "Passages 34, The Feast," 133, 134; "Passages 35, Before the Judgment," x, 127,

131, 136, 138–47; "Passages 36," 178; "The Passages Poems," 52, 114, 123, 138, 189, 190, 193; "Persephone," 6; *Play Time Pseudo Stein*, 186; "A Poem Beginning with a Line by Pindar," 145; "Preface, prepared for *maps #6*," 135; "The Protestants (Canto One)," 6; "Reviewing *View*: An Attack," 12; "Rites of Participation," 19–20, 126–27; *Roots and Branches*, 112; "Santa Cruz Propositions," 13, 142, 168–70, 172–73; "The Self in Postmodern Poetry," 193, 194; "A Seventeenth Century Suite," 161, 162, 167, 172–73, 174–79; "A Spring Memorandum: Fort Knox," 10; "A Storm of White," 35; "Structure of Rime V," 83; "Structure of Rime XXVIII, IN MEMORIAM WALLACE STEVENS," 123; "The Sweetness and Greatness of Dante's *Divine Comedy*," 23–24, 26; "Towards an Open Universe," 193; *Tribunals: Passages 31–35*, x, 127, 127n1, 129–30, 131–35; "The Truth and Life of Myth," 20, 21, 29, 30; "Under Ground," 7; "Upon Taking Hold," 42; "Variations on Two Dicta of William Blake," 53; "The Venice Poem," 64; "We Have Forgotten Venus," 6; *Writing Writing*, 186; *The Years as Catches*, 127n1
DuPlessis, Rachel Blau, 152
Durem, Ray, 98
Durkheim, Émile, 23

Eberhart, Richard, 94
Eliot, T. S., 44, 179; *Four Quartets*, 175
Eliot, George, 171–72
Emerson, Ralph Waldo, 182, 185, 192; "The Poet," 5, 188, 191; "Poetry and Imagination," 191
Everson, William, vii, 2, 6

Faas, Ekbert, 21, 22
Fabilli, Lily, 6

Fabilli, Mary, 6
Fauchereau, Serge, 83
Ferlinghetti, Lawrence, vii, 1, 74, 98
Ford, Charles Henri, 10
Fraser, Nancy, 109n1
Fredericks, Claude, 132n6
Freud, Sigmund, 20, 33, 41, 45, 68, 143, 174; *Civilization and Its Discontents*, 40–41
Friedrich, Casper David, 50n6
Frielicher, Jane, 48
Fromm, Eric H., *Escape from Freedom*, 8n4

Garrigue, Jean, 98
Gelpi, Albert, 83; "Introduction: The 'Aesthetic Ethics' of the Visionary Imagination," 155, 156, 162, 180; *The Letters of Robert Duncan and Denise Levertov*, viii, ix, x, xi, 2–3, 13, 67, 72, 110n2, 129n3, 155, 162, 163, 180, 181, 194
Gelpi, Barbara, 83
Ginsberg, Allen, vii, 33, 66, 67, 97, 98, 111, 142, 184
Golding, Alan, 110n2
Goldman, Emma, 74
Goldstein, David, 85
Goodman, Mitchell, 47, 54, 153, 166, 167
Goodman, Nicolai, 128
Goya, Francisco, 50
Grenier, Robert, 193
Gris, Juan, 172
Guattari, Félix, 19
Gubar, Susan, 56

Habermas, Jürgen, 109n1, 110n2, 117, 123
Hall, Donald, 94, 98
Harrison, Lou, 68
Hatlen, Burton, 150
Hayakawa, Samuel I., 142
H.D., 33, 44, 76, 111, 112, 113; *Palimpsest*, 19; *Trilogy*, 152–53, 154; *The Walls Do Not Fall*, 112
Hejinian, Lyn, 193

Henry, Gerrit, 48
Herbert, George, 177–78
Herring, Terrell Scott, 109, 124
Hesiod, *Works and Days*, 139–41
Hoffman, Abbie, 142
Hoffman, Hans, 48
Homans, Peter, 45
Homer, 97, 140
Homer, Winslow, 48
Hopkins, Gerard Manley, 182
Hopper, Edward, 48
Howe, Fanny, 193
Howe, Susan, 137n10, 193
Hughes, Langston, 94n2, 98
Humphrey, Hubert, 142, 164, 166, 189
Hyde, Lewis, 142

Ibsen, Henrik, 102
Idel, Moshe, *Absorbing Perfections*, 138
Ignatow, David, x, 93–100, 94n2, 105;
    Chelsea 8, x, 93, 93n1, 94, 99, 99n4

James, Henry, 63, 162
James, William, 20
Jarrell, Randall, vii
Jess (Collins), viii, 48, 65–66, 67, 68, 69,
    127n1
Johnson, Lyndon B., 2, 120, 164, 171, 189
Johnson, Ronald, 136, 136n9
Jones, Angel, 81
Joyce, James, *Dubliners*, 171; *Finnegans
    Wake*, 63, 171; *Ulysses*, 63
Jung, C. G., 45–46, 172; *Two Essays on
    Analytical Psychology*, 163
Justice, Donald, 94, 95–96

Kael, Pauline, 6, 8, 10, 11
Kantorowicz, Ernst, ix, 21–24, 26–29,
    64, 105; *The King's Two Bodies: A
    Study in Medieval Political Theology*,
    21–24, 26
Keats, John, 167
Kennedy, John F., 94
Kerouac, Jack, vii, 184
Kinnell, Galway, 94

Kline, Franz, 50
Koch, Kenneth, vii
Kooning, Willem de, 49
Kresch, Albert, 48
Kropotkin, Peter, 9, 11; *Ethics: Origin
    and Development*, 9; *Fields, Factories
    and Workshops*, 9; *Mutual Aid: A
    Factor of Evolution*, 9

Lamantia, Philip, 33
Laubies, René, 50
Lawrence, D. H., 6, 103
Lebel, Jean Jacques, 96; "Coleur de mon
    sang," 96
Lecercle, Jean-Jacques, 19
Leite, George, *Circle*, 12
de Leon, Moses, *Zohar*, 38, 82
Levertoff, Paul, 47, 53, 81, 82, 87, 181; *St.
    Paul in Jewish Thought*, 87
Levertov, Denise, "The Ache of
    Marriage," 47n4; "Advent 1966,"
    161–62, 163, 164, 165, 166–67, 172–
    74, 179, 189; "An Autobiographical
    Sketch," 191; "Candles in Babylon,"
    150; "Clouds," 43, 44, 47, 50–52,
    56–57; "A Common Ground," 113–14;
    "A Cure of Souls," 43; *The Double
    Image*, 192; "During the Eichmann
    Trial," 47n3, 52, 53, 189; "An English
    Field in the Nuclear Age," 88;
    "Enquiry," 170; "For Instance," 86;
    "From a Notebook," 167, 169; "A
    Further Definition," 185; *Here and
    Now*, 1, 192; "Illustrious Ancestors,"
    81; "In California," 87; *The Jacob's
    Ladder*, 47, 81, 88, 99; "The Jacob's
    Ladder," 113; "A Lamentation," 113,
    189; *The Letters of Robert Duncan and
    Denise Levertov*, viii, ix, x, xi, 2–3, 13,
    67, 72, 110n2, 129n3, 155, 162, 163,
    180, 181, 194; *The Life Around Us:
    Selected Poems on Nature*, 192; "Life
    at War," 75, 165, 170, 174, 189; *Life
    in the Forest*, 76; "Matins," 114n4;
    "The Necessity," 101n5; "A Note

on the Work of the Imagination,"
45; *O Taste and See*, 86; "The Old
Adam," 57; "Olga Poems," 58, 189;
Overland to the Islands, 1; "Paintings
by John Button," 54–58; *The Poet in
the World*, 102; "A Poet's View," 191;
"Poetry and Revolution: Neruda Is
Dead—Neruda Lives," 156; "The
Pulse," 83; "The Rainwalkers," 114n4;
Relearning the Alphabet, 157, 167;
"Relearning the Alphabet," 73, 148,
151–55; "The Shifting" ("Turning"),
viii, x, 34–35, 38, 186; "Snail," 157;
"Some Affinities of Content," 191;
"Some Duncan Letters—A Memoir
and a Critical Tribute," 64, 68, 150;
"Some Notes on Organic Form,"
182, 184, 185, 187–88; *The Sorrow
Dance*, 58, 99, 189; "Staying Alive,"
58, 73, 114, 115, 115n5, 116, 118–19,
123, 149, 156, 158, 189; *The Stream
and the Sapphire: Selected Poems on
Religious Themes*, 192; "Tenebrae,"
170, 189; "Testament," 188; "Three
Meditations," 52, 98, 99–104, 101n5;
To Stay Alive, 151, 155, 156, 161, 167–
70; "A Vision," 114n4; "The Well,"
47n3; "What Were They Like?" 165,
170; "Who Is at My Window?" 150;
"A Window," 47n3; *With Eyes at the
Back of Our Heads*, 1, 192; "Writing
to Aaron," 76
Levertov, Olga, 150n1, 170, 171, 189
Lévy-Bruhl, Lucien, 20
Lévy-Leblond, Jean-Marc, 20
Little, Anne, 156
Lowell, Robert, vii, 33, 95, 95n3; "For
the Union Dead," 95n3; *Life Studies*,
95, 95n3
Lowes, J. Livingston, 82

Macdonald, Dwight, 8, 9, 10, 11; "The
Future of Democratic Values,"
8n4; *Politics*, 8, 10, 11; "War and the
Intellectuals," 13

Machado, Antonio, 83
Mackey, Nathaniel, 119–20
Mac Low, Jackson, 8
Malraux, André, *Museum without Walls*,
66
Mann, Thomas, 114
Marks, Saul, 134–35
Martin, John, 127, 129, 131, 134–35, 134n7
Matisse, Henri, 49
McClure, Jo Ann, 33
McClure, Michael, 33, 66, 74, 97
Mersmann, James, *Out of the Vietnam
Vortex*, 15
Miller, Henry, 64
Mondrian, Piet, 172
Moore, Marianne, 33
Morris, William, 136
Mossin, Andrew, 129n3

Nasr, Sayyed Hossein, 130n4
Nerval, Gérard de, 83; *Chimères*, 13, 129
Nietzsche, Friedrich, 96
Nin, Anaïs, *The Diary of Anaïs Nin*, 65
Nixon, Richard, 94, 102

O'Hara, Frank, vii, 48, 72, 109, 124;
"John Button Birthday," 48
O'Leary, Peter, 46; *Gnostic Contagion*,
129n3
Olson, Charles, vii, viii, 7, 12, 33, 37, 39,
44, 44n1, 52, 67, 94, 96–97, 98, 99,
100, 110, 111, 181, 184, 191; "A Discrete
Gloss," 38; *The Maximus Poems*, 97;
"Projective Verse," vii, 133, 169, 182,
188
Oppen, George, 53, 150, 193, 195; "The
Mind's Own Place," 150
Oppen, June, 150
Orwell, George, "Pacifism and the War:
A Controversy," 2n1

Palmer, Michael, 193
Pasternak, Boris, 114
Paz, Octavio, 96

Perloff, Marjorie, 194; "Poetry in Time of War: The Duncan-Levertov Controversy," 115n5, 157; *Wittgenstein's Ladder*, 148
Perse, St.-John, 33
Plowden, Edmund, 29
Pollock, Jackson, 33, 48, 49
Porter, Fairfield, 48
Pound, Ezra, 33, 44, 44n1, 45, 113, 184, 185; *The Cantos*, 139; *The Spirit of Romance*, 12
Proudhon, Pierre-Joseph, 3–4; *Philosophy of the Miseria*, 4
Proust, Marcel, 171

Rainer, Dachine, 8; *Retort*, 8
Raiziss, Sonia, 99–100
Rall, Connie, 7
Rall, Jeff, 7, 11
Ransom, John Crowe, vii
Read, Herbert, "The Cult of Leadership," 9, 13; *Poetry and Anarchism*, 5, 15
Reagan, Ronald, 142
Reid, Ian W., *Robert Duncan: Scales of the Marvelous*, 64, 68
Rexroth, Kenneth, 12, 63, 66
Rexroth, Marthe (Larsen), 63, 66
Rich, Adrienne, 110; "Blood, Bread, and Poetry," 149–50; *What Is Found There: Notebooks on Poetry and Politics*, 148
Riding, Laura, 8
Rifkin, Libbie, 109
Rilke, Rainer Maria, 82, 85–87, 155–56; "Archaïscher Torso Apollos," 84–85, 86
Rocker, Rudolf, *Anarcho-Syndicalism*, 5
Roethke, Theodore, 94
Rodgers, Audrey, *Denise Levertov: The Poetry of Engagement*, 99, 152
Rosenberg, Harold, "Myth and History," 8n4
Rosenblum, Robert, 50n6
Rosset, Barney, *Evergreen Review*, 109

Rothenberg, Jerome, 44
Rothko, Mark, 49, 50n6
Rouault, Georges, 172
Rubin, Jerry, 142
Rumaker, Michael, 110n3
Rushdie, Salman, *The Satanic Verses*, 130n4
Ruskin, John, 36, 45

Sacco, Nicola, 142
Santos, Boaventura de Sousa, 19
Sapir, Edward, 20
Savage, D. S., "Pacifism and the War: A Controversy," 2n1
Shakespeare, William, 23, 24, 26–27, 29; *Richard II*, 26
Scholem, Gershom, 82
Sherman, Leslie, 10, 11
Shurin, Isak, 73
Silliman, Ron, 132; *In the American Tree*, 195
Silone, Ignazio, 173
Simic, Charles, x
Sisko, Nancy, 123
Snyder, Gary, 66, 74
Sorrentino, Gilbert, 53n9
Southwell, Robert, 162, 173; "The Burning Babe," xi, 161, 172–74, 175–77
Spicer, Jack, vii, 21, 63, 64, 66
Starbuck, George, 95
Stein, Gertrude, 33, 38, 171, 186–87, 192, 193–94
Stevens, Wallace, 33
Stevenson, Adlai, 94
Still, Clyfford, 111
Summerskill, John, 142
Sydow, Max Von, 107

Taggart, John, 135, 137n10
Tallman, Warren, x, 66, 67
Tate, Allen, vii
Thoreau, Henry David, 142
Trilling, Lionel, 33
Trotsky, Leon, 11

Tyler, Hamilton, 2, 6, 11–12
Tyler, Mary, 2, 11
Tyler, Parker, 10

Ulpian, 22, 27, 29

Vanzetti, Bartolomeo, 3–4, 6, 13, 142

Whalen, Philip, 67, 97
Whitehead, Alfred North, *Process and Reality*, 51
Whitman, Walt, 3, 21, 155, 184, 185; *Leaves of Grass*, 136
Whorf, Benjamin Lee, 20
Wilbur, Richard, vii, 94, 98
Williams, Jonathan, 1, 66
Williams, William Carlos, 2, 3, 33, 44, 45, 89, 113, 184, 185, 191, 192; *Paterson*, 36

Winters, Yvor, 36–37
Wittgenstein, Ludwig, 148–49, 154, 158; *Tractatus*, 148
Woodcock, George, *Anarchy or Chaos*, 4; "Pacifism and the War: A Controversy," 2n1; "What Is Anarchism," 12
Woolf, Virginia, 76
Wordsworth, William, 187
Wright, James, 53n9, 98, 99; "Confession to J. Edgar Hoover," 99n4

Yeats, W. B., 41, 65; *Autobiographies*, 13; "Supernatural Songs," 40–41
Young, Edward, *Night Thoughts*, 102

Zalman, Shneour, 81
Zukofsky, Louis, 33, 44n1, 184, 193, 195